ALSO BY BARRY GOLSON

Retirement Without Borders

How to Retire Abroad in Mexico, France, Italy, Spain,
Costa Rica, Panama, and Other Sunny Foreign Places
(And the Secret to Making It Happen Without Stress)

Gringos in Paradise

An American Couple Builds
Their Retirement Dream House in a
Seaside Village in Mexico

BARRY GOLSON

Scribner
New York   London   Toronto   Sydney

SCRIBNER

A Division of Simon & Schuster, Inc.
1230 Avenue of the Americas
New York, NY 10020

First Scribner trade paperback edition December 2008

SCRIBNER and design are registered trademarks
of The Gale Group, Inc., used under license by
Simon & Schuster, Inc., the publisher of this work.

For information about special discounts for bulk purchases,
please contact Simon & Schuster Special Sales:
1-800-456-6798 or business@simonandschuster.com

Designed by Kyoko Watanabe
Text set in Stone Serif

Manufactured in the United States of America

1   3   5   7   9   10   8   6   4   2

Library of Congress Control Number: 2006045807

ISBN-13: 978-0-7432-7635-1
ISBN-10: 0-7432-7635-3
ISBN-13: 978-0-7432-7636-8 (pbk)
ISBN-10: 0-7432-7636-1 (pbk)

In this narrative, I am writing about the friends and neighbors who welcomed us into their villages in Mexico. The names, places, and events are real. For the sake of privacy, and to avoid disturbing the villages' tranquillity, I considered changing some names and locations. But there's a published trail of our travels, and I felt that in the age of Google, it would be a futile gesture. So, to the residents of Sayulita and San Pancho: sorry for any unwanted attention this may cause, and warmest thanks for helping us find a new life among you.

For Thia, Blair, and Tyler

For Dad and for Gala

Que les vaya bien

PROLOGUE

We delivered our news at a Mexican restaurant in New York City.

I said, "We're going to live in a small village on Mexico's Pacific Coast."

The table was quiet, then it became noisy, then margarita toasts were offered all around. The dinner was a rowdy, jovial affair; someone among us was finally *doing* it. A grown-up couple was going to do the madcap thing, and run off and join the circus. But afterward, I am told, there were whispered family conferences and long, concerned telephone conversations.

If it sounded to our friends and family like we were being rash and impetuous, it was understandable; and perhaps it was not entirely untrue. They knew that we were at a crossroads. They knew I had topped out, and then bottomed out, on my work. They knew we had wanderlust, and that at my age I probably would not stay around to restart my career. They knew that my wife, Thia, always cheerful and intrepid, was willing to try something new. They knew all this.

But Mexico.

There is a body of escapist literature about people who burn out and leave the career game voluntarily, usually with enough set aside to buy themselves a new life. But in our case, it was the game that left me on the sidelines.

I had worked up to fifty weeks a year for thirty-five years. Although I was one of the fortunate people who liked what I was doing, dues had been paid. Sons had been sent to college. Brothers and sisters had been sheltered and succored. Mothers had moved in with us, at separate times, and had passed their final hours in our home. Our rambling house in the suburbs, and later our apartment in the city, were hearth and haven for a far-flung clan of comrades. But at work, the tradeoff for a stimulating job in the youth-beset magazine business was my double surprise to find that, first, as I passed my mid-fifties, I was no longer as appealing to employers as I had been a decade earlier, and second, I actually *was* the age on my driver's license.

We had lived an active life in New York City and its environs. We were used to going to the theater, to concerts in Central Park, to Zabar's for its pâté, cheese, and thirty different kinds of olives. Though my work was satisfying, it was intense. I was at my office till seven or eight at night, and I often worked on weekends. I almost never felt I could relax, especially not at the crest of my career. I looked around, like a stag at a stream, always making certain I wasn't in someone's sights. I usually was.

When the last magazine I edited was folded in a publishing recession, I expected to get another editing job. But the choices were sparser, the recruiters younger, the salaries smaller. My phone didn't ring. As for Thia, after several careers in teaching, remodeling and editing a newsletter— her true life's work was raising our two boys—she, too, found that her earning opportunities after age fifty-five were greatly diminished.

Maybe life, as John Lennon said, is what happens when you're busy making other plans. But no planning can creep up on you too. Thia and I had put aside some money, though not nearly enough to think about living for long on our savings, much less retiring in anything like the style to which we, like a lot of members of my providential generation, were accustomed. (In fact, many of us will choose not to retire at all; but the problem of living during our later years on a sharply reduced income, whether at work or at rest, is common to many of us. That, not shuffleboard, is what I mean by retirement.)

In the period after the turn of the millennium, it was broadly reported that a majority of our baby-boom generation was not saving enough to live on during its retirement years. That, combined with general insecurity about Social Security, set off widespread anxiety, introspection, and not a little whining. In the last year that we spent in Connecticut and New York City, more and more conversations with friends were about "what happens next" and whether we had "our number"—enough of a nest egg to take us the rest of the way.

The size of the nest egg varied with the family, of course, and some of our more affluent acquaintances declared that it would take several million dollars in the bank, beyond even a house or two, for them to feel set for life. For that reason, they intended to continue working long years and long hours, some at jobs they did not enjoy, until they felt secure. Others, who had toiled at low-glamour service careers with the promise of a good pension and benefits, had begun coming into their own, and we were happy for them. Still others, oldies without goodies, talked of adopting a new financial planning strategy entirely: doubling up on their weekly purchases of lottery tickets.

We had a modest securities account and, after paying retail for two private-college educations, an equally modest retirement account fund. But that was it. No pension, no benefits. I had taken some risks in my career and was glad I had. Some had paid off, some not, but none resulted in payouts or pensions. Our health insurance premiums, now that we were no longer covered by corporate, could make us sick if we thought about them. We had some debts. We owned a small condo in Connecticut, where we could cocoon. In all, nothing to cry about; the world offered far tougher prospects to the vast majority of humankind. But it was nevertheless apparent that we were going to have to look at other places to live, and other ways of living, if we were going to afford a future for ourselves that was anywhere as interesting as the life we had come from.

The other vein I had felt throbbing was a personal pulse, the sense of rhythm we had about our lives and where we were headed. Even without the push, we had spent many nights asking ourselves if this taut, glossy life was something we wanted forever. Our two sons had made us proud, and we had an extraordinarily close and affectionate relationship with them, but they had flown the nest. One was a few years out of college, a reporter in New York, and the other, just graduated, off to study in the Middle East. We knew how fortunate we had been with our kids, how we'd lucked out on the fundamental things of life. We'd always have parenthood.

Now, though, Thia and I were a childless couple once again. It was both liberating and unsettling. How would she and I thrive alone? How much did we have in common now that we were no longer a child-rearing enterprise? Did we want to adjust in place, or move out, try on a different set of experiences that might bind us in a new way? What we needed—what I heard friends of my age say they needed—was a new life that was not just a soft landing but an exploration. Change, we sensed, was not just necessary for economic reasons but to keep people from going stale.

And that Connecticut weather. Glorious in the spring, splendid in the summer, gaudy in the fall . . . and increasingly tough to take in the endless midnight winter. I recognized in myself what I had seen in older friends and relatives: the preternatural desire for sunlight on the face and sand between the toes, not to mention drinks with salt on the rims. Slowly, despite our reluctance to leave family, friends, and the abundance of an anchored life, we began to dream of moving to a sunny place, but one that would be more challenging, better for our sinews, than Florida, Arizona, even California. Oh, and someplace more affordable.

That was when the idea of Mexico began to take hold.

CHAPTER 1

A Rainstorm . . .
A Goodbye Party . . . Crossing Over

¿Es usted norteamericana?
Sí, soy norteamericana.

We are rolling across the republic to the soft droning of my wife's Spanish language drills on the car's CD player. My wife answers with the same exaggerated singsong lilt as the woman on the disc, and it is starting to grate on me. Certainly it is a credit to Thia that she is using our five days of driving to the border as a time to begin learning the language, but it has something of the same effect on me that songs tallying bottles of beer used to have when returning from camp. It is Election Day, and it is pouring sheets here in Ohio as autumn lightning crackles down onto the plains. When we pull off the highway to fill up, I see lines of people outside a school building, holding umbrellas or turning their collars up, waiting to vote. Thia and I have cast absentee ballots in our Connecticut town before leaving, but if there is any astral, or political, sign in our departure, it is not of our making.

The election results unfold for us in a motel in Ohio, where it continues to pour. We wonder, in passing, what effect the lashing rain might have on the voter turnout here. Thia and I resume our drive the next morning, and the weather clears. She puts on her Spanish drills again (yes, she is a *norteamericana,* but I cannot think of a time in Mexico in the next two years when we'll be called that), and we strike a time-sharing compromise: I am finally able to tune into my newest toy, a satellite radio. With 120 channels, it turns a long drive into a continuous sampling of music, news, and sports—Mozart, classic rock, crooners of the thirties, Debussy, even a twenty-four-hour Elvis channel, plus NPR and the talk shows, all thrashing out the election results.

Although we are on our way to simplify our lives, it will not be without some of our society's more useful technology. Mine is the first generation since the rise of the Internet and the technology boom to try out the expatriate life. We may not need our TV—we have not brought along a set—but we *do* want our laptops, our DVD players, our iPods, our Wi-Fi cards.

Our car is a midsize used Japanese SUV I bought recently on eBay. It is hardly a smart choice of car, since it is not serviced in Mexico, and it is not particularly economical or environmentally friendly. But it is a strong, rugged beast, and we didn't want to trade it in for a lesser breed; at least it is a four-wheel drive vehicle. Mexico, as we knew from a previous visit, offered ample opportunities to test a car's constitution. The *topes*—vicious speed bumps that appear out of nowhere approaching towns and villages—were enough to require reinforced shocks, and any detours could involve streams, mud, and rocks.

It also had enough cargo room for the stuff we were bringing for a first year's stay in Mexico. Thia decided suitcases would only be a nuisance to store in the apartment we would be renting, and a pain to pack in the car, so instead we filled sixteen large steel-reinforced plastic trash bags with our (all-summer) clothes, our laptops, a printer, a fan, our flippers, a multitude of CDs and books, a stereo, and a foldable bookcase.

By afternoon of the next day, in Missouri, we switch off the satellite radio in favor of an audio book of Mark Twain readings. As we have planned our rambling route, we cross the big river not that far from Hannibal listening to excerpts from *Life on the Mississippi*. We are in no hurry to reach the Mexican border. We have traveled with our boys throughout the United States and in Europe, and always enjoyed the going as much as the getting there.

To easterners, Europe seems closer than Mexico. In the East, our superficial image of Mexico is shaped by what we read or see on television or when immigration issues are in the public eye: a poor country with good resorts, lousy water, spicy food, dangerous *bandidos,* a colorful history, and a hard-working people—a good number of whom might, at any moment, be poised at the Rio Grande, paying unscrupulous smugglers their life's savings to ferry them across to do America's lowest-paid work. When we get exercised about illegal immigration, as we do every few years, we notice the Mexicans in our midst, laboring in our fields and our cities. But we do not trouble ourselves to know much beyond the clichés about Mexico, or about the Mexicans who remain and reside in their own country. In the East we are exposed to a less nuanced image of Mexico than are residents of California or the Southwest. But it's safe to say that a mix of apprehension and condescension toward our southern neighbor seems to be pervasively, reflexively American. Sorry, *North* American.

In our family, there was a different tradition. It may not have been in our blood—we're pretty much Irish-French—but living in Mexico for a time was part of our family history. My paternal grandfather lived and worked in Chihuahua, in northern Mexico, at the turn of the last century. My father, a mining equipment salesman, was transferred to Mexico City in 1952, and we spent seven years there, leaving when I was twelve. I forgot much of my Spanish and did not return to Mexico until I was an adult.

Though I passed some formative years there, Mexico faded from my mind. My family moved to Europe—I met my future wife's family there—but I went to high school and college in the States and worked in America's big cities. I retained a warm feeling for the years I spent in Mexico City, which was then a balmy city of a few million. It seemed to me, young as I was, a fabled, romantic time of my life. But later, as time went on, I became no less susceptible than other Americans to the drumbeat of press reports about Mexico's unstable finances, poverty-stricken citizenry, and crime in the border cities, to say nothing of the effects of drinking the tap water.

In fact, after we announced our decision to our larger circle of friends, it was surprising how many had their own personal horror stories to relate, and how eagerly they told them. Just before we left, there was a good-bye party for us in New York at our in-laws' apartment. Our friends came to wish us well. One, a svelte, smart New York City judge and an experienced world traveler, told us she had visited

Mexico only once and had been shipped home feet first, retching. A soft-spoken sister-in-law was uncharacteristically agitated when she talked about a friend who had once been stopped by police in Mexico and taken off to jail on spurious charges. A couple of friends from the suburbs mentioned kidnappings in Mexico City and the rash of stories about violence in the border cities.

At the party, after we cut the celebratory cake that was bought for us, several of my male friends put their arm around my shoulder.

"You *dog*," said a lifelong buddy. "We're so goddamn envious."

"You're paving the way," said another friend and fellow writer. "You're going to live the dream."

That is what they were saying. But by the way they squeezed my shoulder, kneading it sympathetically, I knew it was more than happiness or even a touch of envy they felt for us—they were wishing us luck, as if they feared we would need it.

After a final Stateside lunch on San Antonio's voguish riverfront, we are in Laredo, Texas, approaching the border. Thia and I rehearse our plans. The guidebooks and websites have advised us what we can legally take across the border. Among other things, we are declaring only the ten books and twenty CDs we are allowed under a tourist visa, and have written a list to that effect, translating it into formal Spanish on Google's language site.

We are taking a risk by failing to declare the fifty CDs and the sixty or so books we are actually carrying. We will be applying for a tourist visa even though we intend to stay for at least a year, and will wait to get a resident visa at our destination in Mexico. That will eventually allow us to bring over a virtually unlimited number of household goods, but for now we have to make do with what tourists do. We are resigned to what may happen if the Mexican border police give us the notorious red light, which randomly singles out travelers for a major inspection. We know we face duty and a possible fine if our international music- and book-smuggling operation is uncovered.

In downtown Laredo, we pick up our Mexican insurance papers; American insurance is not valid in Mexico. Nasty stories about uninsured accidents in Mexico are a cottage industry online, not least because so many Mexican drivers do not themselves carry insurance—

or driver's licenses, for that matter. In Mexico, we hear, with a legal system in part based on the Napoleonic code, guilt is sometimes assumed and innocence must be proved. If papers are not in order, or there are any discrepancies at the scene of a fender bender, it is not unknown for the police to escort both drivers to a jail until it can be sorted out.

We head for the international border.

In the middle of the bridge spanning the Rio Grande, we pass into Mexico. American customs is uninterested in those of us leaving, while at the Mexican booth, an unsmiling man in uniform peers in at us and nods us through. It's a false positive, we know. The real customs stop is twelve miles down the highway, through a "free trade zone," in which U.S. residents can make casual day trips with a minimum of red tape. Those of us going further face the gauntlet. It is an instructive experience to cross the border by car, unlike flying into a Mexican airport, where you encounter only gradual changes amid the familiar glass and chrome of the arrivals building. In a car, you are immersed in the new culture instantly.

On the streets of Nuevo Laredo, the potholed pavement, littered sidewalks, dilapidated buildings, horizontal traffic lights, and a swelter of unfamiliar signage hit us at once. An old gentleman in a straw hat pulls out in front of us, on the seat of a cart made from a car frame, urging his donkey forward in traffic. The sidewalk action, all bustle and glances, has an edgy cast. In the year to come, there will be stories about gang killings and kidnappings in this lawless border city, and even now I know I want us to do our business and be gone.

We have to get our visas and car papers. Given the millions of vehicles that pass this way, the signs for the Mexican car-permit office are remarkably casual and makeshift. When we find the office, there are lines, and documents to be stamped, and permits to be paid for—in Mexican pesos, not with credit cards. Outside of major hotels and restaurants, we know this is still largely a cash society. This is my first test of patience for the pace of bureaucratic life in Mexico. The American mind begins immediately to make comparisons: God, this is inefficient; in the States we'd streamline this—conveniently forgetting long mornings of waiting in line at a New York City Department of Motor Vehicles. I have to make a conscious effort to adjust—they do it differently here, *relax!*—so I don't start out irritated and annoyed. Our documents are stamped, then stamped again, and then again.

About ninety minutes later, we are on the highway toward the twelve-mile customs station, where the green or red light awaits. We are exhilarated to be headed somewhere we will be calling home, but with a glance at each other, Thia and I know we are feeling the same thing. It is something we would not have admitted to our friends back East: a touch of dread about leaving behind the safe harbor of U.S. laws and norms, knowing that this time in our journey south we are driving deeper, past the point of easy return, to a place that can feel more perilous and alien than most countries we have visited. It's been said that there may be no two bordering countries in the world more different from each other than the United States and Mexico. Mexican author Carlos Fuentes has written that Mexico is far more "intricate and challenging to the North American mind than anything in Europe; a country at times more foreign than anything in Asia."

Still, I remind myself that despite the press clippings and State Department warnings, the overall crime rate in Mexico, at least as compiled by a recent United Nations survey, is ranked at less than a quarter that of the United States. Because public mistrust of the police in Mexico results in crimes being underreported, probably drastically, it's hard to get a true sense of it. But with the notable exception of drug crimes in the border cities, there is a statistical case to be made that in many parts of the country, for many of its 107 million citizens and resident expatriates, Mexico is at least as safe to live in as the United States. It is reassuring to think so.

Approaching the customs checkpoint, we slow down to pass through the lights. Up ahead, a red flash, and a car pulls over to the side and is approached by customs agents. Then a green, a green, and us—green! The very first thing I think after feeling relief is an ungrateful, Damn, what was I worried about?; we could have taken the desktop computer (only a laptop is permitted), and maybe even that old air conditioner we had in the attic in Connecticut. Well, maybe not. We hear later from red-lighted travelers who were delayed for hours while every bag was inspected, with imaginative duties imposed on anything that looked even vaguely new.

The crossing, as I reflect on it, has its disturbing ironies. Here are we, persons born to privilege, now prospective immigrants headed in one direction over a border river that countless desperate immigrants look to cross the other way. We are worried about carrying too many CDs and getting fined; they are, many of them, fearful of being caught, arrested, turned back, robbed, in some cases dying from desert exposure. But something comes back to me: for all the furor about Mexican illegal aliens, which will grow more strident in the months to come, I have also read about Mexican immigrants working in the States who say they ultimately prefer the way of life in Mexico and intend to return here when they have saved enough. Although there's an economic reason I am emigrating to *their* country, I am also hoping to embrace the life and culture they say they miss.

So we are, at last, on our way. Our destination is a stretch of beach villages two days' drive away, about halfway down Mexico's Pacific Coast. We felt it important to settle in the middle part of the country, beyond the reach of the hustle and aggression of the border cities, and outside the periphery of tension and congestion that is Mexico City. We have been to the gentler central and interior parts of the country, and have a sense of how life is lived there.

Still, it is not that we have a dreamy notion of living alone in a rural village or necessarily of living in a more "authentic" Mexico. There are expatriates who seek that out, but we were not looking for a primitive, locals-only retreat. The villages that caught our interest are more prosperous, and more inhabited by Americans, than most. Yes, we want the Mexican experience; yes, we want to engage with a culture that is new to us. But we are going to make a home and do not want to forgo all modern comforts or English-speaking comradeship.

Besides, it seems more interesting to us to engage with a community that is dealing with change, not pastorally preserved in the past. As Mexicans come north to seek a better living, Americans will be heading south in greater numbers to seek a better life. That dynamic—between a purely Mexican tradition and the wave of modernism ushered in by television, tourists, and retirees—will be an increasingly common scenario played out in Mexican towns and villages.

This, at least, is what I found when I took an assignment a year earlier to write about Americans retiring in central Mexico. It was then that I rediscovered my childhood affection for the country and its people. During that trip, I came to feel that the overarching characteristics of Mexicans—amiability, generosity, creativity, honesty, joy in living— were most evident in these smaller towns. As for the Americans, I interviewed a wide range of gringo retirees, in various states of work, repose, and merriment, from Guadalajara to Puerto Vallarta. It was at the end of the trip that, unexpectedly, we arrived at the funky, dusty village that would grab our hearts: Sayulita.

We would not have got there, or done any of it, if I had not first had the rug pulled out from under me. Sometimes you need a shove to discover where you want to go next.

CHAPTER 2

Becoming an Expat . . . Significant Encounters . . . High on a Hilltop

A year earlier, when it became clear that I was not going to be asked to rejoin the New York City fast track anytime soon, we sold our apartment, moved to our small condo in Connecticut, and spent slow mornings over hot coffee talking about the future. Although we got nowhere, it occurred to me that a lot of people in our generation coming up behind us soon would be getting nowhere over hot coffee, too. Perhaps, I thought, we could investigate that very question on a writing assignment. It was a decision that would lead us by a roundabout itinerary to uprooting our lives.

I had written travel articles for many years. The idea of Mexico came up because I knew that a lot of Americans of retirement age had moved to the Guadalajara area, so I pitched a writing assignment to the logical publication: *AARP*, the mammoth-circulation magazine of the retirement organization. The premise of my pitch, approved by *AARP*, was that my wife and I would travel through a kind of retirement belt in central Mexico—the greater Guadalajara area is home to about fifty thousand American retirees—observing, talking, and poking our noses into people's lives. Our itinerary would take us from Guadalajara and Lake Chapala to San Miguel de Allende and then west to the Pacific Coast and Puerto Vallarta. The goal wasn't so much a guidebook collection of facts as a survey of Americans abroad, in their own voices.

Though the scope of the article inevitably would be more about

Americans in Mexico than about the Mexicans themselves, it was going to help that, because of my seven years as a child in Mexico City, I retained some middle-school Spanish. Thia, for her part, was known to use her college Italian in Mexican restaurants, often to intriguing effect, but otherwise did not know a word of Spanish. We were probably not unlike a lot of visiting American couples—some Spanish, and no Spanish. We flew to Guadalajara late in the year with plans to spend about a month in Mexico. I was not yet connecting the trip to the threads in my life, or that of my family's past. It was a chance to see a part of Mexico I had never seen, with a vague idea that it might somehow yield some personal answers.

Traveling through central Mexico for the next month by intercity bus, I met and interviewed the tenacious American residents of Guadalajara; the gated garden dwellers of Lake Chapala; the arty folk and mansion builders of San Miguel de Allende; and the cocktail-on-the-roof expatriates of Puerto Vallarta. (As to the word expatriate: It is remarkable how many Americans living in Mexico take offense at being called expatriates. It is also remarkable how many poor spellers there are. Convinced the word is spelled *ex-patriots*, they get mad if you call them that, and insist they are good Americans who just happen to have a Mexican address.)

From them I absorbed a few of the essentials of retiring or living part-time in Mexico: yes, the cost of living is cheaper, but not always *that* much cheaper. Depending on where they came from, expats' housing costs were anywhere from a quarter to three-quarters what they are in the States. Americans could live on their Social Security checks, perhaps, but mostly if they lived a Mexican life: tacos, not steak. Medical care—a *very* big topic among retirees—was generally praised and is reasonably priced; an important point, since Medicare is not valid outside the United States. Most drugs, except controlled substances, are available without prescription. I was intrigued to find that in some retirement communities—Lake Chapala, for instance—American women outnumber men by four to one; it led me to wonder if that would intimidate, or invigorate, American men I knew.

American retirees in Mexico, I found, are roughly dispersed into two pitched camps: those who assimilate into the country by living among locals, and those who isolate themselves by living inside gated communities or condo complexes. Both types defend their choices and are only too happy to hurl insults about each other online. (By "gringos," I take the poetic license of including the many Canadians here.)

What they agreed on was that expats in Mexico thought of themselves as hardier, pluckier than their compatriots who moved to Florida. Over a breakfast of huevos rancheros in Guadalajara, Michael Forbes, a trim transplanted Brit who edited *The Guadalajara Colony Reporter*, summed up his years of gringo watching: "Mexico can enchant you every day, and it can drive you mad every day: the life of the plazas, the climate, the welcoming, warm people. On the other hand, the crazy driving, the dysfunctional mails, the concept of Mexican time . . ."

"So what motivates the ones who *do* make the move?" I asked.

"Sometimes," he said, "you need to change your life from the mundane, and that can be good for you in your retirement years." That idea—that a retiree needs to avoid living too easy a life; that doing something new, a bit risky, is crucial to avoid stagnation—would come up often in the weeks and months ahead.

We planned to end the reporting trip in Puerto Vallarta; our intention was to stay about a week and head home. I'd been in touch by email with a bed-and-breakfast owner who urged me to come visit a couple of the beach villages to the north of Puerto Vallarta. There was little to suggest this would be a turning point for us, one that would propel us out of Connecticut a year later. Until now, the trip had been a job—informative, nostalgic for me, and ultimately a useful exercise in learning what retirement choices others had made. But it was those two unkempt, unpaved burgs on the edge of the Pacific Coast jungle, and the encounters we had there, that sent us on our rendezvous with dustiness.

But first Puerto Vallarta.

Guidebooks extol the city's blend of old Mexican charm and beach glamour, and we liked the amenities and the shopping. Forty years ago it was a picturesque little beach town. Then John Huston brought Richard Burton and Ava Gardner (and Elizabeth Taylor, in a nonstarring role) down to film *The Night of the Iguana*, giving it a dusting of glitter and steamy tropical allure. In their wake came the paparazzi, the tourists, the cruise ships, and the huge megahotels. It may be the only city whose entire modern urban development was set in motion by a movie.

There is a large, active American retirement community in Puerto Vallarta, an airport twenty minutes from downtown, and plenty of the playtime facilities that spring up around a modern resort. I found a number of hospitable retirees who invited us to their sunset cocktail parties in graceful condos high above Banderas Bay. There is an English-language bookstore, lots of charity work, and a wide variety of good restaurants. It is a city known to be friendly to gays. But we also encountered vendors hawking everything from jewelry to condo time shares—on the street, in the cafés, on the beach. The time-share sellers were exceptionally aggressive, carnival barkers in sunglasses. Tourists from the countless glitzy hotels and cruise ships wandered about.

I would later soften my opinion of Puerto Vallarta, but after a few days we decided to move on. We rented an old VW and drove up the coast to San Francisco and Sayulita, the villages I had heard about, forty-five minutes up the highway. They were supposedly less hectic and more "like Puerto Vallarta was thirty years ago."

We found San Francisco, universally known as San Pancho, to be a gratifying change, a quiet village of unassuming Mexican homes and modest stores and restaurants on a long street leading to a spectacular, surf-pounding beach. Considerably less modest, and more surprising, was what lay at the end of a stony, bumpy road at the north end of town: a colony of elegant mosaic-domed, American-owned Mediterranean villas, which is where Casa Obelisco stands. One of the owners was my email correspondent, Barbara Hart-Kirkwood.

Barbara and Bill Kirkwood, the first of our significant encounters, were former fast trackers from Silicon Valley who had moved to San Pancho for good three years earlier. With another couple, they decided to build a bed-and-breakfast inn over a period of several years—the dream of about every third retiree I encountered, by my conservative estimate. The idea was that they and their friends and partners Judi MacGregor-Levens and John Levens (who arrived later in our stay), would each have their own living wing, and would build four extra bedrooms, a pool, and a cabana for paying guests. The final touches—guest rooms with bedspreads in bright Mexican blues and greens—had just been added when we arrived. As their first paying customers, Thia and I luxuriated in the canopied beds, checking our shoes in the morning for scorpions, and spent an afternoon lolling in the eye-catching pool, which is tiled with a huge mosaic of an *obelisco*, the hibiscus that gave their house its name.

The couples were trailblazers of a sort (though latecomers compared to some of the twenty-year gringo veterans we were to meet later). Foreigners cannot buy land within fifty kilometers of Mexico's coasts, so U.S. buyers had to invest in land via leases and trusts, sometimes relying on *prestanombres* (literally, "name lenders," Mexican citizens who hold the property in their names) and other stratagems. It was our first exposure to the brave new world of property ownership in Mexico: in a country where mortgages are still rare, American retirees hand over large sums and don't even receive title in return.

Bill, a sandal-clad, Hawaiian-shirt-wearing bear of a guy, and Barbara, a petite blonde with no guile, a talent for zingers, and an infectious laugh, were more than good hosts. They spent long hours with us, and their tales about house building, making new friends, and adapting to Mexico's what-will-be mentality were mostly upbeat, but realistic. Unlike many of the part-time residents in the region, they had cut their ties to the States, selling their home and most of their U.S. possessions.

We had long talks around their pool that ranged from police corruption to the excellent plastic surgery that Barbara volunteered she got at a Guadalajara clinic. I mentioned a couple of Puerto Vallarta retirees I had heard complaining derisively about paying cops *mordidas*—bribes. Barbara's take was refreshing. Although she lamented certain "lawlessness" in her adopted country, she said, "Taxes are absurdly low, and so is a policeman's pay. How else can they make ends meet? Just pay it and shut up, I say."

"Absurd is the word for it," Bill, jovial and laid-back, added. "We have a five-thousand-square-foot beachfront house and pay twenty-four dollars a year in property taxes. What kind of protection and services can you get from that?" Bill opened a bar called the Drunken Monkey on San Pancho's main street, though he didn't yet know if it would turn out to be a going concern. "I told Barbara I needed to do something down here to stay out of the bars," Bill said. "So what do I do? I open up a bar."

Despite their perch on Gringo Hill, they were deeply involved in the life of the local community. They employed a number of Mexicans, becoming involved in their families and their dramas. They attended all the birthday parties and fiestas, and on our walks around town, I saw them greet—and be greeted by—scores of San Pancho villagers.

We made plans to spend our last couple of days in Sayulita, five miles down the road. Another beach town, we heard, but with more of a village life. John and Judi went there often to swim (their beach is often too rough), and Barbara swore by the hair salon. Nice little plaza. "Different deal," said Barbara, "same dream." The night before we made our foray into Sayulita, I asked if their family or friends expressed envy for these retirees who, in their early fifties, had made their fantasies come true.

"Yes," said Barbara. "Lots of them come down to visit, look at properties, and get the itch. Then, at the last minute they back down."

"Why?"

"Fear of the unknown. In the States you know there's always a fix. Here, it's fix-it-yourself. You've got to have that spirit."

We came to Sayulita looking for a Sunday breakfast. We had wandered its dusty, cobblestone streets, taken in its pretty little plaza, and had gone for an early swim on its crescent beach with the neat surf break. We heard about Rollie's almost from the moment we got to town. It served only breakfast, from eight to noon, and in the winter season there were often crowds of up to a dozen people waiting for a table. It is up a dirt road from the town plaza, across from the *carnicería,* where chickens are killed and plucked, in front of which an old woman churns a vat of pig victuals to prepare *chicharrón.* And there we had our second significant encounter.

It was a bright Sunday morning, and on Sunday, everyone comes to Rollie's.

Jeanne Dick, dark-haired, cat-eyed, pert in a short jean skirt, wife of the proprietor, came out with cups of coffee for those waiting in line. "I'll try to get Rollie to hurry things along, but . . ." she said, making a *quién sabe* gesture. Inside, past a dozen tables, in the kitchen at the rear, was Rollie, in a T-shirt, apron, and sun visor, flipping pancakes on a large grill.

The menu, a hand-produced manual filled with personal musings, elaborate dish names ("Neoclassicist Eggs: A Revival of Classical Aesthetics and Forms") and earnest annotations ("It speaks to me of glorious mornings"), was unabashedly personal. Bob Dylan's *Highway 61 Revisited* was playing on the speakers. Jeanne the waitress was obviously the starch to Rollie's sugar. She pointed to an entry written by her husband praising his own special half-crepe, half-pancakes ("I have never met anyone who didn't like them"), made a yeah-right face, and said, "I've met *plenty* of people who don't like 'em. Take the Pioneer hotcakes, they're more interesting."

Soon someone shouted, "Sing your song, Rollie!" Rollie, dark-and-gray-haired with a distinguished nose, ambled into the center of the restaurant. "If you're of a spiritual nature," he announced, "a little prayer for me would be in order." Laughs all around. Some of the crowd had seen this before and knew what to expect. Accompanied by a tape of his son, Josh, singing and playing a guitar, Rollie began his breakfast song.

"Bienvenidos a Rollie's Restaurant . . . Aquí vamos a desayunar . . ." As he and his absent son did their Nat King and Natalie Cole bit, Rollie danced around with arms outspread like Zorba, circling the restaurant, taking an older woman's hand and waltzing her between the tables. As the song wound down, he said, "And now comes the hardest part." He began to kneel creakily down, and before he reached the floor, a bemused-looking Jeanne paused with a tray in one hand, and with the other, slipped a cushion beneath his knee. Rollie swept his cap off his head in a bow to the crowd. At that moment, Stretch, their mutt, flashed by to snatch away the cap.

It was all pretty theatrical, and little wonder. Rollie Dick, who was then sixty-four, a former school principal and amateur-theater ham from Salinas, California, was now one of Sayulita's prime boosters, and its gringo godfather. In the time that we spent in Sayulita on our first visit, it was Rollie and Jeanne who most vividly personified the fantasy of giving up one life for another. As we decided to stretch our stay in Sayulita from several days to several weeks, we became friends, and they told us their story.

Five years earlier, Rollie had heard about the village from the family of one of his Mexican students in Salinas and came down for a vacation with his family: Jeanne, also a teacher, and his son and daughter. After ten days, they "fell in love" with the place. On leaving, he asked to be contacted if a place that matched their limited resources came on the market. Rollie's retirement fantasy was to open a restaurant. When word came that a building was available in Sayulita, the Dicks decided to take the chance.

"I flew down," he recalled, "and ten minutes after I got here, I was signing the biggest check I'd ever written in my life to a man I'd never met before, and he was giving me a handwritten receipt in a language I couldn't read or speak." Rollie paid out a significant portion of their savings for a three-story building with a welding shop on the ground floor. "You had to have vision," he said. "Plus, taxes are thirty-two dollars a year." Since Jeanne was still teaching, and the kids were still in school, Rollie made the decision to move down alone. "I lived here for three years without a telephone and without knowing how to speak Spanish. There were times when I was totally terrified, living without my family, but patience is the virtue here . . ." With the help of a Mexican family, he opened the restaurant, and his wife (and kids, part of the time) moved down later.

What appealed to Rollie about Sayulita was the mix of people—locals and gringos—and a certain audacious spirit he found. Also, the politics. "We're on the left politically," Rollie says, "and down here, for the most part, there are lots of risk takers, progressive people who are socially aware."

His political beliefs, Rollie said, led him to make a decision about the ownership of his restaurant. "I'm a socialist at heart and here was a chance for us to put our political, social, and spiritual values into practice. We devised a way for the people who work here to buy part of the restaurant and share in the profits, so we're no longer the sole owners. And oh my God, what a wonderful thing for the Mexican families involved. Their lives are changing."

I asked how Rollie had coped without wife and family for three years. "When I came down here, I had no expectations; I'm on something of a spiritual journey, so I was willing to see what would happen in this new phase of my life. For instance, now I read the Tao, and I meditate every morning—"

"Sits in a chair doing nothing," Jeanne, who had joined the conversation, explained.

"—and I think about what Tao says about doing by not doing. I don't have to worry about the next step, I just take it. You know, that's very Mexican."

"Not doing?" Jeanne laughed. "Seventy hours of work a week. Rollie's a mogul at heart. He plays poker every Wednesday and Saturday; ask him if he shares his winnings."

A couple of days later, Rollie and Jeanne were taking us for a walk through the village. It was Sayulita Days, and the carnival had come to town. A parade of horses, and pickup trucks carrying young women with sashes and costumed children perched precariously on hoods, had just passed by. There were bumper-car rides and sidewalk stands selling spicy delicacies and brass bands competing with each other across the small plaza. Like our San Pancho friends, Rollie and Jeanne were greeted everywhere we walked, by gringo and Mexican alike. But the topic among the gringos today was the lack of water, now going into its third day. Weaving among the festival goers, Rollie explained the finer points of public works in Sayulita.

"The new pump was delivered on the first day of the three-day festival, and they chose to install that day. Of course it blew away the pipes. I asked why, of all times, they'd choose the holiday to install it. They said, 'Because it arrived today.' So when, three days later, there was still no repair work being done, I asked why not. They said, 'Because no one works on holidays.' Makes perfect sense."

Rollie expanded on How Things Are Done Down Here. "There is, absolutely, a mentality here of living in the now. Speaking very generally, it does not involve planning very far into the future. If they tell you they'll be here at nine o' clock, they may or they may not. If they've got money in their pocket from the last job, why come to work today? And you know what? It's wonderful! It's a wonderful way to live, in the now. But it drives some people just wild. I've seen retired CEOs *brought to their knees*! They come down here with some money and think, 'I'm gonna take care of business, get this house built, boom, boom' . . . and they're putty in the Mexicans' hands by the time it's over.

"We made the decision that we were going to live here as guests of Mexico and do things *their* way. A lot of the gringos in town, they want to fix this and sign petitions for that—the roads, the phones. We realize we're in a foreign country—we *really* realize it when we see police pickup trucks roll by with fourteen-year-old boys sitting in the back holding Uzis—yet we've never felt safer in our lives. Yes, we keep our doors locked at night, but as far as walking around at night . . . people are charming, gentle, completely unlike the image you get in the States. There's a *gentility* to the people around here that you don't find anywhere else that we've lived."

A man in a T-shirt called out, "*Hola* Rollie!"

"Armando, the town sheriff," Rollie said. "Also the constable and the judge. Also owns the town's liquor store."

It was another beautiful day. Rollie grinned. "Isn't it great? I spent my whole life in education, but here I've gone to school on my Mexican neighbors. So many of them are so much better off—and I don't mean financially—than people in the States. I'm still an American, still a patriot, but God, life is *so* good here."

We stayed for a month and met many of Sayulita's other gringos and Mexicans. We went out most nights to seafood or taco restaurants, listening to life stories, telling ours, making friends quickly, the way expats do. I found a poker game with a group of grizzled retirees with acerbic senses of humor. Thia met some smart women—a few living on their own. We traveled to neighboring villages. It seemed to us that there was something unusual in these towns, particularly in the way the Mexicans seemed to accept the Americans in their midst, and in the way Americans fell into the rhythms of the Mexican village life.

We knew that we were just seeing the surface, but we liked how people greeted each other, did their shopping, stopped to gossip. This was a prosperous, booming little place where there was plenty of work to go around, and it seemed unlike some other towns where rich Americans, gathered in enclaves, were serviced by poor Mexicans. Though most locals were working people, quite a few Mexicans here were land-rich, and though the town was changing, I felt there was an affable, if pecuniary, parity between the gringos and the Mexicans. And the interesting friction of a traditional culture rubbing up against a modern one.

Then we decided, for the fun of it, to let a real-estate broker show us some properties. To our surprise, and somewhat on impulse—no, *totally* on impulse—we bought a plot of land high on a steep hill above the town. When I say *bought,* I may be overstating the case. The owner had no doubt it was a sale, since he banked our wire transfer. But our New

York attorney, whom we informed on our return, was considerably less certain—no, he was *apoplectic*—because we paid for it in full and got no deed in return, just a power of attorney and a "legal promise" that it was ours. Not to worry. It was the way things were done around here; everything would work out fine.

A year later, on our way back to Mexico to build our home, we are certain that this is true. With one or two misgivings.

CHAPTER 3

On the Road ... Guadalupe and I ...
A Case of Remorse

Thia is on lesson twelve of the Spanish language CDs, and I am whistling "Ob-La-Di, Ob-La-Da" to distract myself, waiting for the drills to end so I can tune into the satellite channel that plays old-time classic radio shows. I stroke my sparse mustache, which I began to grow a couple of weeks ago. I am convinced it gives me a desirable touch of Pancho Villa bravado. The toll highway south of Laredo heading toward Monterrey is smooth and encourages speed. Outside, sagebrush, juniper trees, and arid plains stretch to the wide horizon. Montana's Big Sky is no bigger. Thia, who was born with the gift of zest, pauses the CD player every twenty minutes or so to eagerly point out a new sight—"Look at—!"—a patch of tiny yellow flowers, a field of planted purple maguey.

We also see the remains of a picnic come sailing out of the window of a car ahead of us. It's startling the first time it happens, as is the amount of trash that accumulates along the side of the road. It will take some getting used to for Thia, but it's interesting how quickly I assimilate the sight. Mexicans toss around quite a bit of litter on the highways, and it does not seem to bother anyone much. It did not bother Americans much either until the late fifties. What is interesting about Mexico is that this trash-friendly nonchalance coexists with the civic attitude of a Querétaro, the lovely colonial city of courtyards and wrought-iron balconies that we stopped in during our first trip. In its central neighborhoods, Querétaro is the cleanest city I have ever seen anywhere in the world. Uniformed sweepers are at work virtually all day, and its streets are as shiny and spotless as Disneyland's.

Tolls are steep—a stretch of one hundred miles can cost ten dollars—but the free roads, which sometimes run parallel to the toll highways, are much rougher and often clogged with trucks and buses driving ninety miles an hour. ("Why does a bus pass on the curve?" goes a joke one of my Mexican friends told me. "Because usually there's no one coming.") In the late afternoon, we pass a green van we recognize—one of the rescue vehicles known as "Green Angels," which patrol the roads constantly for drivers in distress. It's a free service, no membership required, and is a wonderfully reassuring sight. Before leaving Connecticut, on the advice of the online bulletin boards, I stocked up on extra air filters, oil filters, puncture kits, warning flares. But sailing along the well-maintained highways, with plenty of Pemex stations whizzing by, it's hard to know what the road paranoia is about. I never *did* feel it.

From 1952 to 1959, we lived in a pleasant neighborhood of Mexico City called Lomas de Chapultepec, populated mostly by Americans and middle-class Mexicans. Life in the Mexican capital then was a near paradise of clean blue skies, Sunday lunches in Xochimilco, and bougainvillea on the terrace. My father was the sales manager of a mining equipment firm, and I remember going with him, joyously, on business trips to northern Mexico in our old Ford. Though his salary was modest by stateside standards, my mother had a Studebaker and ran a household that included four children and a cook, maid, and gardener. The cook, Rita Gonzales, and the maid, María Luisa, her daughter, treated us like kids, not little masters, and we respected and loved them. We kids could drink the water out of the tap; our parents never could.

I attended the American School of Mexico, which had the enlightened policy of holding classes in Spanish until lunch, then in English the rest of the afternoon. Outside the school, we traded baseball cards and bought jicama spears with lemon and hot chile powder from the vendors waiting for us. Conversations with American and Mexican kids my age slipped seamlessly in and out of either language. I was in the Boy Scouts of Mexico with my friend Julio and an altar boy with my friend Enrique. I went to Mrs. Plum's dancing class to learn how to waltz with American girls my age; I also did the *jarabe tapatío* with my

younger sister for family visitors, who enjoyed the authenticity of seeing the Mexican hat dance performed by a red-headed girl of six and
her blond-haired brother of nine.

My birthday is December 12, which happens to be *el Día de
Guadalupe,* the holy day and feast day devoted to the Virgin Mary. It is
Mexico's most important religious holiday and is celebrated with fiestas, parades, solemn high masses, and fireworks in the *zócalos,* the main
squares and cathedrals, of every city and town in the country. My
mother always said she attributed my self-esteem entirely to the fact
that I awoke every birthday to the sounds and sights of an entire country celebrating, apparently in my honor.

Thia and I stop at a Pemex, one of Mexico's ubiquitous state-owned
petroleum stations, for gas and coffee. A uniformed attendant smiles
and waves me over to a pump. He points at the display to show us that
the peso counter is on zero. The travel websites alert you to a common
rip-off, by which attendants start fueling with the last gas purchase still
displayed to overcharge liter- and peso-addled gringos. This attendant
wants me to know this is an honest station, and I feel a little sorry that
he thinks he must. While he washes bug blat off the windows, I go in
for coffee. The girl gives me a cup of hot water and a packet of Nescafé.

As I pay for the gas, which has rung up a charge of almost 300 pesos,
I hand the attendant two bills: a 100-peso note and a 200-peso note. I
look away for the moment, and when I look back he is holding two
bills, but they are now the 100-peso note and a 20-peso note he has
substituted for the 200-peso bill. He stands there expectantly. Ah, too
bad, I sigh to myself, a scam after all. There's going to have to be a confrontation.

"I gave you a two-hundred bill," I say, pretty well, in Spanish. I point
to his pocket, where several large bills protrude.

He looks at his pocket, he looks at his hand, and he nods. Without
losing his poise, or in any way acknowledging that he has been caught,
he gives a friendly smile and steps aside for us to leave. It is mildly
unnerving, but the entire transaction is so matter-of-fact, so sweetly
unthreatening, so lacking in ill will, it is as if we both agree it was worth
a try, no hard feelings.

Not ten minutes later, when we are confused by a turnoff, we stop by a parked truck and ask for directions. An old gentleman, pulling at his mustache, begins telling us how to get back on the highway. Then he stops, gets into his truck, laboriously turns it around, and drives forward, waving for us to follow. It takes five more minutes before we are back to familiar ground, but he has hung in with us, and finally he points to an on-ramp. I try to get close to give him a tip, but he waves us away, shouting, *"Ándale!"*—Go along! The two incidents, so close together, are an early nudge to me that this country will resist easy generalizations.

As we come off the highway to drive through a couple of good-size towns, I become adept at Mexico's infamous right-for-left-turn, a major difference in driving customs. It is potentially fatal if you forget it: to turn left on highways and major avenues, you must first pull over to the right, onto a service road if available, and either wait for a traffic-light arrow or let traffic pass by before driving across the lanes. A left-hand car signal on a main road means, Pass me. The carnage can be spectacular.

People are helpful and friendly with advice and directions, and the dire warnings we have heard about police looking for payoffs, about cars being broken into at lunch stops, about hostile squeegee men at intersections, all fail to happen. A single gas station attendant, a palmed note, a smile—I have had worse taxi rides in Manhattan.

The car trip is not without its anxiety, however, and it is entirely of our own doing. We have a bad case of buyer's remorse. In the period of time it took us to decide to move down here, we began admitting to ourselves that we had severe second thoughts—not about the move, not about our plans, but about the property waiting for us. We had been warned about this by expatriate friends. Older hands have seen a *lot* of intermittent remorse.

Despite the fact that life in a Mexican retirement town is by definition low stress, the expats say there is a recognizable kind of gringo who can, at any given moment, be recognized walking along the streets, staring at the cobblestones, muttering aloud, clenching and unclenching his fists. Chances are, he is swearing at himself for taking the first price offered, for accepting the blandishments of a real-estate broker, for leaving his brains at the border, for agreeing to take legal documents he would not have accepted in the States, for—let's face it!—for *throwing their life's savings down an iguana hole!* Perfectly normal. Happens to everybody.

Still, we have good reason. The more we thought about why we were coming down to live in Sayulita, the more we realized it had to do with the desire to be a part of village life. Yet we had chosen a piece of land in splendid isolation high above the village, on a hill no one else had yet built on. We must have thought we were fated to own it.

. During our earlier reporting trip, on the day we arrived, we were driving around in our rented VW, and on the north end of town we noticed a very steep cobblestone hill that climbed up to . . . nothing. The road apparently had been built for future use by a developer with land to sell—no public-works road would ever be built at such a steep angle. We drove the VW up the road, tires spinning a couple of times, and turned around at the top.

"I wonder who owns this?" I said.

"Somebody lucky," said Thia. We stood there, sunstruck, inhaling the high breeze and taking in the arc of the sea and the jungle below.

So when, a couple of weeks later, accompanying our friendly real-estate broker, a highly talkative, highly bald Canadian named Harvey Craig, we found ourselves being shown that very parcel of land, we decided it was kismet. We had come upon it originally ourselves, it happened to be available, and now we had the opportunity of a lifetime. *This* is where we would build the sweeping terrace, *there* is where the infinity pool would go, and over there, at the cliff, we would have an outside shower done in fine Mexican tiles. Someday.

Now, speeding down the highway, that fantasy has flown. The reality is that we will be arriving in our new home town as owners (well, with a *promise* that we will be owners) of a piece of property unsuited for us. Besides the prohibition against foreign ownership of coastal property—it must be held in trust by a bank—this piece of land was until just a year ago part of the *ejido*, the system of communal ownership designed to keep land in Mexican hands. Now it is "regularized," meaning a trust can be purchased in one's own name, though the process was not completed when we bought it. We had a *compraventa*, a binding contract from our seller and an irrevocable power of attorney, but we did not yet have the bank trust certificate.

Besides its unorthodox documentation, it is too far from the village for us; when it rains, it requires a four-wheel-drive car to get up its near-vertical approach road; it would be expensive to build up there; we would have to build retaining walls just to get started. Who *exactly* thought this was such a good idea? The discussion is taken up in the car once again. Didn't every guidebook, didn't good sense say that we should have rented before we bought? Wasn't it true, really, that one of us had persuaded the other to buy? And wasn't that person, really, my wife, who had been perhaps quite a bit more eager than I, and hadn't *that* tipped our decision? My wife's recollection differs, which she makes clear as she points out to me, not unreasonably, that I am a blithering idiot.

We drive on, stop our Lucy-and-Ricky bickering, and spend the night at a motel near Aguascalientes. It is a so-called no-tell motel, which lets us into a locked, enclosed parking area, offers complete privacy, hourly rates, round beds, and porn on television. We didn't know at first what we were checking into, but it turns out that these motels are highly secure havens to sleep over with an SUV filled with stuff, as well as adding a dash of local spice. Listed on the room-service menu, besides enchilada dinners, liquors, and toothpaste and toothbrushes, are such useful items as "soft lube" and Viagra—fifteen dollars a packet, no prescriptions needed. Certainly, the women in purple eye shadow, exposed lace bras, and three-inch heels entering and leaving with their Mexican male friends are a break from the usual travelers we see. As I survey the scene outside our bedroom in the corridor, my wife tells me, again not unreasonably, to pull my head back inside the door. We watch some stimulating television together.

As we head south and west the next morning toward Guadalajara, we circle Mexico's second-largest city with surprising ease. We used taxis the last time we were here, but I find the driving better marked, and less intimidating than I expected. A couple of hours west, on the road toward the Pacific Coast, following the signs for Tepic and Puerto Vallarta, the jungle begins to creep up. The foliage has changed to lush tropical forest, as fields of mango trees alternate with pineapple groves and jungle palms.

We are about to enter the small state of Nayarit, which, along with the coastal region of Jalisco, contains one of Mexico's most unusual environmental anomalies: a one-hundred-mile stretch of dense jungle growth, the first truly tropical stretch south of the United States, the only one before the equatorial rain forests of Central and South America. Here can be found wild parrots and jaguars and wild orchids and boa constrictors. Not to mention gringos clearing their yards with machetes.

We are now on Mexico's main north-south coastal road, route 200, which will take us past San Blas, and then to Las Varas, La Peñita, Rincón de Guayabitos, and finally San Pancho and Sayulita. We have put aside our property fears for now, and I get to choose what we listen to on satellite radio. And while that moment back on the Mississippi— the one we shared with Mark Twain—was planned, this one happens just by chance: on the channel devoted to old-time radio serials, we tune in just as the Cisco Kid is being chased, along with his sidekick Pancho ("Ehhhh, Ceesco!"), by a band of nasty bandidos, and the two of them are galloping away to the safety of their mountain hideaway. For which, I can only assume, Pancho owns the deed.

CHAPTER 4

Arrival in the Dust . . .
The Zen of Garbage . . . Way out of Africa

Sayulita's charms are more apparent at second than at first sight. Though it enjoys a splendid location on a curved sand beach surrounded by ruffled green hills, it can seem like a scruffy kind of place when first approached from the highway. The one-mile road to the village is lined by litter, a tire shed, a cantina—that is, a legal whorehouse—and a number of unimproved homes and stores. As we rattle our way over the small bridge into town, onto its streets, which are a mixture of cobblestone, packed dust, and shock-shattering ruts, it is clear that this is a town under massive, unrelenting construction. There is a large mound of dirt from a sewer dig piled up by an intersection, upon which an old pickup truck has parked, its hood sticking straight up into the air. It looks a lot like the one that was here when we left last. There are bricks and blocks and gravel and mounds of cement everywhere.

Little Sayulita has been discovered and is bursting like an overripe mango. Since we were here, it has been written up in the *New York Times,* in other big newspapers, in magazines. Just a few weeks before we leave, *Entertainment Weekly* puts Sayulita on its "In" list without saying where it is or identifying it in any way. And then there was that retirement article in *AARP*. Our emails from friends and real-estate agents informed us that prices have spiked in the last year as scores of retired or near-retired people stumbled into town looking for property to buy. It is a stretch to call it the "quiet little fishing village" described in even the most recent guidebooks.

Sayulita is a young town. Forty years ago it was a group of thatched-roof palapas along a river that emptied into a cove, with a few hundred inhabitants who made their living mostly as fishermen and farmers. It got its name from a rich general from Sayula, Jalisco, who adopted it as his beach getaway, and began calling it little Sayula. It had five main families who were the powers in the Sayulita ejido, and whose many interrelated descendants still run things behind the scenes. Indeed, almost all the Mexicans in this town seem to be related.

Bumping down the Avenida de la Revolución, past the *Borracho* Tree, the Drunk Tree, where older Mexican gentlemen quench their thirst while watching the parade jolting by, we see women outside their stores misting the dusty street with hoses trailing out their doors. On the right, a small open-air market of tents and trinkets, with tables set up to sell handcrafted jewelry and gewgaws. Annie Bananie, a blonde Canadian *gringa* with an overbite and a quick line of patter, sells her own handmade jewelry, and is in the same spot in which we saw her last. She waves, apparently recognizing us. On the left, right next to a new antique store, the first of the town's many casual eateries that spill out onto the streets. It is known as Red Chairs because most other restaurants use the familiar white plastic chairs. (The invention of these ubiquitous stackable chairs created its own little revolution in Mexico. New restaurants spring up at a moment's notice, and in Sayulita there are dining establishments of one table and two plastic chairs outside houses that serve literally home-cooked meals.)

The streets are host to an astonishing number of dogs, not all of them scrupulously groomed, who lie about snoozing or scratching themselves. Drivers in town do not brake for animals; the assumption is that the dogs in this town are professionals and should know how to avoid moving wheels. ("There are no dumb dogs left in Sayulita," a Mexican friend told us.) A chicken darts out in front of our car, pursued by a rooster. A child darts out in front of our car on a plastic scooter, pursued by her sister. Cars and SUVs, many dusty and beat-up, are parked haphazardly. On the sidewalk, a horse is tethered to the clasp of someone's front gate.

There are the usual grocery stores, real-estate agencies (five of them on or just off the main street), a dental clinic (with a sign showing a big pair of juicy red lips and large teeth), a couple of pharmacies ("free medical consultation!"), uncountable signs for yoga, massage, or whatever-therapy, and a good number of restaurants. Nothing out of the ordinary. It is only as the street reaches the town's broad, open square that a visitor might begin to suspect Sayulita has something else going for it.

The plaza is a mix of curved concrete benches, and planted palms with a bandstand in the middle, and definitely not the usual sleepy town square. It is, even in the late weekday morning of our arrival, packed with people passing through, milling about, sitting on benches. It is a curious blend, not easily characterized: tourist couples in cargo shorts; blond surfer dudes and dudettes carrying long boards; a couple of Mexican fishermen toting their mahimahi catch in a basket between them; teenage girls in bikinis and Teva sandals; a dignified Huichol Indian man in his embroidered costume; Mexican kids with blond-streaked hair setting off small firecrackers; a sleek city couple, probably from Mexico City, in matching gold lamé beach wear; rumpled gringo seniors in comfortable cutoffs; schoolchildren in maroon-and-white uniforms; a pony-tailed guy with an iPod wired into his ears, obliviously swaying through the crowd to his own beat.

La Hamaca, a posh arts and crafts store with a floor of soft sand, is just off the plaza, and next to it is Choco Banana, the breakfast and luncheon shop, "a tradition since 1991." There are no fewer than four ice cream shops and, since we were last here, a sleek, new delicatessen, and a couple of new Internet cafés have sprung up. Gentrification is in full, artificial-flower bloom, but, *gracias a Dios,* there are enough funky local Mexican stores and roadside vendors, not to mention dust and dog droppings, to keep it from going over the edge into chic.

Rising behind the square is the unique topography that makes Sayulita, at last, so appealing: within a bowl created where the jungle slides into the sea, perched upon steep hills ringing the town, is a profusion of homes, many created in a distinctive style of curved white concrete and palm-frond roofs, with bougainvillea and hibiscus spilling over terraces. It is a kind of sylvan amphitheater, with the hillside houses as box seats surrounding the plaza stage. Just down the street, a couple of dusty blocks away, is the Pacific.

It's been a long ride from the chilly East Coast; we want a brief moment at the warm beach before heading to our rental apartment. November is early in the season for this region; though the plaza is full, the sand today is sparsely dotted with umbrellas and sunbathers. A number of fishing boats draped with nets are beached toward one end. Pelicans and frigate birds wheel over the crescent bay, sweeping low over a dozen surfers waiting for waves at a neat surf break about fifty yards out. We recognize a couple of friends on the beach, but keep quiet, taking in the scene. Just then, a man on horseback with a droopy mustache and a cowboy hat appears carrying a child on the saddle in front of him. His horse is cantering along the water's edge, hoofs splashing through the shallow surf, and the man is singing a *canción ranchera*, joyfully.

We're back.

We head up past the plaza toward our rental apartment. We run into Mike Scannell, one of the guys from the twice-weekly poker game I joined during our first visit here. He is a land developer from Washington State who moved to the village and is—like many others—in the thick of buying, building, renovating. He has a deep chocolate tan, wears the regulation shorts and T-shirt, and has curly brown hair that makes him look a decade younger than his sixty-some years.

"Hey, welcome back, Thia! Who's that with you? A *pistolero*?"

Ah, excellent. My Villa mustache.

"Just be sure you bring money to the game," I say. "I want it all."

I may get it, too, as I recall. Mike, who has an easy way about him, signals the hands he holds by clicking his chips when he is about to bluff. We ask about families, about who's in town, who's coming later. We agree to meet at dinner during this, our first week.

Up a dirt road is our temporary home, an apartment a couple of blocks off the square. We will be living on Calle Niños Héroes, a name that a gringo resident must conjure with from history: the boy heroes were the military cadets of the Castle of Chapultepec who threw themselves to their deaths rather than surrender to the invading U.S. troops during the War of 1846, which resulted in the annexation of about half of Mexico.

As for us, we come in peace.

The real-estate frenzy has made rentals as well as purchases pricey by Mexican standards, but we got lucky. We had been emailing Jeanne and Rollie Dick, and they told us about a rare find: a two-bedroom apartment in town owned by an absent American friend at a reasonable long-term monthly rent. With an equally rare rental bonus, a working telephone! Our plan is to live there while we build our own house; the one, I am anxiously reminded, that is literally and figuratively up in the air.

*   *   *

We're settled in; the garbage bags are neatly tucked away, the SUV is already gathering a film of dust outside. The apartment has a pleasant living and dining room with a Mexican-tiled kitchen attached, a terrace overlooking dense jungle foliage just twenty feet away, and oversized bedrooms. Outside, we feel the remainder of fall weather in these parts—hot, muggy, moist—while inside, the whirring ceiling fans keep the rooms cool and dry.

Thia is a nester and in a short afternoon has given our rental apartment the feeling that we have lived there a while: brightly colored cushions and a serape draped on the couch and chairs; a mosaic-edged Mexican mirror she has found now hanging in the hall; sprigs of tulipana in a jar on the table. I take off with a list of staples. There is a small grocery store a couple of hundred yards from our apartment.

I introduce myself in my jagged Spanish and tell the store proprietor, a round-faced woman in an apron, Sandra, that we are not tourists.

"We will be living here, down the street. We are *vecinos*," neighbors.

"Qué bueno, qué bueno," she says, beaming. *"Bienvenidos."* Her store is the front room of a cement-block house; her kids dart in and out through a curtain separating living room from storefront. She has modest amounts of a wide range of fruits and fresh vegetables. Avocados, which cost two dollars the last time I bought them in Connecticut, are twenty cents apiece. Oranges are six cents apiece. As I leave with a bagful of groceries, she says, *"Que le vaya bien,"* which is unique to Mexico, and as common as "Have a nice day" in the States, but sounds more heartfelt. What it seems to mean to me, loose translation: "May your life turn out really well."

I linger outside our apartment, putting a tarpaulin on top of the car. Dust begins settling on the car's finish almost immediately; there are workers upstairs, finishing off a second story, spattering cement about with abandon and cheery curses. A short man with wiry black hair and an enormous beach ball of a belly walks over to help me adjust the tarp. He is our next-door neighbor, and he introduces himself as Gaby, Gabriel Ponce Muñoz, a construction worker. He has the habit, common in these parts, of rolling up the front of his T-shirt to pat his ample stomach contentedly. He is curious about us, and not the least bit formal, which makes it easy. He has a wife and small daughter, and his parents, he tells me, live next door to him in their own very modest home. Above his door is a religious inscription, and there is a chatty parrot in a cage hanging from a window.

"Señor Gaby," I say in my hesitant Spanish. "Can you tell me about *basura*—garbage? How often do they come by?"

He rubs his belly and thinks for a minute. He says, "Three times a week, but . . ." At this point, another neighbor, a woman from across the street, happens by with a friend and overhears. She says Monday, Wednesday, and Friday are the days. Another older woman from the small house several doors away is intrigued by the conversation, and volunteers that Tuesdays and Saturdays are equally good days to try. Gaby's opinion is expressed by arched, what-do-you-expect? eyebrows and a shrug that says this is a question to which there may well be no answer. It turns out the garbage collection schedule, while thorough, is as elastic as many other time-sensitive activities. People don't get upset about it, apparently; they live with it. Gaby tells us about his work-around, which is to take his stuff down to a larger street in the early morning of any weekday, because on that street the collectors come by "some days, for certain." Mexicans, we are to learn, are masters of the work-around.

It is later that afternoon, and I am out on the terrace. Thia comes out of the apartment with a puzzled look.

"The water's off. What do we do now?"

"I'll check with the neighbors," I say, and go outside to rejoin the people I had met, many of whom are still in front of their homes, talking.

"Our water is off," I say. "Is it just us, or is it the town?"

This sets off a new group discussion with various proposals being put forth. One woman says it may be because of our construction, but then again maybe it is not. Another says her water is off too, and not to worry, because this happens all the time. The water will come back on by itself.

"When?"

Another excellent question, worthy of philosophical shrugs all around. Gaby gives his belly an extra pat and eyes me. This new gringo neighbor of his is going to keep things hopping. I look to the side of our apartment, where workers are mixing cement. In the States, a water turnoff would mean that the union guys take a contractual break until the authorities do their part. I don't think Mexicans, who have a long history and excellent reason for distrusting the system, wait for authorities to do much. The workers here have formed a short bucket brigade to a nearby creek and are passing up pails of water for the cement. The work, and the work-around, goes on.

The problem for Thia is her hair. It is dank and dusty, and she would very much like to wash it. But without water . . .

We look around the apartment and see that the only water available is in one of the huge plastic bottles of purified water that are ubiquitous in Mexico. They are blue tinted, and they rest upside down in a plastic stand with a simple faucet on the side. They can be bought for about $1.50, and you swap your empty bottle for a full one. Upending it into the stand is a learned craft: you tear off a plastic cap, grasp it from the bottom and at its throat, and in one practiced swing, you propel the five-gallon bottle into the opening of the stand as the water begins to pour out, hoping this won't be the time that you misjudge   leaving you with a huge puddle of water on the floor. With good aim, a kind of vacuum is formed, the bottle gives a mighty glug, and stasis is achieved as the plastic stand and the upside-down bottle precariously become one.

There is about a tenth of the bottle left.

"I need it," says Thia. "I can use what's there, and then you can go get us a new one at the place down the street."

My wife leans over the sink and flips her hair forward. I now have to reverse the usual procedure and swing a nonempty bottle out of its perch over to a point above my wife's head, and pour . . . gently, so it doesn't just wash the soap away.

Thia makes a moaning sound.

"What is it?" I grunt, the bottle swaying as I try to keep it trickling out and positioned just right.

"Remember the hair-washing scene in *Out of Africa*? Meryl Streep and Robert Redford up by that gorgeous waterfall? Redford scoops a gourd into the water and washes her hair himself? And remember how he rubs her scalp sensuously, intimately, as she just holds her head back and lets herself go in ecstasy?"

I tell her that I believe that I was out getting popcorn during that scene. I let the last of the water pour out, leave my wife with her hair hanging ecstatically into the sink, and walk out carrying the empty bottle. Shortly, I return from the store, now carrying a full bottle over my shoulder, the wildebeest I bring back in triumph from the hunt, my prize from the wild, sensuous Mexican savanna. My woman awaits.

That evening, fresh from our water shortage frolic, we go over to Rollie and Jeanne's. Hugs all around. Both Thia and Jeanne are exuberant, and jump up and down like schoolgirls. Rollie and I are guys, so we har-rumph and clap each other on the back. We go to dinner, across the bridge to the northern part of the village, which is quieter, less jumpy. We sit down at an outdoor palapa restaurant called Terrazola, where Onton, the owner, brings out a sizzling platter of mahimahi, cooked in butter and garlic with a dash of *salsa picante*. We talk about our trip down, about Rollie's plans for his new nighttime restaurant, about the newest gossip. A plan for Thia to help out at the restaurant at night, which will be fun and draw us into the town's life, is nailed down. The waves lap at the shore a few yards away, and an orange November sun sets over the hill across the bay.

CHAPTER 5

Iguanas and Orange Juice . . .
Doña Lety . . . A Grave Decision

The next morning dawns to a chorus of roosters competing from one end of the village to the other. The one under our window lets loose, then a cock from down the street responds, then one from up the hill, and so on, ricocheting back to our own bantam, who is not about to let the crowing go unanswered. But there's something else: it's not yet seven, and the harsh vibration of jackhammers starts, right on top of us. Our landlady warned us about the floor she was building above us, and one reason we got a good deal is that her crew will be busy till Christmas, six weeks away.

It's all right: we came down for the life, not isolated tranquillity. That is why, talking about it late last night, we have definitely decided to sell our hilltop lot. We ought to be able to get a good price for it. Then we can begin thinking about purchasing a new lot closer to town for our permanent home; *that* will be a challenge in a frenzied market.

We get up, put on our shorts and sandals—the only clothes we intend to wear in the daytime from now on—and head for a morning walk and swim. We take the back way to Playa de los Muertos, the insider's beach in Sayulita, so named because it cuts through a graveyard now festooned with colorful wreaths, plastic-wrapped floral bouquets, and votive candles—the Day of the Dead is just past. There is a gravestone of one gringo who died here: "Woody: Gone Surfing." The beach is deserted, and the waves this morning are calm and cool. It is our first morning swim on the first morning of our new life. We run into the surf holding hands, looking, I'm certain, like a suntan-lotion commercial for the pre-golden-years crowd.

Back in the apartment, I squeeze a half dozen oranges, Thia fries up some huevos rancheros, and we sit down on the terrace. It looks directly onto jungle growth, a canopy of palms and mangoes and thick underbrush. As we dig in, we look up. Not one, but two iguanas are making their way along a palm frond. There's a brightly colored, big ugly guy, resplendent in shades of green and yellow, shaking his wattle, his head straining up to the sun. Behind him, a smaller, grayer one, clearly his significant other. They will become regulars. As one sun-seeking couple to another, we name them Iggy Pop and Iggy Mom. Corny, but we're not in Manhattan anymore, and that makes our humor more accessible. *We* think it's funny, anyway.

We have to make a quick trip this morning into Puerto Vallarta, forty-five minutes away, and we are on the two-lane mountain highway that winds through the thick tropical forest, past colorful little shrines to dead motorists, toward our appointment with a financial officer at Lloyd's, the investment firm most Americans use. Lloyd's specializes in keeping funds in dollar accounts for Americans and Canadians who are afraid that the peso will plummet.

That a bank appointment is one of our first chores speaks to the challenge of staying solvent in this part of the country: there are no ATMs in Sayulita or San Pancho. As we found when we were here last, virtually everything is done in cash—only a few restaurants will take credit cards—and that means foraging down the jungle road pretty regularly to hunt and gather ATM pesos. The nearest machine is in Bucerias, the closest midsize town to us, on the highway to Vallarta. It's really the only way to get spending money in Mexico, since the exchange rate is the best available.

A few kilometers before Bucerias, where the highway widens to four lanes, we roll to a stop at a speed bump and stare out the window at a couple of young soldiers in dark green uniforms cradling automatic rifles. There are signs in Spanish and English advising us that this is a military checkpoint. Drugs are presumably the target here, but drivers in private cars are rarely pulled over. Trucks and buses are sometimes flagged for a thorough check, though what the efficiency rate must be is hard to tell. As I will learn, the soldiers are regularly off duty, and it seems that for a *narcotraficante,* it can't be too great a mental burden to pull off and wait till the soldiers leave for a break or retire to their barracks at night. With the inspectors putting in bankers' hours, this is not what I would call bulletproof interdiction.

We are waved through and a few miles beyond pull over to the pockmarked service road in Bucerias. Finding a spot, I park and stand in a motley line of Mexican laborers and sleek gringo matrons, and wait my turn at the dingy but highly popular ATM. Most days it dispenses all the working cash for three towns, except when it does not. I pocket my pesos, ten and change to the dollar, and we take off again through the jarring potholes that take us back to the highway.

We will need more than an ATM can dispense when we are ready to build our house. This must be done, we are told, entirely in cash, including architects, labor, and materials. So with the prospect that we will be building on *some* sort of lot in the near future, we are opening our Lloyd's account now, to give the paperwork time to clear. Though wire transfers work fine, a personal check on a U.S. bank deposited in your Mexico account can take eight weeks to clear.

To reach Vallarta, we must leave the state of Nayarit, and set our watches ahead one hour. This business of switching time zones every time we make a shopping trip or a visit to a doctor, I will find, can be maddening. When friends or family fly down to visit, the schedules are always on Vallarta time, and we residents of Nayarit must calculate not only our driving time but the time-zone difference. The arrivals terminal in Puerto Vallarta always has at least a few passengers out on the sidewalk, sitting on their suitcases, with puzzled looks on their faces.

We pull in at the Vallarta branch office on the outskirts of the city and inside are introduced to Rosie Rubio, a thin young woman in a trim uniform with serviceable English and a wide smile. She helpfully explains the bank's policies to us as we make arrangements to wire transfer money from our New York account. She tells us about the various funds, foremost among them the dollar account, which offers 1 or 2 percent in interest—it's the safest for Americans queasy about devaluation—and the liquid pesos account, which offers a more attractive 5 or 6 percent. (At this time, U.S. banks are offering about 1 percent in the money market.) I inquire about one of the other funds.

"Oh, that is our stock fund," Rosie Rubio says. "It invests in Mexican stocks."

"What types of stocks?"

"All—how you say—blue chips. Excellent, but the yield, it varies very much."

"What is the current yield?" I ask.

She looks it up on her computer screen. "Up sixty-seven percent, annualized. But the yield, it varies *very* much."

On the drive back to Sayulita, Thia says, "I *know* what you're thinking."

"What?"

"Don't even *dare*. I know every line you'll use."

So sad. To dismiss my argument for a *surefire 67 percent profit,* without a hearing. Is this the beginning of too much togetherness?

Back in Sayulita, we take our first afternoon stroll through town. We stop at a window in a wall where a sign says, Doña Lety's, advertising *tortas*—hot sandwiches on a soft roll—and fruit drinks. She is a stout woman with a pleasant face and intelligent eyes. She works out of the front room of her home and hands out the orders on a shelf over the sidewalk. We order a couple of tortas and introduce ourselves.

"A great pleasure," she says in Spanish. "Will you be staying here a while?"

We're pleased again to say that we are residents.

"Ah," she says. "Someday soon, Mexicans—" she waves a hand northward "—all up to *El Norte,* and Americans—" a wave in the other direction "—all down here."

I'm going to like Doña Lety. If I have heard a more cogent take on the dynamics of immigration between our two countries, I don't know of it.

Munching our tortas, we walk past a realty office where we first were gripped by land fever, the impulse to buy that led us to our present quandary. We look idly at the flyers advertising real estate. Inside, the office is packed with visitors in shorts. The first flyer we see is for a walled lot, and the picture shows an attractive large, black iron gate surmounted by a small tile roof.

"I recognize that," Thia said. "It's on the north side, by the school."

"You want to start looking already? We've got months."

"It will be a nice walk."

It is about a seven-minute walk from downtown. The lot is surrounded by a tall, thick hacienda-style wall, and the gate is even more imposing. It is a block from the beach. It is a tidy size, about six thousand square feet. This lot has no view that I can tell; there are two groups of two-story bungalows on the beach side of the street and very tall palms in the way. It is an attractive location, but it makes me soften a bit toward our hilltop albatross, not far away on the north side, with its cardiac climb and panoramic view. That was, after all, part of the original dream.

"What did the flyer say this was going for?"

Thia remembers, and I whistle.

"My God, they weren't exaggerating. The prices have gone nuts. We got twice as much land up there for less than that."

"A year ago."

"Yeah, well. It just goes to show we're going to have to be smart about how we sell our lot and smart about what we buy this time. That's our advantage. We can take our time, speak to people in Spanish, learn to bargain. We're not on vacation, and we're not flying off somewhere, for once."

We decide to put off real estate for another day, another week. By American big-city standards, real estate here is still cheap. Land on or near a beach is prohibitive in the States, but local Mexicans, until recently, couldn't be bothered with seaside property. Too hot, no grass for the cattle, no room for a hacienda, bad for plaza life. Mountains and valleys, that was where the pesos were. That has been changing, especially since the gringos began coming down. So, for an American enamored of living near the beach, it's still cheaper down here but not as cheap as it was. In Sayulita, it's more than that.

We walk back to town and stop several more times to greet people we already know. It was part of what charmed us the first time we were here: everybody is out and about in Sayulita, and a stroll—even one with a purpose—hardly ever goes by without several stopovers. On the bridge, we run into Señor Gonzales, an elderly gent who wears a huge straw hat, has strong Indian features, and looks like a character out of *Treasure of the Sierra Madre*. He runs the local laundry and remembers Thia.

A bit farther on we run into Ian and Kerry Hodge, a young couple from Oregon, formerly in software, who came down a few years ago to live and make their fortune. They were working at a real-estate office here, where we first met them, and showed us a number of lots that we did not take. Kerry, a striking blonde, ran the rentals department and Ian, tall and rangy, sold the land with American-style hustle. He had helped me put together our deal, though he asked if Thia and I *really* wanted to climb that hill. They were fair and friendly with us, and we like them. We make plans to meet for dinner tonight. That's how dinner dates get made here—on the way to somewhere.

Mike Scannell pops up again by the plaza. We stop for coffee with him at Choco Banana, and tell him about our first day so far. He knows about the land we bought, and when we tell him we are going to look to sell it, he is surprised.

"Are you going to buy somewhere else?"

"After we've really looked over what's out here, yes."

"Where?"

"In town, or a quick walk. Near the beach."

Mike shakes his head back and forth slowly.

"What?" I ask.

"There's nothing left by the beach. Everything's been snapped up. Everything else is overpriced. Keep your place. The walk up that ridiculous hill will make you strong."

I want to tell him that at my age, everything that does not make me stronger will kill me. I say, "Well, the only thing we happened to look at today *is* by the beach. That walled lot?"

Mike nods; he knows it.

"And you're right, it's overpriced," I say.

"No it's not," he says. "Not by today's standards. And it's the *only* property left a block from the beach. I know, because I've heard that several people are interested in it. It just went on the market. It'll go like *that.*"

A shame about the timing. We first have to find a buyer for our property, and after that we are going to do what the books all advise, what we should have done the first time: rent before we buy. Thia and I walk back to the apartment, disheartened and jittery. Though the news is apparently good for sellers, it's tough for buyers. If we take our time and get a good price for the hilltop lot and expend the same effort to find a new lot, maybe we can find something decent. But it will take a careful investigation to find a good purchase in this atmosphere. And we have come down here to construct our dream house affordably. We are back at the beginning, only with higher real-estate values, in some part a direct cause of my *AARP* article. Ah, I thought we had left real-estate fever—and irony—back in Manhattan.

Over dinner at the Sayulita Café, chiles rellenos all around, we catch up with Ian and Kerry. Since we saw them, they have left the real-estate office and started another business. Using his old software skills, Ian has created a website, SayulitaLife.com, that posts news and information, and does a good business matching—what else?—real-estate sellers directly with buyers. It cuts out the middlemen, the real-estate agencies, so Ian admits he may not be the most popular guy in town with them.

We tell them about our plans. I'm going to be writing freelance articles, and Thia will be helping out with Rollie's new nighttime restaurant. We will travel around Mexico, get to know the country, figure out if we like semiretirement.

"Well, we retired at thirty and never looked back," Ian says. "Wouldn't do it any other place. We love it here."

"Some retirement. You're both entrepreneurs."

"That's what I mean: retirement—lots of work."

I compliment him on his website. He tells me the sellers love it; they pay a fee to post their ad and do not pay a broker. He occasionally takes a fee for handling the challenging paperwork. He was smart enough to realize that most Americans are daunted by the legalities in buying or selling land in Mexico, especially near the coast, and learned his way around the system. He says he is about to handle the technicalities for a sale by an American woman who has a choice parcel of land, a walled lot—

"A walled lot?" I say.

"A walled lot?" Thia says.

Ian says that the woman bought it for two-thirds its current price about a year and a half ago, it's about the only reasonable lot near the beach, and there have been two or three serious inquiries, offers, what-have-you—

"Offers?" I say.

For asking price, he says, and wonders why we're so interested.

Thia and I look each other. We have lived together for thirty-five years. As she often notes, when I am thinking about something, she generally knows exactly what I am thinking about. As a member of the male species, I am less sure what she is thinking, and I am especially not sure now. It can't be. We're *not* thinking the same desperate, ridiculous thing, are we?

We've come down here to live; we regretted the first time when we bought something on the spur of the moment. We're prepared to take our time this round, to investigate, to find a bargain, to live on our diminished means in this affordable country. We cannot possibly buy anything until we sell the first lot, because if we did, we'd have to pay for it all in cash, of course, and be tapped out and be unable to build until we sold the first lot, which might—*might*—be a pig in a poke. To say nothing of what might happen if in the meantime the peso fell or the market tumbled or bodies of narcotraficantes started washing up on Sayulita's lovely shores. So after less than twenty-four hours in our promised land, we're not thinking exactly the same thing, are we?

Dessert is a particularly good version of flan—all desserts in Mexico appear to be versions of flan—but I am not in a mood to savor it. Without saying more than a few words to each other in a whisper, Thia and I have told Ian that somewhat on impulse—no, *completely* on impulse— we have decided to buy the lot. We ask him to call the owner and tell her we will meet her asking price and wire her a down payment the next day. Ian is amused by this, but not surprised. He has seen it all before. The boomers are coming, and he is there to receive them. Another member of Generation X getting rich on his elders. He agrees to call her. We have coffee, strong.

So ends our first full day in paradise, in a land where no one is in a hurry, where everything can be put off, where a couple of our age and temperament has semiretired to take it easy, to live off the quiet wisdom we have learned and earned. And here we have gone and bought before we rented—*twice*. I am a wreck. I am clenching and unclenching my fists. The cobblestones slap against the soles of my sandals on the way home, and I trip on the front step and fracture my toe in two places.

CHAPTER 6

We Go to a Doctor . . .
Gaby the Blowfish . . . Getting It

My middle toe, which was twisted at a right angle over my fourth, must be attended to. Because of the trauma, it did not hurt that much last night. I wrenched the toe back into position and fell asleep to nightmares of a walled lot pressing in on me. But it is morning now, and it hurts. Thia makes a phone call to our friends Barb and Bill and finds that my best bet is to drive to San Pancho, fifteen minutes away, and check into the emergency room of the clinic there.

We call ahead, and the San Pancho emergency-room doctor is not in yet, just an attending nurse. When will he arrive? "Soon," we are told. We figure early afternoon at the soonest, and I try to walk. It is a serious fracture, obviously, and I cannot walk without support. I look around, and I see only my golf clubs. I extract two irons, hold them by the blades, and begin to hobble around with some success.

We spend the rest of the morning making calls about the walled lot, lining up the wire transfer, conferring with Ian. By noon the pain is too much, and we drive over to San Pancho. We arrive at a long one-story building with a couple of dusty ambulances outside. The doctor is in, a friendly man with a casual manner. He says it is probably a severe break and points me toward the X-ray room, to which I hobble, still gripping my golf irons. No crutches here, unfortunately. My X-rays are taken by a nurse-technician wearing a uniform consisting, for unknown reasons, of white hip-huggers and backless stiletto heels.

When I get back with the X-rays (in Mexico, you own the film and must take it with you wherever you go), the doctor confirms the double toe fracture and says I will have to wear a cast and stay off my feet, and away from sand, water, or cobblestones, for three to five weeks. I have taken exactly one swim in Sayulita's waters.

We pay at a cashier. No question of insurance here, of course. Cost for the X-rays, the medical attention, and the cast: thirty-eight dollars.

We haven't yet gone over for a real visit to Bill and Barbara's or John and Judi's, our B-and-B friends in San Pancho. I cannot now, because the steps to their house are too steep for me. But over the phone, after happy greetings and condolences, they recommend a Dr. Mauro Malja in Bucerias. He treats all the Americans, speaks English, and is widely respected. We make an appointment to meet him for a follow-up to my emergency care.

As we've learned, health is much discussed among expatriates. I already have a positive view of medical and dental care in Mexico. On our first trip here, I came down with severe pain in my gums, where a molar had been extracted. On the recommendation of Rollie, I drove into Puerto Vallarta and was examined by a dentist in a gleaming new suite of offices, as up-to-date with digital X-rays as my dentist's office on Madison Avenue. He diagnosed bone slivers working their way up through my gum, and said I would have to have oral surgery to get them out. A specialist from Guadalajara came through once every two weeks, he said, if I could wait that long. I said I was in pain. Without hesitation, he began the procedure himself.

I had only one uncomfortable moment: as he was slicing away some gum, I heard him murmur to himself cheerfully in Spanish, "I don't get to do this much." By the time I left his office, I was feeling better. The bill for the diagnosis and an hour's oral surgery session was one hundred dollars. When I went home to the States and checked in with my superb New York dentist, he looked it over and pronounced it a job well done.

We researched medical care in Mexico before driving down and came to a couple of conclusions. Generally, the quality of medical care is good, and so we were prepared to rely on it. Guadalajara has first-class care and facilities, and Puerto Vallarta has several decent hospitals and a good number of big-city-trained, English-speaking doctors. Locally, in the small villages, care is far more rudimentary. Sayulita has a small government-sponsored clinic, as do most villages in Mexico, often staffed by a recent medical school graduate doing a term of "service." These *saludes,* or health clinics, are very plain affairs, but they provide basic treatment not always seen in small localities of more prosperous countries. The San Pancho clinic is several notches above that.

As to insuring ourselves, Barb and Bill told us earlier that they did not feel it necessary to sign up for Mexico's national health service. Barb had looked into private insurance in Mexico and found it reasonable—several hundred dollars a year—with one hitch: Bill, who had a couple of prior conditions, was ineligible. But after tending Barb's sick father down here, they found that out-of-pocket medical costs, even for serious procedures, were very reasonable. So Barb signed up for private Mexican insurance and said they were keeping "a reserve" of thirty thousand dollars for Bill in the bank for worst-case scenarios. Otherwise, it is pay as they go. "Unlike the States," Barb said, "there's almost no case I can think of where you could go bankrupt here with a major medical condition. Two words: *no liability.*" By comparison to the Unites States, we find, Mexicans rarely sue one another. It can make for a personal form of score settling, but at least the private economy is not distorted by the fear of liability lawsuits. Other things, maybe, but not lawsuits.

For all those reasons, Thia and I, with a small black bag's worth of prior conditions—underactive thyroid, high cholesterol, among others—decided to drop our very expensive American insurance as soon as we crossed the border. We signed up with a U.S.-based international "travel insurance" program, which reimburses costs in foreign countries above a large deductible and, for extra reassurance, provides emergency evacuation back to the States. (Barb has perhaps the most interesting wrinkle on this: She moonlights several times a year in the States as a sales trainer but is a resident of Mexico. So her Mexican policy evacuates her back to Mexico, where her private insurance will cover her if something serious happens to her while she is traveling in the States.) U.S. Medicare, of course, is not valid in Mexico, but that does not mean much to those of us under sixty-five. We have to come up with a work-around.

When a day later I finally get to see Dr. Mauro, as he is universally called, who works out of a modest office down another bumpy street in Bucerias, I find a soft-spoken man of youthful middle age. His English is good, his medical degree is from Mexico City, and he examines my toe with a gentle hand. Thia has driven me and is sitting in. Dr. Mauro takes the time to talk to us about our general health, asks some astute questions, and writes a couple of prescriptions for us. Though there are others waiting, he seems in no hurry, and we talk personally for about fifteen minutes.

He tells us he grew up poor and so had his medical education subsidized by the Mexican government, which meant that he owed it a longer stretch of service in a location of the government's choosing. (All physicians owe some public service.) He ended up, as it happens, in San Pancho's clinic, where he treated locals and gringos alike for anything that came up. He moved into private practice in Bucerias several years ago.

I ask him if, given the respect in which he is held, if it is possible for him to prosper or to move his practice wherever he wants.

"No, not at all," he says in unaccented English. "It's government policy here to turn out large numbers of doctors, so there isn't the natural supply and demand you have in the States. There is a doctor in every town and village, some of them young postresidents living in small clinics to serve out their obligation. This is for a just cause; in a poor country, the government's policy is very popular. But I'll never be able to just find a new practice somewhere or charge what I think I may be worth. So I'm content doing what I do."

He goes into a closet and brings out a worn pair of crutches. He tells me to use them free of charge for the next month and to bring them back when I am ready to take off the cast. I ask him how much the office visit is, and he asks for the equivalent of sixteen dollars for both of us. I hand him a two-hundred-peso bill and feel dreadful taking the change from him.

Back home, I spend some time getting used to my crutches. I sprained an ankle about twenty years ago, and I remember getting around on crutches with ease, bounding along the sidewalks. Now I'm feeling my age and my weight, to say nothing of those slippery cobblestones. Our wire transfer for the walled lot has gone through, and we have to wait for the sale paperwork to be done. I amuse myself in the kitchen by trying a few Mexican recipes that can be cooked on our gas burners. The borrowed crutches are too small for me, so we drive to Vallarta and buy another pair in a medical-supplies store. In a few days, my spirits start to lift as I begin to accompany Thia part of the way down the dirt road to the beach on slow, crutch-swinging walks.

A few of the town's foibles begin to show up. The water goes off again—more sewer lines are being dug up—and for most of one night the electricity goes off. I think about the reaction when that happens in the States: call Con Edison, demand to know what the *hell* is going on and when the *hell* the lights are going to come back on, and hang up mad. Around here, the village goes dark, candles flicker on, and the dark hills sparkle in pin lights. Nobody gets upset, neighbors walk in the moonlight, candles are brought out to the café tables, and if any-one asks—few do—nobody can really say when they'll come back on. The flash point for irritation is different in Mexico: there is nothing that can be done, so you let things happen at their own pace. And you improvise, like those waterless workers and their bucket brigade.

I can already see how this is a great country for improvisers. Where money is scarce, why pay for something when you whip it up on your own? On a walk, I see two long boards leaning vertically against a home under construction. Two rows of cement blocks have been stacked from bottom to top against the boards, and wooden slats are wedged hori-zontally between each set of blocks and held tightly by the weight of the blocks. It is a small engineering feat that makes for an entirely secure-looking ladder. At a restaurant, the waiter makes a fine show of lighting crepes at the table; what makes it different from a dessert light-ing in New York is that here the waiter is heating the pan on a circle of upright empty beer cans—and says, "See—Mexican genius." I already know there is no gas station in or near the village, but no matter: at the corner of the plaza, out of a storefront, jerricans of fuel are sold at a markup. A driver parks in front, a woman comes out with the jerrican and a large plastic Coke bottle that has been cut in half to a cone shape and pours the gas. It is not just the improvised fuel-business model that stands out, but the fact that the capital expense of a hardware-store fun-nel has been successfully avoided. Mexicans make do.

In the first week or two, we begin getting to know our neighbors better.

Gaby, my large-bellied neighbor, is a cheery, Falstaffian fellow. Almost everyone in town has a nickname, and Gaby's is *el Botete*, the

Blowfish. Though I have heard others call him that, especially when his shirt is riding high above his proud stomach, I would not presume to. I am walking back to the apartment on one of our first mornings, and he is sweeping in front of his place, and he continues cleaning up in front of ours. Perhaps it is that I am on crutches, but the gesture touches me. I am not such an invalid that I cannot do some one-armed sweeping myself, and I return the favor a couple of days later, sweeping up the mango leaves and discarded candy wrappers in front both of our homes. He comes out and watches with what I gather is a look of satis-faction; the gringo is doing his part.

He calls me over to make introductions to his parrot, which hangs in a cage by his door. It is a talkative bird, just a few feet from our door, and we hear him squawking most mornings. We don't mind a bit. Gaby explains that he has taught the bird to speak, drilling him in Spanish phrases. I ask Gaby what the parrot has learned. Gaby leans his face close to the cage, and he and the bird croon back and forth to each other: *"puto, puto, puto,"* or, "male whore, male whore, male whore."

Gaby loves music, and it is clear from our first weekend that Sunday is an especially musical day. Inside his open door, we see him sprawled in the aluminum lawn chair in the middle of his cement-floor living room, soaking up the sounds of ranchera music blasting from his stereo. We don't mind that either; we like his taste. Over time, the strains of an afternoon Mozart clarinet concerto from our satellite radio will mingle with the plangent moans of a vaquero done wrong by his woman, and the blend seems almost natural.

One of the acquired habits one learns in a Mexico town is a far greater tolerance for sounds and noise. Gaby's parrot is our first wake-up call, and we have become used to the roosters before dawn (actually we get used to roosters at *all* times of the day and night; in this village, it is always fiesta time for roosters). We are likewise entertained by the village-wide colloquy that goes on among resident barking dogs at night. And we have come to expect the grating cement mixers to lull us out of sleep. What takes getting used to are the number of morning pickup trucks that come by, their loudspeakers on a tape loop, touting a remarkable array of products and services. But that's how news gets out in smaller towns; it fuels the economy.

Throughout much of Mexico, one of the most celebrated sounds of the morning is the cry of *"El gas! El gas!"* announcing propane delivery.

Everyone's hot water and stove runs on propane (electricity is one util-
ity that is expensive in Mexico), and we learn that we should flag down
the gas man when our tank needs switching. But there's more on the
concert program.

On our morning walks during those first few days, we are passed by
loudspeaker trucks going in both directions; so many services are being
advertised they begin to sound like overlapping rap songs.

*"You need oranges, you need tangerines, you need fresh pineapple! You
need oranges, you need mangoes!"*

*"Penetrating cream, for rheumatism, arthritis, for young and old, for
aches and pains and anything that ails you—twenty pesos a jar!"*

*"Shrimp! Shrimp you can fry, shrimp you can broil, shrimp you can boil,
the best shrimp you can buy anywhere!"*

*"Metals, aluminum, tin, and we'll buy any metal you no longer need, like
your old car radiators!"*

There is even a loudspeaker truck piled high with mattresses—*"You
need mattresses, fine mattresses, mattresses you will sleep well on!"* and so
on—but it is difficult to understand the marketing strategy of this particular business. Are there enough people, out for a morning stroll or on
their front stoop, who flag down the truck for a quick mattress purchase
with their pocket change and then haul the thing into a waiting bedroom? What do I know? I probably wouldn't exchange a used radiator
during my morning walk either, but I may not yet understand the local
economy.

Thia is not bad at keeping up her own contrapuntal sound track. She
is in her element on our morning walks, thrilled with the luxuriant jungle vegetation we pass every day, hovering like a hummingbird to sniff
at flowers, exclaiming in delight at the sheer variety of it all. In our life
together, we have never lived in a sunny climate; she has never had the
kind of garden she dreamed of. My wife, quite literally, stops to smell
the flowers.

One morning, we run into Chuck and Teke Mohill, who own a posh
hillside home on the north side of town, beyond our lot. We know them
a bit, and Chuck stops his Jeep in the middle of the street to say hello.
Behind him, cars pull up and just hover; nobody blows his horn. Here,
traffic yields to conversation, excepting an occasional ill-humored

honk. Chuck greets us with a hale hello. He leans out of his window and says, "Isn't this a wonderful way to be living our life?"

Anywhere else, we might wonder if he was on furlough from a feel-good cult. Here, that kind of greeting is fairly common and spontaneous. At our poker game, which I have rejoined, one of the guys will say, "Can you *believe* we live here?" and it will not seem an unusual comment; there will be smiles of agreement around the table as the cards get shuffled. It is not just about the pure pleasure of our tropical setting; it is more like a recognition that with all the hassles and inefficiencies, so inexcusable to some foreigners, life in these parts—to us— is both sweeter and more piquant. Expats here have a saying that sounds smug to an outsider: "Either you get it or you don't." So far, we get it.

CHAPTER 7

Dialing for Pesos . . .
Courtesy Calls . . . It's Harvey, Eh?

Despite my handicap, our little routines become a schedule. In the morning, Thia leaves me to my own gimpy pace for a stretch and marches ahead for a swim at the beach. We come to know the people on our route. Many of the neighboring houses have chickens and roosters running about; one has an old hog rooting around the yard. As to the chickens, they aren't just a good source of drumsticks; I hear they gobble down scorpions, which makes them attractive neighbors as far as I am concerned.

After our walks, we come home to coffee and fresh orange juice and an omelet with peppers and manchego cheese, or sometimes oatmeal with bananas we pick from a small tree behind our apartment. After breakfast, we sit out on the terrace and discuss what we want to do with our day. As always, we watch for Iggy Mom and Pop, who usually tree-waddle up the palm as the sun begins to warm. Across the foliage, a few palm trees away, is the back of Rollie and Jeanne's restaurant and domicile, a three-story brick building with a small viewing palapa on the roof. Early in the morning, before they open for breakfast, we see them during their meditative moments under the palapa, and we wave. They will be opening the dinner restaurant in a couple of days, and Thia is getting ready for her winter debut as a four-times-a-week waitress-hostess. Americans are not supposed to work in Mexico without an employment visa, and that is predicated on not taking work that a Mexican might do.

Rollie has a large Mexican staff, but he needs an American waitperson and greeter for the large number of English-language-only tourists who come to nosh. Thia's role is to be informal, and strictly because she wants to volunteer and stay active.

Late mornings we reserve for domestic tasks, meaning mostly that we wave a cloth ineffectively at the swirling dust that comes in from the open vents. We have not yet decided on what every gringo agrees is a big drawing card in Mexico: reasonably priced maid service. It is a bigger decision than foreigners suppose. If a domestic worker spends most of her week working for a single employer, the employer must pay her social security taxes and becomes liable for paid vacation and severance. Inevitably, say long-timers, your maid's personal dramas become yours, giving you an instant extended family that carries unexpected responsibilities.

I also spend my time calling to settle bills and past obligations. Like most active consumers, it is stunning to us to find how much paperwork follows us around, even if we think we have closed down our old life. The mails in Mexico are notorious for nondelivery and pilferage, so we have signed a contract with Mail Boxes, Etc. to have our stateside mail forwarded to a Laredo mailbox, from which it is sent by some modern equivalent of the Pony Express to a Puerto Vallarta office.

Thank God for the telephone. Until just a couple of years ago, private telephones were still at a premium here. For years, there was one telephone on the plaza, and residents lined up to use it. To take an incoming call, the caller would be told to redial in ten minutes, and a kid on a bicycle would ride up to someone's house to alert them. For a long time, residents put their names on a list for installation, but there was general consensus that the list was less than binding. Jeanne Dick remembers that when the telephone installer's truck would come into town, people used to rush around telling their neighbors, "He's here!" and go accost the man with all manner of blandishments.

Now that phone service is available, as it is in our rental apartment, the trick is to make certain it remains available. Phone bills must be paid in line, in cash, but in Bucerias, and if one doesn't know the date by which this is required—which happens to be the twenty-seventh of every month—phone service is cut off like a dropped call. Nothing works as punctually in Mexico, I am told, as cutoff of service for nonpayment.

I am almost startled to find that not only are telephones more available, but high-speed Internet access has arrived too—and it's even wireless. It takes a trip into Bucerias and a wait in line, but soon our bedroom has a blinking modem in the corner, right above the shelf where we store candles for general blackouts. After a few telephone calls to English-speaking operators—my Spanish is not up to reboots and configurations—it is giving me better access than our Connecticut provider. On the other hand, rarely did I walk into my Connecticut den to find a rooster pecking angrily at the modem lights.

What this access will mean to me, during my toe period and beyond, is that I will not have to sit at the Internet café listening to electronic trance music while I read my email, and that the *New York Times* online will be available to me every morning in my bedroom. The Internet is, I believe, *the* big change in the expatriate life, ending the kind of what-month-is-this isolation of the past, as well as making the separation from family and friends bearable.

Afternoons are reserved for the "errands" of our life, and they generally involve walking somewhere in the village to do something vital and being waylaid by myriad friends and acquaintances and fresh gossip. There is no such thing as a straight line from home to destination. We are learning the protocol of greetings as we go. With gringos, it's "Hi." With the Mexicans, we are beginning to recognize, it can be *"Hola"* but often is more elaborate. There is a three-part greeting ritual to be followed: *"Buenos días,"* which must, in fact, be spoken at the correct time of day; if it is a few minutes past noon or dusk, it may be gently rectified by the recipient; followed by *señor, señora,* or, most trickily, *señorita,* which is often a judgment call and may also be corrected; and *"¿Cómo está usted?"* which in Mexico may suggest a courteous pause to listen to the answer, which will often involve matters of health or family. A couple of times a day we pass Gaby's parents, an old, dignified, and somewhat worn-out couple who spend most of their afternoons on chairs by their front stoop, but the routine is invariably the same.

"Buenos días, Señor y Señora Ponce. ¿Cómo están ustedes?"

"Buenas tardes," Señor Ponce corrects, pointing up at the sun for emphasis. *"Estoy bien, pero mi pinche pierna . . ."* "I'm fine, but that goddamn leg of mine . . ."

*   *   *

Today I am to swing my way down to García Realty to have my first serious discussion about our hilltop lot with Harvey Craig, our ever-informative broker. It is not quite fist-clenching time, but I have been having ungrateful, senseless, perverse thoughts: Wouldn't it have been nice to find a way to hang on to the lot as an investment, to sell it a few years from now as possibly the only nest egg we would ever have? It's senseless and perverse because we need the money now, to build on the walled lot.

Besides, the hilltop property is still in a limbo created by its prove-nance as a lot still officially owned by a Mr. Chiripa, but subdivided by a Mr. Fernández, who sold the rights to it to a Mr. Mejía, who then sold those rights to an impulsive American couple on their way back to Con-necticut. Not a real problem; it is the way things are done here. And it is somehow comforting to know that we are the end of a line of Mexi-cans who have profited nicely from each sale of the land, and that we have thus contributed to the swelling local economy. But in the end, maybe it is a far better thing to extend the line of ownership to another proud possessor. Because there will always be another one. As Jeanne says about Sayulita, "Unpack bags, buy land."

I stop briefly to talk with Enrique Ortega Rodríguez, "Cocula," as he is known, owner of the only hardware store I know of named Jacque-line. He also runs a small bungalow complex, likewise named Jacque-line. The store, named after his daughter, is a dark and somewhat dingy place, but Enrique works each day at a counter fronting upon the side-walk, from which he dispenses nails and screws and local political advice. His father was the first *ejidatario,* and politicians from across the state who visit Sayulita respectfully come knocking at his door. Rollie put us onto him during our earlier trip, when we were first looking around for land.

"Have Enrique the hardware owner show you some," said Rollie at the time.

"He's brokering for someone?" I asked.

"No. He *owns* more land than anyone in town."

During a bumpy tour he gave us of the jungle coastline south of the village, Enrique, waving casually from the wheel of the pickup truck he was driving, would point to this or that entire hill, saying in a matter-of-fact way, "I own that," "That is mine," and "I am selling a few hundred acres of that." I calculated what I understood land to be worth and figured Enrique for a multimillionaire—in dollars. There was nothing small enough he had to offer us—he was showing us around as a favor to Rollie—so he dropped us off by his hardware store. I bought a package of nails from him.

Today he is solving a cement problem for a couple of construction workers, and we exchange greetings as I limp by. The town center is being torn up by bulldozers; mounds of cobblestones have been removed while the sewers are replaced, and are lying in heaps along the sidewalk. I make my way slowly up the stairs to Harvey's office. He is a smart, loquacious Canadian, and is rubbing his shiny bald pate as I walk in. He gives me a cheery greeting.

I tell him that I am interested in selling our lot because of a new development in our lives, and he stops me.

"I already know, the whole town knows, you bought the walled place, which I sure would have liked to sell you myself, of course I know it was multiple listed and you did it yourself through Ian's website, I personally don't have a problem with that, I want you to get the best price, and now I'm gonna be honest, because if I get you the best price, I'm gonna make a good commission, and I'm not getting any younger, we're both not getting any younger, I have to provide for my old age, how've you been, how's your lovely wife, what are those boys of yours up to, eh?"

I ask Harvey what he thinks we could get for the hilltop lot. He tells me that the market is crazy, that things are nuts, that he thinks we could get a good price for it, though of course there's the matter of the bank trust not being finalized, which is the fault of that goddamn lawyer he has emailed me about, only the good news is he's no longer using that goddamn lawyer, and he thinks that any buyer would understand that a Sayulita property without a final trust document is just the way things are done down here, he personally doesn't see a problem with that, the buyers are looking for anything, and he thinks he can get me the best price of any broker in town.

I am summarizing his response.

The kernel of Harvey's news, of course, is that we can get a good price for our lot and that he thinks he can sell it quickly. It's true that it's a seller's market, and it's true that we have property with a view to die for, but the challenge will be to find someone who can move fast, not sweat the small stuff (such as a clear title), and pay us in full and in cash in time for us to start construction in the walled lot. I ask Harvey what the chances are of his finding someone to fulfill those conditions.

Harvey begins his next State of the Union address, and as he does, a thought strikes me. If it's true that we could get more than what we paid a year ago, what about selling just half of the lot and holding on to the other half? It would yield a good part of what I think we will need to begin building our house, we could take out a home-equity loan on our little Connecticut condo for the rest, and we would still have a nest egg . . .

I interrupt Harvey in midstanza and put the idea to him. This stops him, and he rubs his head. Harvey is smart and knows the system. He thinks for a minute and then says something unbelievably concise.

"Why not?"

On my way home, swinging on my crutches over a couple of open sewer ditches, I stop at Doña Lety's for a torta. She knows me by now, and I look forward to her crusty wisdom. She always knows what is going on. Though she comes from a humble background, she speaks Spanish elegantly, even eruditely. I ask her what she knows about the construction in town.

"My information is that it will take five months," she says, shaking her head. "They will replace the sewers, grade the streets, cement the cobblestones back in; that will take most of the time and money. It will run into Christmas, New Year's, and even Easter—our earning season. It is absurd, because the loose dirt from the hills will sweep down during the rainy season, and we will have mud and dust again."

I ask her what could have been done that made more sense.

"They could have done something more *primordial* and diverted the dirt from the hills, put in more street lamps, done something fundamentally useful. But someone decided they were going to use three million pesos of public funds, and put away two million"—she makes a hand-in-pocket gesture— "and spend the other million tearing up the plaza. Next year, there will be work again for the street construction crews. It's an old, old story, and we know it well."

$\mathcal{A}$ $\mathcal{L}ittle$ $\mathcal{H}istory$ ... $\mathcal{I}$ ♥ $\mathcal{T}enochtitlán$ ... $\mathcal{I}nvaders$ $\mathcal{R}eturn$

Despite my increasing skill on crutches, I can't walk long. So for much of my first six weeks in Mexico I stay at home with brief forays for exercise and meals. The upside: lots of reading time. This is a town of readers. Television, dining, and talk aside, there is not much else for the older residents in the way of entertainment, so you see scads of foreigners clasping books on their way to the beach or the taco stands. Many of the inns and restaurants have shelves of used books for lending or exchanges. In the coming months, I will get around to Galsworthy and Updike and García Márquez and, always, Twain. But for a month or so, toe splinted, I focus on the history books I have brought with me for research. In my early schooling in Mexico City, I was brought up on legends of the conquest and the heroes of Mexico's revolutions. I am curious to learn what new scholarship has produced, and what I might learn as an adult about our new neighbors.

To a citizen of the United States, which has been invaded just a few times in its history, it is difficult to comprehend a story like Mexico's. (To Canadians, who had no revolutions or conquests since the fur traders pushed around the Inuit, it must be even more difficult.) Stripped of myth and legend, the history of Mexico has been one long, bloody land grab. In four hundred years, Mexico had four conquerors: the Aztecs, the Spanish, the Americans and the French. Between the defeat of the Aztecs in 1521 and the Revolution of 1910, Mexico had just one administration—Benito Juárez's—that fairly represented its people. For much of the rest, the country was ruled by Spanish monarchs, weak presidents, corrupt despots, or foreigners, with an assist from the Catholic Church, which at one point owned half the land in Mexico. Indians, and to a slightly lesser extent, the mestizo mixed breeds (by far the majority of the country), were kept in poverty and ignorance while their country was plundered of its wealth. Only early in the twentieth century did this begin to change.

My first reading goal is to drill down into Mexico's transforming encounter, between the Spaniards and the Indians. I figure the more I know about that long-ago cultural collision, the more I learn about Mexico today. Hugh Thomas's magisterial *Conquest,* all eight hundred pages of it, traces that encounter in splendid detail. For several weeks, I lose myself in this and the other histories.

Tenochtitlán, today's Mexico City, was founded on a lake island in the valley of Anáhuac. In 1519 it was a city of 250,000 (when Spain's biggest city was Seville, with 80,000), with soaring temple-topped pyramids and floating flower gardens. More than one conquistador compared it to Venice. The Aztecs, more properly called by the tribe's original name, the *Mexica,* migrated from the hot lands to the west (right here in Nayarit, where we now live).

The Mexica of Tenochtitlán lived in a complex society with a rich, flexible language, Nahuatl, and an intricate economy propped up by slave labor and tribute from conquered tribes.

The great humanist missionary Bartolomé de Las Casas believed that, human sacrifice notably aside, the Mexicas' forms of government, education, religion, science, and arts met Aristotle's definition of a civilized society. In Tenochtitlán, art, poetry, mathematics, and music flourished for centuries—and were eradicated in a matter of months in 1521.

The Mexica believed the reason for their existence was to serve the gods. They believed that the world would end in earthquakes and apocalypse, and that human beings would be turned into animals. For this reason, human blood had to be spilled so the gods could retain their strength, the sun would rise again, and catastrophe put off. Thus, human sacrifice (and cannibalism) became integral to the society. As many as twenty thousand beating hearts, "precious cactus fruit," would be extracted in a single year atop the bloody temples.

This need for an unending supply of captive sacrifices was to become crucial in the Spanish Conquest. In my early school years in Mexico City, we were told stories about the Mexica believing that Cortés was Quetzalcóatl, a fair-skinned god-king who opposed human sacrifice and whose imminent return had been prophesied. Cortés, as it happens, was fair-skinned, showed up on schedule, and opposed human sacrifice by Indians—which he emphasized, logically enough, by killing thousands of them. Even by the rough standards of the day, the Spaniards were extraordinarily cruel conquerors.

But it is also worth noting that the fabled emperor Moctezuma II was a total ninny. He wept at every report of the Spaniards' approach, tried to buy Cortés off with slaves and women, and wailed to his advisers that he wanted to run away. He was indecisive and weepy right up to the time the Spaniards invaded Tenochtitlán and captured him. The Spaniards began destroying cultural artifacts and erecting Christian crosses at the tops of pyramids. Moctezuma, identifying with his captors, was killed on the roof of a temple, probably by a rock thrown by a Mexica, during one of the many insurrections against the Spanish occupiers.

There are statues today in Mexico to both Moctezuma and Cuauhtémoc, his cousin and successor. But it was Cuauhtémoc who was the true hero, a resistance leader who mounted counterattacks on the Spaniards, and believed them to be neither invulnerable nor gods, but "political terrorists." Cortés captured, tortured and hanged Cuauhtémoc, subjugated the Mexica, and razed much of Tenochtitlán.

During my broken-toe period, I also happen across a popular work titled *There's a Word for It in Mexico*. It is a small-press book by the unlikely sounding Boyé Lafayette de Mente and is a cult favorite of expats in Mexico. It takes over one hundred words or phrases spoken in Mexico—*abrazo, amigos, machismo, familia*—and uses them as jumping-off points for scathing essays on the country's history and development since the conquest, which he sees as four hundred years of unbroken oppression, cruelty, and effective genocide.

There are more evenhanded accounts of Mexican history and culture, but the book popularizes for gringos the revisionism of many recent historians. Taking the point of view of the victims—Mexico's Indians and mestizos, the Spanish-Indian population—it makes the case that few people on earth have been so badly governed and so cruelly oppressed. De Mente gives little quarter to the Spaniards, and almost none to the church. He believes that knowing this is essential to an outsider's understanding of the Mexican people and to getting a peek beneath the masks that today they habitually wear:

> The paradoxes of Mexico—the omnipresent trappings of Catholicism, the pagan soul of the people, the savage brutality of the criminal and the rogue cop, the gentle humility of the poor farmer, the warmth, kindness and compassion of the average city dweller, the perverse masculinity cult, the sensuality of the culture—are glimpsed and touched only in passing, and if considered at all are usually misunderstood.

The argument of this school is that the Spanish so systematically stripped away the cultural and religious foundations of a sophisticated native population that their society disintegrated. Forced to "convert" to Catholicism, kept in perpetual bondage as serfs, the Indians and many mixed breeds lived under a despotism that was far more brutal to the vast majority of its population than, say, the English in North America (Indians and blacks always excepted).

Spaniards awarded themselves *encomiendas*, vast plantation estates that included virtual ownership of all who lived on them. Indians worked sixteen hours a day in newly discovered gold mines without pay and could be punished or killed at the whim of their masters. As Indians began to die from overwork and disease, the Spanish found another source of labor they could work and suppress: the offspring of Indian women they were encouraged to impregnate. These became Mexico's mestizos and were similarly kept down by the Spaniards, who went on to create a caste system of sixteen distinct "breeds" apart from their own pure-Spanish race. Thus an entire population was relegated to second—through sixteenth—class citizenship.

Only the few Spanish-born had political rights; trade with other countries was forbidden. Colonists could not raise their own grapes, olives, or silkworms, all of which were reserved for Spain. Indians were forbidden from walking in town squares and ordered to wear identifying clothing and were denied schooling or decent health care. De Mente writes, "The Spanish viceroys as well as all of the larger land-grant holders maintained their own armed guards and small private armies, and in close collaboration with the Catholic Church, ran Mexico as a virtual prison colony."

This may be overheated, and it doesn't take into account the humanitarian work of the Catholic missionaries, beginning with the Franciscan de Las Casas, who treated the Indians of New Spain with greater tolerance than their Protestant counterparts did the Indian tribes of the British colonies. (Spanish Catholic missionaries encouraged dance and music and fiestas, which they adapted from Mexica practices to help convert the Indians; Puritans, famously, banned all such pleasures as sinful for all.) Though they were discriminated against in the public arena, Mexico's Indians were granted more rights under the law, and integrated more fully into society, than were America's Native Americans, who were concentrated and exiled onto reservations.

But there has nevertheless been a shift away from the triumphalist history I learned as a child. I recall the rationale used to justify harsh Spanish rule over the natives: that at least they were bringing civilization to a heathen race that practiced the savagery of human sacrifice. However, the ritual of sacrifice by the quick knife, bloody though it was, can also be seen against the backdrop of the civilizing nation's own practices. Its priests ran the Spanish Inquisition, which may have put half a million people to death, many burned slowly at the stake. Its conquistadors, followed by Creole grandees over the next centuries, routinely killed, mutilated, and tortured, including the practice of oiling the Indians' feet so they would burn better.

What is less known is that little of this stopped when the legends suggest it stopped: at Mexico's Revolution of 1810, supposedly inspired by the American and French Revolutions. Mexican children are taught about Don Miguel Hidalgo, and José María Morelos, and other legendary heroes of their war of independence. But Mexico's founding heroes were killed within a year of the revolt, and the war continued largely as a battle for power between Mexican-born Spanish and the viceroys. After independence was proclaimed, Indians and mestizos were kept in the same poverty and powerlessness they had experienced for three centuries.

Mexico was governed for yet another hundred years by corrupt presi-dents and óligarchs, one after another, and experienced fraudulent elections, armed coups on schedule, and corruption at all levels, which became a part of the national fabric. Reforms by the few liberal-minded leaders would sputter alive for a few years and then die out. Foreign powers such as France and the United States invaded at will. France installed the Austrian-born puppet emperor Maximilian in 1864 and then, in its inimitable Gallic way, abandoned him to his execution. The United States sent troops down on flimsy pretenses in 1846, stormed the halls of Moctezuma and the hills of Chapultepec, and, in their man-ifestly American way, took over half of Mexico's national territory: Texas, New Mexico, Colorado, Utah, and then Arizona and California.

Mexico's presidents began a tradition, observed up to very recent times, of amassing enormous wealth before stepping down and retiring to enjoy it in splendor—or exile. A handful of owners still held most of the land. There was a stretch when an authentic folk figure and reformer, the Zapotec Indian lawyer Benito Juárez, was elected president in 1867, but after his death in 1872, Mexican politics went back to the usual dic-tatorship and exploitation. It took a second revolution a century after the first, in 1910, the revolution of Francisco Madero, Pancho Villa and Emiliano Zapata, for a modicum of reform to creep in. Only then, and not even really then, did something like a tentative democracy begin to emerge. Almost another century more would pass before Mexico's citi-zens could cast a meaningful ballot for a candidate outside a single party.

With my foot propped up on a chair, gazing out at my neighbors like Jimmy Stewart in *Rear Window,* I continue to read and think about what I've begun to observe in Mexico. When I compare its history to that of the United States, it is not difficult to imagine why—besides language—the differences between two countries sharing the same continent should be so pronounced. The United States has its own brutal story of oppression against African-Americans and Native Americans, but the majority of our people were not held in the kind of iron grip by a class-obsessed elite that Mexicans experienced for four hundred years. Our (white) settlers more or less ran their own affairs in America, start-ing with the Mayflower Compact and running to Virginia's House of Burgesses. Our revolution was essentially the rebellion of a colony with democratic institutions from a home country with semidemocratic institutions, governed more by Parliament than by King.

Mexico's revolution is ongoing.

It is no wonder, then, that despite my early years in the country, I experienced the sense of dislocation when I crossed the border into Mexico. I think about my Mexican neighbors, and I feel both respect for their survival skills and sympathy for their harsh historical experience. Whatever faults the American system has—and this part of Mexico has its share of gringos unhappy with the role the United States is playing in the world—the Mexicans did not get our breaks in self-governance. Mexicans have a profoundly rich art, culture, and family life, richer than ours in many respects, but in politics they were saddled with thugs and thieves from the very beginning of their history. A twentieth-century president, populist Lázaro Cárdenas, reversed the trend in the 1930s when he expropriated foreign oil and redistributed land to the peasants. Vicente Fox, the twenty-first-century president holding office as we arrived, broke the tradition of one-party rule and raised hopes with his campaign against corruption. Some long-timers believe they see progress, others think Fox was unable to make much headway. The 2006 election to succeed him resulted in demonstrations and demands for a recount, but it also proved domination by a single party has effectively ended.

None of which goes to the point of what Mexicans—or Americans—have made of themselves out of their respective histories. In my earlier residence here, and in the short time I've been living here now, it seems to me that the Mexicans I have encountered appear better-adjusted, happier than their northern counterparts. Though I caution myself that a foreigner does not necessarily know what is behind their smiles, Mexicans nevertheless appear more cheerful, less anxious, and more at ease with life's flow than many Americans. (A recent global survey polled citizens' stated sense of "happiness" in seventy-five countries, and found Americans down the list at number fifteen, while Mexicans ranked number two; other Latin American nations scored high as well.) So it is hard to avoid the impression that Americans, who have the pursuit of happiness enshrined in their founding document, look for happiness as individuals, outside themselves, and find it elusive; while Mexicans, from a foundation of oppression and powerlessness, in a political system that has worked only fitfully, have found a high degree of happiness within themselves and their families.

Of course, the emigration numbers paint a less happy picture, with entire towns being emptied of their young men who go north and send remittances home. Joblessness and corruption are Mexico's scourges, but Mexican history is again instructive. After centuries of indentured labor and forced tribute to an overlord class, Mexicans have more than the usual aversion to paying taxes and vote accordingly. The ripple effect is pernicious: low tax compliance, which leads to poor funding for teachers and police, which leads to erratic quality of education and civic corruption.

The economic weakness that causes Mexicans to leave their country is one facet of Mexico's reality. It can lead some dismissive Americans to believe that there is not much else *besides* poverty and unemployment. But another facet, obvious but often overlooked up north, is that Mexico is of course inhabited by its millions of citizens (including a rising middle class) who are *not* fleeing, who believe their culture and way of life is to be admired and cherished.

I reflect that as an American, I am blessed to have been born in a prosperous country in which education is supported and the rule of law generally prevails. But I temper my comparison with the little matter of America's own kettle of contradictions, including tax breaks for the wealthy, vast pay gaps between workers and chiefs, and rampant lobbyist corruption. I conclude, as I often will in the months ahead, that the high ground is not always visible from here.

I am impatient for my toe to heal, to get out around town again. I have a feeling that I will see my neighbors in a somewhat different light, limned by the thought that none of us can entirely escape his history. Mexicans have seen a lot of invaders in their time, and I have to wonder what traits will show through, which masks they will wear or drop, in this new invasion of retired foreigners. Most of us gringos are less rapacious than the conquistadores, but our skin is fair, we are riding our SUV steeds, and we are coming—as we prophesied to ourselves—to a promised land.

CHAPTER 9

We Meet Eagle George ... Thia Starts Work ... We Look for an Architect

My cast is finally off. I take the crutches back to the medical-supplies house in Vallarta and thoughtlessly ask the attendant if I might sell them back to the store. She hesitates, then says, "Well, there is an old woman, crippled for life, who came by and could not afford to buy crutches. We told her we might be able to sell her a used pair if we got some back." She asks if I would be interested in selling them to the old woman. I feel like a crumb for not having thought of donating them, and do the right thing.

Back at the village, I take my first swim and stay out in the surf for an hour. Floating close to the break, I can watch Sayulita's beach life: Mexican families, unlike the Americans, smartly out of the sun under umbrellas and jerry-built palapas; white-costumed Indians selling jewelry and serapes; a couple of fishing boats surrounded by bathers who are buying *huachinango*—red snapper—fresh from the nets; brown-skinned surfers riding the waves; Manuel the horse guy with his wraparound shades and ponytail leading a chestnut mare; white-skinned girls in small bathing suits, down for a week at the women's surfer school, plunging into the waves with their short boards. A pelican whizzes by me a foot above the water, going north.

Ian Hodge has suggested we meet our future next-door neighbor, so we make a date and walk across town to the house next to our lot to introduce ourselves. George Newman, an American who has lived here for thirty years, was the original owner of our lot before it was sold several times. The Newman place, Casa de Jorge Aguila, is an idiosyncratic blend of hacienda, Western ranch house, and garden cottage. Built on one level, it is a kind of open ranch (the Western kind, not the suburban), divided into two parts, each with its own outdoor thatched palapa.

George is eighty-three, tall and lithe, is wearing a genuine Stetson and a Western shirt with pearl snap buttons, a belt with a big Western buckle, jeans, and cowboy boots. As he shows us around, I ask George about the two wings, and he explains that he and his wife, Shirley, had different architectural points of view, so each of them designed and built half their home. "She thinks everything I build is *tacky*," he explains.

Shirley's side has the living quarters, done in beams and tile, and a small pool. George's side is the outdoor Mexican kitchen, a large palapa with an *equipale* seating area, and a bathroom he constructed outside for the convenience of his many guests, with a small Moorish cupola on the top. There is an old saddle on display in the front of George's wing, and equally old photographs of heroes of the Mexican Revolution of 1910, Villa and Zapata and others, mounted onto the palapa posts.

George has a parade of visitors nearly every day. He knows everyone in town, and everyone knows him. He has a large eagle tattooed on his chest, a souvenir from World War II, and thus is universally known as Eagle George. He arrived in 1968, one of the first gringos in the area, and has lived here ever since, except for the summers, which he spends up in British Columbia.

We sit down with Eagle George and the shy, introspective Shirley under his palapa. He tells us that he is very happy that we have bought the property because he was beginning to think some developer would buy it. Also, he has affection for the property and is pleased to see it go to a couple of young'uns like ourselves. We are, of course, pleased at the welcome and the accurate reference to our youth.

He tells us that we have a fine, fine property, complete with electricity, cesspool and a giant *aljibe*—a water storage tank—that will make us independent of the town water system. We know this already, but it is good to hear his enthusiasm for our purchase. He says he will only offer advice if we ask for it, to which we reply we want all the advice he can give. So his first suggestion is that we build without an architect, as they did. We could hire our own construction team, and they can build our home from our sketches, as many people have around Sayulita.

"We're not quite that adventurous yet, George," I say. "We've never built anything before."

"Aw, if you can show a Mexican builder what you want, he can build it. I did it without even speaking Spanish. That's how things get done around here."

He tells us that he first owned our lot, as well as much more along the beach. "I guess you could say we owned the land where all the five-hundred-thousand-dollar houses are now," he says, referring to the stretch of expensive homes in the northern part of town, both on the coastline and on the hills above. "My friend Vicente Pérez built the first brick house in Sayulita twenty-five years ago; he built our place here; and he's the one who built the wall around your house. He and his family are A-number-one quality people."

He says he has watched Sayulita grow from a few palm roofed huts, and he is delighted with the progress, despite more crowded streets and the rising prices. He has traveled all over the world and all over Mexico, and he settled here because he knew it was a special village. "There are other towns around here where you walk around and no one's out. Here, there's life on the streets, and everyone visits with everyone else. The gringos and the locals generally get along real well. We have shysters and con men, split between gringos and Mexicans, but I've enjoyed living here better 'n anywhere else." He says he and his Mexican friends predicted that people would discover the village, and now that so many locals are prosperous on raw land sales, he's not surprised that so few have sold their homes, preferring to stay with family and roots instead of selling out for cash.

"It's hard to assimilate into a culture, but you need to have Mexican compadres," George says. "You can't just hang out with gringos. There are a lot of things you don't do for yourself, and you have to know who in a village knows how to get things done. It's not always out on signs for you to read." He says the people he's known here for thirty years are "A-number-one quality people, except for a couple of snakes."

Eagle George brings out a couple of beers, and soft drinks for himself and Shirley, and, with a little prodding, tells us his story.

He was born on a Kickapoo Indian reservation in Oklahoma and was raised mostly among Indians. He had a '34 Packard and went to stomp dances—also called powwows. George grew up a rambling man. "I just loved taking off and going places. On December 6, 1941, I stuck out my thumb and headed west. The next day was Pearl Harbor." He enlisted in the navy, qualified as a gunner on a submarine, and was wounded off Guadalcanal.

One night in Hawaii, he imbibed most of a bottle of Great Island gin and found a tattoo parlor. He told the tattoo artist that where he came from, eagles were important—for war bonnets and so on—and he wanted a nice big eagle on his chest. He then commandeered another bottle of Five Island gin and several hours later went home and passed out, the bearer of a fine eagle whose wings spread from one pectoral to the other.

George stayed in the navy after the war ended and was stationed with the Asiatic Fleet in Qingdao, China. "When we went on leave," he says, "we saw the Nationalist Chinese troops, the Communist troops, the Japanese prisoners of war, and the U.S. Navy, all in one town in China . . . and everybody got along! That stayed with me." When he left the navy, he began traveling again, drifting in and out of Mexico and Canada.

He prospected for a living and kept up his rambling, solitary ways, trudging through Canadian snows. "I never had a tent. I'd just use a piece of plastic and pull it over myself in the snow and burrow in like bear." He began driving down the Baja Peninsula and Mexico's Pacific Coast. He would wander into small villages and find lodging and stay a while. Then he would move on, to places Americans generally did not visit in Mexico. And on a long drive down the rough road south of San Blas, he came across a sweet-water creek that he followed to a few palapas by a beach.

"They were exceptionally friendly people, these Sayulita folks, even to a gringo who no habla much español. What I liked about the town is that people generally got along, even when different kinds and nationalities began coming to town: surfers, RVers, Mexicans from other parts. I felt the way I did when I was stationed in China."

We are meeting a surveyor at the lot, so we excuse ourselves. We agree to come back and hear more about his adventures in Sayulita. He reminds us that among his many jobs, he used to build septic tanks.

"That's a great A-number-one cesspool you've got there. Don't let anyone tell you to rebuild it."

* * *

Thia has begun her volunteer work at Rollie's at night. Rollie and Jeanne have bought the small house next door and expanded the restaurant into it. Out front, they have built an open-air caged stove for their paella, which is one of Jeanne's recipes and the restaurant's signature dish at night. Despite standing-room crowds for breakfast, the nighttime business begins slowly. Thia's last job some years back was mostly desk work. Now, standing and rushing around a restaurant for five hours a night, even with a moderate number of customers, comes as a calf-stiffening surprise to her. The first night, she comes back to the apartment at around nine and flops down on the couch exhausted. I place my still-tender foot up on the coffee table, she puts up her shuddering thighs, and we look at each other, models of the new, active, healthy retirement.

Within a couple of days, however, she begins to come home a bit less worn out.

She tells me about some of the locals and tourists she is meeting, and I tell her about the conquistadores I have encountered in my nighttime reading. One night I go to dinner there myself and sit down at one of Thia's tables. I hang around till closing time, and I get lucky: I go home with the waitress.

One reason Thia wants to work is so that we can meet as many people as possible and keep informed on village life. The restaurant—with masterly input from Jeanne, who is every bit as gifted at dispensing information as paella—is a fine way to do that. Rumors, speculation, and necessary news bulletins are swapped from table to table. Someone at table three wants to know who the best yoga instructor in town is; table six knows. Table four is looking for a maid twice a week. Miguel, the charming flat-topped waiter, happens to know that Eva, in the kitchen, has a cousin who is looking for work.

This is how we go about the professional task of finding an architect and a builder.

Despite the fact that we have not sold our hilltop lot—either in whole or in part—we decide that we at least need to begin talking about what kind of house we would like to build. Though I have wire transferred the 10 percent cash deposit for our new lot, we have not yet closed. But prospects do appear promising for selling half the hilltop property, so in order to straddle ownership of both lots, I have arranged for a home equity loan on our condo in Connecticut. I would rather wait to have the money from the hilltop lot, but real-estate fever is still rising in the village, and both architects and builders are going to be increasingly difficult to hire.

We like the thick, handsome hacienda wall around the property that Vicente Perez has built, and we decide that we would like to build a house in a similar style: hacienda, rancho, a touch of Spanish villa. Most of the gringo homes in the area, especially those designed by the town's leading architect, Estela Gayosso, are beach modern, or "art gecko," as we've heard it described: curved, rounded concrete lines, open terraces, and palapa roofs held up by vine-entwined palm trunks. The style is idiosyncratic, even whimsical. One flamboyantly curved home is known as the Flintstone House. Another house, in the expensive north side, has an undulating orange roof and is known naturally enough as the Ronald McDonald House. Nicknames aside, it is an evocative, vivid design suited to the Mexican tropics.

We want to build in more of a traditional Mexican style. From my childhood memories, I summon up images of traditionally elegant wood-timbered homes that we visited in Cuernavaca, the even-then-fashionable retreat outside Mexico City. Thia has long dreamed of building a home with a garden, a courtyard, a fountain. We see brick, roof tiles, a whitewashed exterior, squared edges, flower boxes with cascading plants. In our previous life, we have bought and sold homes, but we've never built anything beyond a tree house from scratch. This is our chance. I begin sketching ideas, and I fall asleep at the table, the fan whirring above me.

After a few more late nights, and some reconnoitering around the village, Thia and I find we are in basic agreement. We have been warned that planning a house is stressful on a couple, but so far so good. I do not understand her obsession with toilet placement; she is less than tolerant of my imaginative ideas for a large den. There are several snappish moments—"That's plain *weird*," "Oh, we're comparing architectural knowledge, are we?"—but overall, we see things the same way.

All the gringos in town seem to be building something: a casita, a villa, a rental unit. It's a tight labor market, and we are warned by a gringo old-timer, "Every guy around this town who owns a pencil is an architect, and every guy who owns a trowel is a contractor." So it is essential that we check credentials carefully. There is no chamber of commerce here, no *buen* business bureau. We ask at the real-estate offices but cannot be certain who is being recommended or why. Estela is out of our price range. So we turn to the only reliable source of information in town. After several days of diligent research, we compare recommendations from tables seven, nine, and twelve at Rollie's and narrow down a short list of three candidates. We get phone numbers for all three and make appointments to meet them on different days.

The first architect shows up three hours late, the second shows up two days late, and the third shows up on time. He knocks at the door one morning, doffs his flat-brimmed hat, and announces himself: "Aurelio Carrillo, *su servidor.*"

CHAPTER 10

Aurelio the Architect . . . A Parade in San Pancho . . . Triny and Gloria

Señor Aurelio Carrillo has worked as a designer and builder in Sayulita for twenty-five years. He is a dapper man with a ruddy complexion and a small mustache. He wears a flat-brimmed straw hat with its thin leather thong behind his head—he is rarely without it, we are to learn. He greets us at the door with a bow and a low sweep of his hat, like a caballero at the royal court, revealing a shock of white in his curly black hair. There is a slight grin as he does so; when he says, "*Su servidor,*" meaning "Your humble servant," I feel the grin is balanced precisely between playful respect and irony.

We sit down at our rented *equipale* stick-and-leather table to tell him what we have been thinking. We speak mostly in Spanish, which I attempt to simultaneously translate for Thia, but when I stumble, Aurelio has enough command of English to fill in. He tells us in his circumlocutory way that he is not a licensed architect—he dropped out during a family emergency and never completed his degree—but has designed and built many homes in the area. We tell him about our hacienda dreams, about our vision of a little courtyard, about wanting to build in brick and tile. Our lot is modest, and we don't want to use all the space, so we tell him that we are debating whether to build up to two or even three stories in height. I give him a little sketch I have made and ask him a couple of questions about his experience. As we do with the other two candidates, we offer him a preliminary fee of $250 to give us a sketch of a floor plan and an elevation to give us an idea of his style.

"You cannot always depend on the tongue for information; sometime it is better to see with one's own eyes. I, Aurelio Carrillo, invite you, Señor Barry y Señora Thia, to accompany me while I show you some of my work." Aurelio has a courtly, deliberately formal way of speaking, which he undercuts with sly looks of amusement. He can become animated, using both his hands and his arms expressively. "Please," he says, sweeping his outstretched hands toward his red truck parked outside, "allow me to convey you."

As Thia and I begin to clamber into his truck, Aurelio rushes around to our side to hold open the door for Thia. He drives us up to several houses he has designed "with the owners" and built with his crews. We stop at one of the houses he built in stages, beginning in 1984, for Sayulita's best-known resident artist, Evelyne Boren and her husband, Michael Sandler. It sits high on a hill, directly above the fishing-boat side of the town beach, and it is an early version of the now-familiar rancho-beach style, combining tiles and beams, open spaces and sweeping vistas.

Driving over in his pickup truck to see our lot, he speaks about his affection for the village, his hope that the streets would not be paved anytime soon ("Look how natural this looks, how much a part of the earth"), and says that it is his job not just to design what his clients say they want, but what they feel.

"I want to let their horses run free," he says.

At our lot, we walk around the property, talking about the dimensions of the house and whether there might be a view if we built high enough. I look up to see Eagle George, wearing his Stetson, loping over from next door to join us. I am about to introduce the two men, but he and Aurelio have known each other many years, and they embrace each other. Aurelio has one of my pencil sketches in his hand, and now Eagle George leans over to confer with us.

Our iron gates are now open, which is an invitation to enter, to stop in. A Mexican who is strolling by and an American couple wander in, to look the place over, to offer advice, and at one point there are six people gathered around Aurelio, nodding or stroking their chins as they look from my sketch around the lot. As we all file out, Eagle George takes me aside to say that Aurelio may well be an A-number-

one-quality kind of person. But he may not know about septic tanks
and cesspools, George says, so we should remember to consult him.

Aurelio drops us off, and we agree to see each other in a few days,
when he has sketched a floor plan and a rough map of our lot. Thia and
I have concurred that if his sketch is competent, Aurelio is the one we'd
like to work with. The other two candidates seemed more conventional,
but we ask them for sketches too. (We also have not yet adjusted to their
relaxed sense of time and appointments.) The going price, after the preliminary sketch, for full architectural plans including floor plans, eleva-
tions, plumbing, and electric grids: $1,500. The engineering report will
be extra. I sit down and make more sketches until late afternoon. I am
trying to let my horses run free.

We run over to San Pancho—finally—to spend part of the afternoon
and evening with our Casa Obelisco friends. San Pancho's quiet streets
are usually a contrast to jumping Sayulita's, but today is Revolution Day,
and a fiesta and a parade are scheduled at dusk. San Pancho has an
unusual history. Like Sayulita, it was no more than a few hundred huts
and palapas in the 1960s. Then in 1968, Luis Echeverría, future president of Mexico, took an interest in the village and built a scenic estate
nearby. Echeverría, who thought of himself as a man of the people,
decided he would make San Pancho into a model village of the future,
a small center of industry and crafts. He built several factories, a
museum, and a hospital; he even brought in Japanese fishery experts to
teach the fishermen modern techniques for their catch. The streets of
the village were named after significant places of the underdeveloped
world: Calle Cuba, Calle Nicaragua, Calle El Salvador, Calle Cambodia,
Calle Saigon . . . and for some cryptic reason, Calle Tahiti. The main
street in town is Avenida Tercer Mundo, or Third World Avenue.

People here still remember what it was like: full employment, factories humming, the village prospering. Then Echeverría, elected president, in the tradition of many predecessors, left office under a cloud and
fled the country. The heavily subsidized factories of San Pancho closed
down, the museum was shuttered, and people were out on the Third
World street. (The hospital, which I went to for my broken toe, sur-
vives.) It is not until recently, with the arrival of gringos and tourism,
that the village has regained its footing.

We will have ringside seats for the parade at La Ola Rica, the town's best restaurant. Barbara, Bill, Judi, and John are waiting for us. Effervescent, truth-telling as ever, Barbara hugs Thia and looks me over. My mustache makes me look older, she says; doesn't like it, when am I shaving it off? Bill, who's put on some of the same weight that I have, in the same places, hugs us and waves us to our seats. Judi, dark haired, with a Boston accent, and John, trim, quiet, and silver topped, are also here to review the parade. We make small talk, order margaritas, and sit back to watch.

Revolution Day celebrates the Revolution of 1910, so the streets are filled with little Pancho Villas and Emiliano Zapatas. The parade has several marching bands, white-costumed riders on horseback, toddlers crowded into the back of pickups, a couple of young women perched on the roof of a truck cab. There is even a homecoming queen—here, the Queen of the Third Age, elected by collection boxes around town—who is an old, wizened woman seated on a plastic chair in the back of another pickup truck, surrounded by women friends of a similar age, similarly balanced precariously on chairs as the truck bumps along. She is waving to the crowd with the back of her palm, like Queen Elizabeth.

But it is the kids who are the stars. The young boys, with large curly greasepaint mustaches, are marching along in white cotton suits, bandoliers across their chests, and carrying toy rifles. The little girls are in traditional *tapatía* hoop dresses with sashes proclaiming them princesses of this or that block.

"See how clean the streets are?" Barb observes. She says she organized a trash clean-up the day before by offering T-shirts to the kids who brought in the most trash; several of the kids went into people's homes and brought out trash to add to their stash. "There's a ninety-year-old couple in town," says Barb. "One of the gringos here pays them to pick up trash on regular days," she says. "They don't want charity, they want to earn their keep, so you see this old man bending over to pick something up while his wife holds onto him so he won't topple over. Sweet, sweet people."

I mention the toddlers in the truck, the girls perched on the roof, the old women teetering in chairs in the back of the truck.

"In the States," says John, "there would be lawyers running alongside them, hoping to get them to file a lawsuit if they happen to topple over."

"Yeah," says Bill. "The entire country is a fantasyland for negligence attorneys—open holes in the sidewalk, kids running between cars, parades with disaster waiting to happen—but it's not an issue here."

"Two words," says Barb.

"No liability?" I ask.

"You're assimilating," says Barb.

Thia comments on the large number of young mothers with one and even two children.

"Of course, many don't marry," says Judi, "but it's not like it is in the States, where a single mother is on her own. Here, more often the father lives with her and supports her; they just don't get married, maybe because it's such a hassle to get divorced."

Bill tells us he has, alas, closed down the Drunken Monkey bar that he had been running out of a second-floor porch in a building near the entrance to town. "I was just breaking even," he says, "and I was getting ragged trying to be a good barkeep and still help out with the bed and breakfast." He says he got a lifetime's education in running a business in Mexico. "It took me a full year to get the government to accept our taxes," he laughs. "I told our accountant that I wanted to pay our fair share, no matter how difficult it was. He said, 'Why?'"

At a nearby table, we overhear two gringo couples, probably retired, complaining about a number of things: the water, their maid, the condition of the streets.

The implication, of course, is that it's all so much better back home. As I'm beginning to do by reflex, when I hear a gripe—or think of one myself—I find myself making a quick mental check on its equivalent in the States. Don Adams, who wrote the funny, informative *Head for Mexico: The Renegade Guide,* coined the term "gringo amnesia," by which Americans, criticizing some aspect of life in Mexico, conveniently forget about life back home in the States—where electricity was *never* suspended, the telephone *never* went dead, there was *never* a speck of trash in the streets, the sewer *never* backed up, and so on. Why Americans would choose to live somewhere that they constantly criticize is befuddling—and profoundly irritating—to Mexicans, as I will learn.

The evening ends on a somber note, discussing the private lives of Mexican couples the four of them have known.

"Even though Mexican men treat their kids wonderfully," says Judi, "when it comes to how they treat their women, there's still a certain amount of, well—"

"Wife beating," Barb says bluntly. "We've had temporary female help come to work bruised and bloodied. The nicest, gentlest men you could imagine when you meet them can become tyrants at home. It's an old macho legacy, and they haven't shaken it yet. It's gonna take time."

I hear evidence of this from Mexicans themselves fairly often—a local radio show regularly features advice to men on treating their wives better—but my comparison reflex still kicks in. It is certainly less culturally acceptable for men to beat their wives in America, but I reflect on some of the deeply vicious, wounding spousal warfare I've seen in the States—including a recent rash of empty nesters in our age group—and I stifle the impulse to patronize. It's enough to think wife beating in Mexico a bad thing; I'm just not certain, as I might have been before coming here, that my culture is the one to teach the necessary moral lessons. Still, I admire the fact that Barbara and Bill and some of their Mexican friends have begun, well behind the scenes, to organize an effort to provide counseling for battered women.

I watch a young Mexican couple walking home from the parade with two children holding balloons, one child riding her father's shoulders, the woman leaning into him with another child in her arms. I may not be getting the whole picture, I may not know what happens when the doors close behind them, but it's the image I take home with me that night.

The next afternoon, I return to La Ola Rica. It is owned and run by Trinidad "Triny" Palomera Gil and her domestic partner, Gloria Honan, who are close friends of Barb and Bill's. Triny has a rare stretch of time off; she and Gloria make the hour drive to Puerto Vallarta every day to pick up produce and supplies, then run the restaurant from six to closing time, six days a week. Once a week they drive to Guadalajara, three and half hours away. Triny handles the front of the restaurant—the waiters, the customers—while Gloria does the cooking.

Triny is a small woman in her midthirties with a dark, cherubic face that has Indian features. She was born in San Pancho, where her father had a small coconut-oil business. She knows (and is related) to most people in town and has watched the influx of foreigners into San Pancho with a bemused eye. We sit at one of her tables and talk.

I ask her about the reaction of townspeople to the Americans' arrival.

"Mostly it was for the good, but the Americans caused some resentment and envy—all that money, when Mexicans had so little. It was too bad, because some of our villagers had become lazy about working hard, and spent their time being envious of Americans."

"So how did the Mexicans and Americans get along?"

"I'm sorry to say I know some Mexicans who take advantage of Americans. They say American, they think money. But I know Americans who take advantage of Mexicans; bullying them, sometimes humiliating them. Sometimes I hear jokes about Americans among my Mexican friends, but it is usually because of how some Americans act—always complaining, for instance, about Mexico. What is difficult for us to understand is, if there are so many things some Americans don't like about living here, why are they living here?

"Once I saw a petition being passed around by Americans in Sayulita, to get the disco to shut down earlier, to keep the music down. But look, this is our culture: our roosters crow, our dogs bark, we play our music loud, we have loudspeakers at fiestas, our workers shout at each other, our families are loud and demonstrative. And Americans want to change this? If they don't like it, why do they want to live here? It's a puzzle. An American woman not long ago walked into a cantina with a loud jukebox—and unplugged it! There was another woman who moved in downtown, near the church, and didn't realize there was an early Sunday service, with lots of people gathering and talking before mass. Well, she got up one Sunday morning, took her hose, and squirted water on all the churchgoers. The people really stared at her."

"What did the churchgoers do?"

"They laughed."

"What about temptation?" I ask as we watch a rare rain squall. "Does living around these rich people change Mexican behavior?"

"There is some dishonesty, sure. But the vast majority of people are honest. Much more honest than Americans seem to think."

"How about pressures to sell out, to sell one's property?"

"Well, it is a great temptation, especially when real-estate prices go up so much. And the real tragedy is for the Mexicans who sold out for a low price, because it was more money than they had ever heard of. For some, it meant buying a truck and a big-screen TV—and all of a sudden it's gone, and they're on the streets, without a home, without land."

"Do you think everyone eventually has his price?"

"I'd like to think it's in the character of the Mexican to resist, to keep their homes—and many will. But how many? I don't know."

I ask Triny about her personal journey. She sighs, apparently wondering if she should discuss the topic. Nodding, her decision made, she tells this story:

"Gloria and I have known each other eleven years. Back then, my family had the only telephone in town—everyone used it. Gloria came for a vacation visit with her three kids; two daughters and a son. She came over to use the phone. I got to know her and the kids. Gloria and I began to know each other, to talk, and then there came a crazy moment when . . . we began a relationship. We moved in with each other, but no one here would accept us, not even my family. Gloria's family back home—her husband, her parents—well, it was bad, it was very tough on everyone."

"She left her husband, her children, everyone, to live with you?"

"Yes. And it was so difficult, we had to move to Puerto Vallarta to live there. Then we went to the United States to talk to Gloria's family, and then back to Puerto Vallarta. We moved into a tiny apartment, ate beans and tortillas. We sold things on the street. When we returned here to San Pancho, we bought this little place that was just a room. We thought of opening it as a coffeehouse, mostly for the Americans. I got a table from my mother and four chairs from somewhere else."

"Was your family starting to accept the situation?"

"Yes. Here in San Pancho, there are a fair number of gays, openly so, and it seems to be accepted and tolerated within the Mexican community—except, oddly enough, in a gay person's family. There it can be a scandal, as it was for us. But things got better."

"Having a successful business must have helped."

"Yes. In time, we decided to expand to dinner service, and then Americans began to come. They accepted us and liked our food—Gloria's food. Eventually, Gloria's kids came to accept the situation, and one daughter even moved down here to live."

I ask Triny if she runs the restaurant exclusively for the American trade.

"We're running it mostly for Americans; they are the ones who can afford it. But more and more Mexicans have begun to come too. For the poorer customers, I adjust our prices."

I ask her about how Americans mix with the townspeople.

"My biggest surprise," says Triny, "is Americans with too much money who come down here and live in a bubble of their own. They don't want to go out, to meet Mexicans, to learn the culture; they don't want to grow. And that's sad. In the past, there was one couple with a lovely baby, and they made it known they did not want a Mexican to *touch* her. Too afraid of dirt and disease, I guess. On the other hand, a couple like Bill and Barbara, who got out, who met people, absorbed our culture, who hug our babies and join in on trash pickups—the Mexicans *love* them."

I tell her that it seems to me more and more Americans will be living among Mexicans, that it is one of the few growth businesses for a town like this. How do Mexicans talk about that?

"There is more and more acceptance," she says. "This is what I hear. There is work. They can live better. One of the things that surprises Mexicans in a healthy way is to find that not all Americans are rich; some are even poor. But let's face it, we are conditioned to say that gringo equals money."

"What parts of American culture do Mexicans adopt?"

"It's all about television," says Triny. "Mexicans want to imitate what they see of the United States on TV: Jennifer Lopez, the girls' shirts cut high on their stomach. They even name their babies after American names they hear on TV. There are now lots of Mexicans named Johnny or Charley."

"What American traits do Mexicans dislike?"

"Our mentality isn't to look at someone and want to change them," says Triny. "Mexicans certainly imitate a lot of what they see in Americans, and there are modern things—in the way they build houses, for example—that they have been happy to adopt. But I remember how I felt when I went with Gloria to the States and saw my first American suburb. I looked around, saw the immaculate lawns, and said, Where *is* everyone? Where are the children? Where are the dogs? Where is the noise? We Mexicans don't want to imitate how you spend your time—rushing to work, rushing home for a quick lunch, family rushing off in different directions. Nobody wants *that*."

CHAPTER 11

Defining Mañana . . . A Perfect Marriage . . . Sunday at the Rodeo

For quite a while, the big topic around our breakfast table is how high to go with the house? Sayulita's ring of hills tempts home builders with commanding views. There is frequent friction in town over one neighbor obstructing another's view; the polite thing is to check your plans with your neighbors first. However, we are on a flat piece of land, with a palm-blocked vista. Great location, but it's doubtful we will have a view, even from a second or third floor. If we *could* see the ocean, we might build up, and add a viewing palapa on the roof. But there are no houses around our lot with second or third floors that would give us a perspective on what we might see. In the States, before making a major financial decision like this, we might consider hiring a crane to rise to a third-story height and give us an assessment. Surely science or engineering has a solution for us here.

It comes to me: there is a tall mango tree in the middle of our lot. If someone could somehow get to the top of it . . . well, we're in Mexico; time to improvise. I approach one of the younger workers building on the floors above our rental apartment. His name is Enrique, and he is seventeen. I ask him if he climbed trees as a kid. Of course, he says; he would shimmy up palms all the time. I make him a proposition. I tell him to ask his boss for a half hour off and ask him to wait for me.

I duck into the apartment to tell Thia what I am doing.

"That's ridiculous and dangerous," she says. "Do you realize we'll be responsible for him if he falls?"

I remind her of how little scientific exploration there would be without boldness of purpose. I look around the apartment for instruments that will accompany me and my assistant on our Balboan quest for a sight of the Pacific. There is a large ball of twine, which I take. For a plumb line, I will need some weight. I assess the tools available and take the can opener, then tie it expertly to the twine. I string out the twine against our tape measure and make a couple of knots at twenty-five and thirty feet. We set off.

At the lot, Enrique slips out of his sandals and climbs barefoot in less than thirty seconds almost to the top, and drops the plumb line. He calls down to me, *"No se puede ver."* Can't see the ocean. Disappointment. I ask him to climb higher. He does, and repeats his call—no ocean view. Finally, I say, go as high as possible. The plumb line now measures thirty-three feet from Enrique to can opener.

He suddenly cries out, like a sailor spotting a spit of land, *"Agua!"* Water!

I ask him how much water he can see, and he leans down toward me and holds his thumb and forefinger an inch apart. *"Vista muy pequeña."*

It's not much to pin our hopes on, but I pay Enrique and go home to present Thia with the fruits of my research. It pains her slightly to acknowledge that I found the right empirical method of measuring our view, but we decide, yes, we are going for the extra height. At least we will have a way to rise above our little walled compound and feel the sea breezes and gaze down at the town. At best, we will have a tiny glimpse of the ocean. I recall a *New Yorker* cover cartoon called "Partial View," which shows a minuscule sliver of blue peeking through a mass of dark high-rises. With a pavilion on our roof, we might even be able to do better. I make a couple of elevation sketches to show to Aurelio.

It is now becoming winter on Mexico's Pacific Coast, which means the temperatures are above eighty during the day and drop down to sixty or less in the evening. We are invited to two Thanksgiving parties: one at Chuck and Teke Mohill's, up on their spectacular bluff, with an infinity pool that disappears straight into the sea; the other at Dick Dobbeck and Cheryl Vaughn's, right on the beach, with terraces and gardens and

a great carved wooden gate. We have stuffing at one party and cranberry sauce at the other. It is a change from the diet of tacos and tamales
that we have for at least one meal every day.

Thia has been thriving at the restaurant, meeting everyone in town,
impressing the Mexican staff at Rollie's with her exuberance. Everyone
gets a nickname sooner or later in Mexico, and Thia's already been
given one by the night shift: La Luz—"the Light." Her Spanish lessons
have slowed, but Thia uses what she has, and a fair amount of Italian,
to get by at work. She says *"Buona sera"* and calls the men *signor* and the
women *signorina,* and it's close enough. At one point during her first
week, La Luz tried to thank the staff of this new establishment for their
patience with her, and it came out in Spanish that she was thanking the
patients of this new institution, for which she got a nice scattering of
applause.

As for my days, I stay busy in my semiretirement. I exercise, talk to
my neighbors, read my books, do errands relating to home building,
worry about problems relating to home building, take short day trips to
surrounding villages, meet someone for a fruit drink, then go online to
research and pitch freelance articles. In the evenings, when Thia is
working, I write. There is a local preservation group I am taking an interest in. I also take care of our burgeoning real estate interests ("Hello,
Harvey—any offers yet?" "Well, funny you should ask, because I gotta
tell ya, no firm bites yet, but I have no problem with that, here's my
thinking . . ."). All in all, it may not sound like a very full day. But there
are things that need doing here, everyday things. One of Bill Kirkwood's
mantras is, "I got up this morning with nothing to do, and by the time
I went to bed it was only half finished."

As almost everyone will admit, doing the ordinary errands of life—
ordering, repairing, picking up, delivering, repainting, replacing—takes
more time and demands more ingenuity in Mexico. It is a truism that
Mexicans have a fundamentally different sense of time, inherited (or so
it's said) from the Toltecs and Aztecs. Time is circular, not linear, so
there is the expectation that if something does not happen as scheduled, it will happen when it is meant to, as fate will have it. It is true
that one can spend a lot of time in Mexico waiting. *Mañana* is a derisive
cliché to Americans, but that is because we choose to take it literally, in
its dictionary definition. Yes, it means "tomorrow," and yes, it also
means "morning," but in accepted practice it can as easily mean the day

after tomorrow, possibly in the afternoon, possibly later. It is not a noun but a conditional future. It is *not today*. Mexicans, a polite people, do not like to disappoint. Mexicans, a proud people, do not like to say they do not know. Americans who don't get it are constantly frustrated. Americans who *do* get it don't let the long waits and the missed dates bother them; they know that life is long, and that someone will arrive by and by, in his or her own sweet, circular time.

Beach scene:

Late in the morning, the fishing boats come back toward Sayulita beach, one by one. There is a routine: A friend of the fisherman clears a little patch of beach by asking sunbathers to move to the side. Then the man in the boat revs up and smashes over the waves and lifts the motor at the last second so that the boat runs up the beach to a stop on the sand—simply unimaginable on a crowded public beach in the States. Then, sunbathers and fishermen place themselves in position around the boat and begin pulling it up the rest of the way to a safe spot on the beach. When that is done, some of the same sunbathers, and a few of the girls who have been watching, gather around and point at the freshly caught mahimahi and red snapper, some still flapping in the bottom of the boat, and take away their lunch or dinner, wrapped in newspaper.

Village scene:

Because of the building boom in the village, construction workers stream in every morning by the truckload. A pickup truck parks by the town bridge, and as many as twenty workers jump out of the back, many holding lunch in a tied handkerchief. I see a broad, scowling bull of a man with a scar running down one side of his face, a couple of glinting silver teeth, and hair that already seems dusty. He is wearing worn shorts and shoes with flapping soles, as well as an impeccable powder-blue beach sweatshirt reading Beverly Hills Polo Association.

Apartment scene:

Though we've been in no hurry to hire domestic help, the war against dust is getting to us, so we give in. A young woman who calls herself Yoya now comes in to sweep and dust a couple of afternoons a week. One day I am at home, writing, lifting my feet off the floor when she mops under me. A minute later, I hear her say, "Oooh, a little amigo . . ." She is holding a small, brown, dead scorpion by the tail. It was on our bathroom floor. It's the light-brown dangerous kind. If you get stung, you drink a lot of water, take an antihistamine, and wait a few minutes to see if your arm or leg is getting numb. If you do feel numbness, someone drives you to the San Pancho clinic for an antihistamine IV. People without specific vulnerabilities don't die from them, but Yoya's little amigo reminds me that I have been remiss about shaking out my shoes in the morning.

I play poker with Doc Forbis, the regular host of our game, and I occasionally meet with him on slow afternoons in his casita in the heart of town. Doc wears his salt-and-pepper hair cropped short, is a steady player, and is half owner of the real-estate agency that Harvey works for. The other owner is his wife, Reyna Garcia. They have an unusual marriage: Reyna speaks no English, and Doc speaks no Spanish. It is a good marriage, by all accounts.

Doc came down in 1990 with three old classmates from Sacramento State College, and all of them ended up buying land here—which back then was even riskier, if far less costly, than it is today. He was, frankly, looking for a wife. He was living a hippie life in Sayulita—which was then mostly a few palapas, horses, and the occasional Jeep—and had come to town with a list of attributes he wanted to find in a wife. As he was reading them one day on the beach, a friend from the village said, "That sounds like Reyna."

Reyna García was born a few miles away from the village and belongs to one of the "five families" who settled Sayulita. Dark and slim with coal-black hair to her shoulders, Reyna is related to dozens of people in the town and was as well respected as any of the town leaders—"and that's saying something," says Doc. She is a licensed nurse and worked for twelve years at San Pancho's clinic. Every day she walked from Sayulita out to the highway, where she caught a bus to the highway drop-off into San Pancho, then walked to the clinic—about ten kilometers a day in all. She sent four brothers to college on her earnings.

When Doc was looking for a wife, Reyna says she was looking for a husband—preferably an American, because she wouldn't consider the local Mexican men she knew as potential husbands. Too macho. Doc, who does not flinch from sweeping generalizations, says, "Most Mexican men treat their wives humiliatingly." He spoke no Spanish, and at fifty-two, didn't have the ear to learn it. Reyna was no better at English. He courted her for six months in the Mexican style: never alone with her, always accompanied by female relatives, her brothers keeping a watchful eye on him. He would sit at a table with her, spreading out his dictionaries and phrase books, picking out one word at a time. When it came time to pop the question, he had a bilingual friend write out his proposal in Spanish; then he took Reyna out on the Sayulita beach, got down on one knee, and asked her to marry him, pronouncing the words phonetically. She said *sí*, and became his wife, real-estate partner, and, in time, his tender nurse.

Doc has had five ruptured-disc operations on his spine, each worse than the last. He is in pain every hour of the day and constantly on medication. He can no longer move around the village and spends most of his time in a dark room with the windows open and the fan turning above him. Reyna tends to him and brings him meals and gossip about the agency and the village. He calls to her in the next room during a conversation he and I are having.

"Mi amor. Hambre." Doc's way with Spanish today is to pluck one word—the key infinitive that he knows—while ignoring all other syntax or vocabulary. So: "My love. Hunger." Other times, I hear him say, *"Mi amor, abrir* window?" which Reyna knows means, "My love, can you please open the window?"

Doc says, "We communicate on a *deeper* level because we don't know each other's language." Later, when I talk to Reyna about it in Spanish, she says the same thing. As I leave on one of my early visits, I hear her ask him how he is feeling: *"¿Cómo te sientas?"* He says, *"Dolor, mi amor—malo."* Pain, my love—bad.

We have not yet officially chosen Aurelio as our designer and have tabled the other sketches as we try to make up our mind. Aurelio seems to listen well when he is not talking a kilometer a minute, and is spirited without being insistent about what he believes would be a better idea. When I thank him again for sending in his sketch and being so prompt, he laughs and says, "When you are selling tamales—*sell* the tamales."

This leads to a discussion about different nationalities and their concepts of time and money. I ask him about his experience with a variety of clients, and he says that Germans, by far, are the hardest to build for; they are so exacting about organization and time, it can be overwhelming in this climate. Next, he says, come Canadians, because their currency is weak, and they are always looking for a deal. Next toughest (more so than Americans) are the Mexican clients, who want everything but everything on the cheap. If an American wants to build a house in ten months, Aurelio has learned that it is an economic agreement, and the American will abide by it, and expect you to abide by it, all the way to the last day. If a Mexican wants something in ten months, says Aurelio, it is more of a wish, and the terms may change halfway down the road.

We are beginning to question our three-floor idea; Doc Forbis says the mistake Americans make is to build too big a house. And three stories *is* a long way to go for a bitty view. But though we are planning to build up, it will be a small house: two thousand feet maximum. So for now we stick with it and have some new ideas for a living room area. I ask Aurelio to give us a more detailed sketch with a location for a small pool. I remind him that we are trying to keep to a budget, and that he should squeeze the square feet where possible. Aurelio agrees, reminding us that a sketch is *borrador* in Spanish, which means something that can be *borrado*—erased. So there is no problem in going over and over a sketch, he says. The challenge will be—and I can see that he is giving us fair warning—to stick to an idea once the plans are final and construction is under way.

Rollie tips me off to a Sunday event I should not miss: the Sayulita Rodeo. It takes place every Sunday in the fall and winter at a small ring just outside the village. It is a concrete stadium in some disrepair, with just three rows of continuous round stone benches overlooking a six-foot drop into a matted grass circle, and a small grandstand to the side. Advertisers have panels along the ring: Lesy Groceries, Tepatco Butcher. As I arrive, music is blasting from loudspeakers at the business end of the ring. Rodeo-goers are in their Sunday *vaquero* best: the men in white straw-brim hats and boots; the women, many of them, in low-cut black-lace blouses, tight jeans, and tightly braided, swept-back hair with spit-curl accents. There is a festive air in the stands. Toddlers, babies, and dogs roam freely about the benches.

There is beer everywhere. One brand, Modelo, apparently has the franchise for these affairs, because it is being hawked, passed, tossed, shared, guzzled, and emptied everywhere the eye can see. Inside the ring, the action has yet to begin. Four *charros* on horseback circle the ring, nudging their horses into little sideways dances, and are evidently there to distract the Brahma bulls when riders are thrown or dismount, and to keep some kind of order in the crowd. It is good to know there is some kind of security in the ring, for this—the crowd, the beer drinking—looks a bit casual for a sport involving a group of thousand-pound angry, bucking male cattle and no guardrail at the edge of the seats.

There is a band on a platform taking up most of the available sound, a dozen or so extremely enthusiastic musicians in white jackets playing guitars and trumpets, singing upbeat ranchera songs, while they do dance moves straight out of the Temptations. In the center of a ring, a small ten-year-old boy in an oversized black cowboy hat dances around in place while the charros, the riders, circle with their dancing horses.

It is hard not to notice that the charros inside the ring are drinking beer, too. People are buying beers for the four horsemen, passing down cans to them into the ring—sometimes two at a time, sometime a six-pack. As the afternoon sun begins to set, and we still await the first bull event, the ring charros are downing beers at approximately the same pace as the crowd, which pace is quickening. The charros take the beer as their due, then make their horses spin around fast in a tight circle, at the end of which both the horse and rider appear giddy. As they finish their beers, they toss them onto the ground of the ring beside them.

The riders of the Brahma bull event, which is in fact the *only* event at the Sayulita Rodeo, are announced. "Let's hear it," shouts the announcer, "for the Monster, who is so ugly, even the bulls turn aside." A cowboy who looks about fifteen takes a bow. "Let's hear it for el Güero, the Blond, and *quién sabe* how *he* turned out that way!" Another fifteen-year-old in boots, stringy blond hair, and cowboy hat, takes a bow.

Then another twenty minutes of singing and drinking pass while the athletes prepare for their moment of truth. There is some clattering at the cattle gate; suddenly, a huge bull with a small cowboy attached to it comes bounding out of the pen and, in what can only be a couple of seconds, throws the rider. The crowd gives the kid a hand, and more beer is purchased and passed around. The drinking now gets serious, as does the dancing. More Modelos are bought for the spinning horseback charros, and piles of cans begin to collect beneath the horses, who must dance even faster just to stay off the cans. Fans emulate the charros by tossing *their* beer cans, some half-finished and spouting geysers of brew, along with lit cigarette butts, into the center of the ring. I've not seen an athletic field used as both ashtray and garbage dump in this way before, but I make no judgments.

There are another fifteen minutes of music and dancing and beer throwing, until a new rider is announced. Bull and rider come out of the gate, the bull instantly throws the rider, who is warmly applauded, and the festivities continue. Men and women, little boys in boots and little girls with hoop earrings, get up to do a cowboy two-step on the stone seats. A fistfight breaks out, which the band changes tempo to accompany, but it is a half-hearted fight that ends up in *tu-mamá-también* insults and laughs.

Another fifteen-year-old rider, another bull, another cowboy flat on the grass, applause. This continues until the crowd is more or less universally drunk, with perhaps a hundred beer cans lying in the ring, and until one of the charros has fallen off his horse from too much spinning. A stout rider and his horse are leaning at rest against the side of the ring, in recovery. The band does its synchronized Temptations moves until late in the evening.

It may not be the Ballet Folklórico, but I don't think I've seen a more authentic entertainment relished by so many people of so many ages. I am among the last to leave, and I sit watching the Sayulita Rodeo, with all its cowboys and cowgirls, flicker out like a doused campfire.

CHAPTER 12

A Birthday . . . Eagle George Hits the Road . . . A Surprising Phone Call

December 12 arrives—my birthday, or, as I think of it these days, my very own Mexican Day of the Dead. We more or less observed it at the party in New York before we left; I see little reason to celebrate it here, though Jeanne sent a chocolate soufflé home from the restaurant the night before. But when my sister Michele calls me and says, "Hi, Lupe," I remember that here above all there will be no ducking the festivities, if not for me, then for the Lady of Guadalupe. The familiar iconic image of the Virgin Mary surrounded by a halo will dominate the day, which is scheduled to have parades, fiestas, bands, masses, and the running of a fireworks bull after sunset.

I recall Rita Gonzales, the Indian woman who cooked for, and lived with, our family in Mexico City for seven years, taking me down by bus one afternoon in the 1950s to see the old basilica. (Even then it was sinking into Mexico City's watery soil. It was replaced by the new basilica in 1974.) Walking past hundreds of pilgrims, many on their knees, who were making their way toward the inside of the church, I saw the "miraculous portrait" supposedly imprinted on the cloak of the Indian Juan Diego in 1531. Rita told me I was lucky to have been born on such a day. On the way home, she explained that the Virgin was a more important religious figure than Jesus, and that Jesus might not have gotten into so much trouble if only he had listened to his mother.

Here in Sayulita, I am reminded of Rita, whom I cherished, when I see a box of matches called Clásicos. Catching sight of them on our kitchen table, when I light the gas stove for the first time, I get a Proustian jolt, a remembrance of a moment past: the design on the Clásicos matchbox is of the Venus de Milo, with a train locomotive, for some obscure reason, coming out of a tunnel beneath the statue. I must have been about nine, and had been taught something about Greek statuary by my father. We were in the family kitchen at our home in Lomas de Chapultepec, and I asked Rita why the statue shared the matchbook cover with a train. Rita bent over to me, pointed at the Venus de Milo and said, "See this woman? She discovered the locomotive, and for that they cut off her arms." I have remembered that all my life, not only for Rita's cheerfully cynical attitude toward authority, but also, I think, because I was awed by her power of invention.

After Sayulita's parade of floats and pickup trucks with their shaky cargos of waving, sash-wearing celebrants on chairs, we attend a mass in the small church just off the plaza, then come out to watch the running of the bull. A man puts on a papier-mâché bull's head bedecked like a pincushion with fireworks of all sorts. He then runs around the town plaza, shooting off sparklers, Roman candles, and rockets that whiz around the square, scattering children and old people, occasionally caroming off someone's head, or skittering along the sidewalk, before flying off to lodge in a straw palapa roof, causing the owner to run out with a bucket of water. There is screaming and laughing and running around for most of an hour. It's not Pamplona, but it's not Palm Springs, either. The Palm Springs Chamber of Commerce long ago would have sued the parade leaders, banned the bull, and arrested the guy inside.

In the course of visiting our lot one morning, I see that Eagle George is out in front of his house with a pick. He is wearing cutoff jean shorts and is bare-chested, the faded tattooed eagle covering most of the front of his torso. He is the leanest, fittest eighty-three year-old I have ever seen. He is swinging his pick at a rut in the road. If I am not mistaken, he is not so much filling in the rut as deepening it. The rubble and ruts are becoming rougher with each thud of the pick.

"Good morning, George," I say. "Trouble with the road?"

"Yep," he says, wiping his brow. "Too smooth."

"Ah," I say. "You *want* to make the road rougher?"

"Sure. Discourages traffic. Let 'em go around the other way." He swings the pick with authority.

A few minutes and several loose rocks later, he invites me in for juice under his palapa.

"Anyone ever complain?" I ask. "The police, the public-works department?"

He laughs. "We take care of our own public-works problems. Always have."

It is a warm morning, and he brings out freshly squeezed orange juice. I ask him if he feels like continuing with his personal history.

"I'm far too busy doing nothing," he says, and starts in.

When George first arrived in 1968, Sayulita wasn't even a one-horse town: it was a burro town. "The streets smelled of burro urine," George recalls. "We would sleep with rocks next to our cots, and we'd throw them at the burros to shut up their braying at night. The town was full of burros until the price of dog food went up—" George laughs loudly "—and we haven't seen a burro here since." George gathered shellfish. "It was back before they overharvested the oyster beds—we picked so many oysters from the rocks we could hardly sell them." Entertainment was a traveling gypsy troupe that showed open-air movies on strung-up sheets. "And every Saturday night, we'd go dancing in the dust, down where the plaza is today. We used to have great fiestas; we'd roast two, three pigs at a time."

I ask him how he made his living.

"I was an entray-pre-noor," he says, giving it an Oklahoma twang. "I took pigs to market, sold oysters, and began buying land from the ejido and building houses. I started the first real-estate business here." He says he bought his first house on the beach and paid $800 for the land. "I spent forty thousand dollars in construction, all because it had a lot of antiques, stone carvings . . . I sold it recently to an American couple for four hundred thousand."

I bring up the subject of land scams in Mexico.

George says most of the scamming has been around foreigners buying lots in communal ejido land. He praises the ejidos for once being "the right thing, a powerful force when Zapata started the Ayala plan, breaking up the big properties and letting everyone share in the land." But, he says, corruption became rife, adding that the recent changes—

the government-mandated conversion of certain ejido land into "regularized" property that foreigners can buy through a bank trust—is a good thing.

"I owned ejido land under a prestanombre and never had a problem. But some prestanombres got greedy and either scammed people or outright stole land. You know the saying about why God invented cows and gringos? To milk 'em. But as far as the vast majority of Mexicans' reputation goes, they're honest, honest people. Lots of A-number-one quality people. Many more of the crooks have been gringos than Mexicans. There are some Americans, a couple of them still here, who are so crooked they'd steal the diamonds out of their mothers' teeth."

"Why did you never have a problem?" I asked.

"I've been fortunate. I've done things you shouldn't do. I loaned Mexicans money when they needed it without any paper or collateral. Twelve years ago I loaned a woman three thousand dollars, and just the other day she came in and put the money on my table—three thousand dollars. I've looked out for other people in their need, and other people have looked out for me. My oldest Mexican friend, Vicente Pérez, drives me into Vallarta for my doctor's appointments."

He says that for the most part, because of a long history of doing things for themselves, people in Mexican towns create their own way of taking care of one another. "We didn't have a secondary school here," he recalls. "The women in town were upset that they had to bus their children out of town every day. Well, there was this box factory that was going nowhere, and we had a big fiesta, the Mexicans and the gringos, and together we paid to convert that box factory into a school. We got everything in one night! People here take care of their own."

I ask him how he feels about all the growth, the traffic, the land speculation.

"I feel positive about life," George says, "and about the way things have turned out for this village. There are a few drug problems, people growing *mota* [marijuana], cocaine use, but generally far fewer people go out and drink away their money than in other places in Mexico. All this progress is good. People have pickups, they have television sets, they are educating their children. Today we import over two hundred people a day for work!"

What about health care, especially as . . . well, time passes?

George laughs. "Yeah, you know you're gettin' on when undertakers call you up and say, 'How you *doin'*, Eagle George?' But I think the care here is excellent. I had to get some surgery, Dr. Mauro put me on his table, took care of it. Would have taken six weeks in Canada, where we spend our summers. Would you like to wait two years for a hip replacement in Canada? Nurses go on strike there twice a year. In the North, they restrict your freedoms. Here they value their freedoms more.

"I've never liked insurance. Never carried collision on any car. I'd rather die here in Mexico because you get a much better funeral. One of the town leaders, Luis, said to me, 'You old so-and so, you've been here so long, we're going to give you a free parcel of land.' I said, 'Great, how big is it?' He said, 'Two meters by one meter!'"

Thia and I have been enjoying our time alone. During the afternoon, and after she comes home from the restaurant, we are thrown into each other's sole company—and we are liking it. We do not have television, so we talk. There is a scene in a movie we both love, *Two for the Road*, in which Audrey Hepburn and Albert Finney, playing young unmarried lovers, see a silent couple eating dinner. "What kind of people eat a whole meal without talking to each other?" Finney asks. "*Married* people," says Hepburn. We had quoted those lines to each other when we wondered what it would be like when the kids were no longer our main conversational topic. It is a relief to find we have plenty to talk about. Certainly the fact that we are absorbing this new culture, building in unfamiliar territory, improvising our life together, all play a part.

Among the friends we happen to spend time with, there is less drinking than I might have thought in a tropical setting. Of course, it's possible that many *had* to stop drinking altogether. Not only is there a well-marked meeting place up the road for English-speaking AA members, but one evening I wander out to the plaza to see about one hundred Mexicans gathered around a speaker's stand. It is an open-to-the-public outdoor AA convention, and I watch as speakers began with, "*Me llamo Roberto, y soy alcohólico.*"

At the same time, in this progressive town, there is an easy tolerance toward pot smoking. Thia and I have not smoked since the seventies, so it is at first surprising to see a good number of American grown-ups in Mexico enjoying the weed. But it is so readily available here, and so commonly shared, that we occasionally have found ourselves at retiree cocktail hours on someone's terrace, catching the sweet odor of marijuana smoke. However, it is a bit peculiar to see gray-haired people giggling and making a dash for the fridge to root around for munchies.

As I say, we are enjoying our time together.

Then, one night, comes the phone call.

Our older son, Blair, twenty-five, has been reporting for a New York weekly newspaper for three years. We know from his emails and phone conversations that he has been getting restless, but that evening in mid-December we are unprepared for what he says to us.

"Dad, Mom, I have an idea, but I want you to be completely honest with me."

We are listening together on the speaker. "All right," I say.

"How would you feel if I quit my job and came down to live with you guys?"

Silence from our end. Then: "What an idea," says Thia.

"I know this is *your* adventure," he goes on. "But since I was contemplating a change anyway, I thought, When will I ever get a chance like this again? To live with you guys, to learn Spanish, and to think about where I want to go with my life—and do it in paradise!"

It sounds pretty good when he puts it like that. And the truth is, once the surprise wears off, we are flattered and pleased that a son thinks well enough of us to join us in this way. While it is true that adult children boomeranging back to live with their parents is not so uncommon these days, Blair is not doing this out of economic necessity but as a way of rethinking his career, of learning a new language—and because he thinks he'll have fun with us. Our other son, Tyler, twenty-two, is in Damascus, Syria, studying Arabic, and we have bought advance discount tickets for both the boys to join us for Christmas in Sayulita. Blair will simply stay on. Over the next week, there is a flurry of telephone calls from Blair telling us he has given notice at his paper, that he has stashed his sports jackets, that he has gotten a six-month visa, that he is *really doing it.*

Yes, it is flattering, and it will be good to get a younger person's perspective on our adventure, as he calls it.

But still. Just when we thought it was safe to be alone again . . .

*   *   *

The celebrations on December 12 are just the beginning. For the two weeks leading up to Christmas, Mexico celebrates Las Posadas—literally "the inns." This is when children from different neighborhoods each have an evening to re-create Joseph and Mary's journey to find shelter at an inn. A couple of kids are dressed as Joseph and Mary and the other neighbors—adults as well as children—parade after them, holding candles and singing the traditional birthday song, "Las Mañanitas," as they go from inn to inn, being ritually turned away. On the night before Christmas, they find shelter, and the kids get to break a piñata.

In this village, tradition and spirituality coexist with the Christmas vacation rush of a resort at peak season. So the kids' posada processions must weave their way through families in bathing suits and sandals, teenagers carrying boogie boards, college-age kids carrying beer bottles, and a slew of tourists, both Mexican and American. At Christmas, there is no more room at any of Sayulita's inns, and many are turned away.

Five days before Christmas, our sons are scheduled to arrive. Thia has fixed up the extra bedroom, and we have hidden the Christmas gifts we smuggled in, anticipating their visit. Thia is working at Rollie's tonight, so I will drive to Vallarta to pick them up.

I meet the boys at the airport; they are both fit, handsome, and buoyantly happy to be here. On the drive back to Sayulita, they lapse into dueling quotes from *Ferris Bueller's Day Off,* and I consider the moment's unreality: Here are our sons, bantering in the car as they always did in the States—on the way to soccer or Scouts—only this time I am driving them to our new home village *in the Mexican jungle.* When we arrive in Sayulita, driving through its dusty streets, Tyler says, "Hey, this reminds me of Syria." Fresh from Damascus, he will amuse himself in the days ahead finding traces of the Arab conquest of Spain in its language. He points out that a sign on the local mayor's office, *"Alcalde"* comes directly from Arabic—*al-qadi*—and is a term of respect.

"With respect, dude," his brother says, "surf's up."

Blair has in fact surfed a few times in the past, and takes it up with passion. Tyler is happy to sleep hard for the first few days; he has flown a long way. Sayulita is a major destination for surfers: there is a famous women's surfing school, and two sons of a prominent Sayulita family are Mexican surf champions. With its steady break about fifty yards out, Sayulita is a perfect place for novice or midlevel surfers. It is part of the seascape here, the constant speckle of shiny-haired surfers bobbing out beyond the break, waiting to catch their wave and ride it to shore.

We take day trips to the Thursday market in La Peñita, where vast numbers of vendors sell everything from fresh vegetables at incredibly low prices—two dozen oranges for nine cents—to trinkets and CDs. For contrast, we visit the all-gringo luxury enclave of Nuevo Vallarta, where glittering shopping malls are indistinguishable from those in upscale American neighborhoods. Then we drive to the statue-lined beachfront of Puerto Vallarta, where art shops and jewelry stores alternate with Señor Frog's and Hooters. The time-share hawkers are patrolling the *malecón*—the oceanfront sidewalk—with a vengeance, but by now we have come up with a response: "*Non, merci,* we are French Canadian." There are three classes of people, we hear, who are ineligible for the "free" tours and giveaways that are offered as come-ons to get visitors to sign up for time-shares: people who do not have credit cards, people who already own Mexican property—and French Canadians. Whether it is because Canadians are thought to be stingy (and Quebecois partic ularly so), I do not know, but it works for us. The time-share sharpies slink away without further proffer.

In the months to come, we will change our minds about Puerto Va-llarta, mostly through our growing friendship with Dick Dobbeck and Cheryl Vaughn. Dick, retired from the mental-health field in Detroit, is affable and social. Cheryl, a teacher, is a shy woman with an entre-preneurial and artistic streak. She runs a small Spanish-language school in Puerto Vallarta and paints. They will become good friends of ours, sharing generously of their time, showing us the "real" Puerto Vallarta that lies behind the glitzy malecón. A few streets back, the old city has been preserved, and the plazas and cobblestone streets winding up the mountains retain their authentic character.

The day before Christmas, after shopping in Puerto Vallarta at the Gigante supermarket, our family heads back at dusk. We stop to pick up a potted baby palm tree, about four feet tall, for eighteen dollars, and some Christmas lights. We think it is important to have a Mexican Christmas and to celebrate with a local Mexican tree. I ask the nursery man for the name of the palm we have bought, and he says it's called a Jorge Washington palm.

The palm goes up in a little pot on the low credenza by our window, and Thia festoons it with colored sparkling lights. She packed some of the boys' favorites—Hershey's Whatchamacallits and Slim Jims—back in the States for the occasion and bakes Christmas cookies. Thia has become Mexican enough by now to improvise the next step: she takes our snorkeling fins and leans them against the credenza, flippers down, then inserts the candy into the fins' openings as stocking stuffers.

Our rubber stockings leaning by the Christmas tree with care, we go out to the plaza where carolers—both Mexican and gringo—and churchgoers mingle in the warm evening. As we look in at Christmas mass, we hear, improbably enough, an organ version of the Beatles' "Let It Be," with the parishioners singing words in Spanish. The plaza is strung with brightly colored lights. We have our Christmas Eve dinner at Alberto's excellent Sayulita Fish Tacos and make our way home. The next morning, the boys open up packages beneath the tree to find the iPods we bought in the States as a final act of extravagance and smuggled in with the rest. Tyler has brought us an inlaid wooden box from Damascus, and Blair a framed photograph of himself and his girlfriend.

New Year's Eve here does not have quite the ball-dropping champagne tradition it has in the States. We have gathered with Rollie and Jeanne, their actress daughter Jodi, and several neighbors. We have a spirited game of charades. ("Quetzalcóatl!?" Jeanne shrieks. "Who could have guessed *that*? Not fair!") We even have our own fireworks: Blair takes off his shirt, puts on a bandana, and whirls fire poi—cords attached to burning fuel-soaked balls—to the electronic thrum of trance music. We are pleased that the cost of a couple of Ivy League educations has produced at least this one practical skill. It's not Guy Lombardo, and it's not even Dick Clark, but at midnight Nayarit time we are out on the terrace, toasting with plastic cups and a local wine, thinking about our New York friends and family, now asleep in their cold domain.

CHAPTER 13

Art on the Beach . . . Half a Lot . . . An Aurelio Moment

Thia and I decide to give each other our holiday gifts in the old-fashioned Mexican manner—on Three Kings Day, which falls in the first week of the new year. This is when children traditionally put shoes, not stockings (or flippers), outside their doors so that Melchior, Caspar, and Balthasar can leave presents for good little Mexican boys and girls. A week or so before Christmas, before the boys arrived, we stopped along the seafront sidewalk in town to watch an older gentleman painting. We liked his work—primitive beach and jungle scenes with an impressionist's eye— and we realized that we had seen some of it framed on the walls of several friends, including Bill and Barbara, and Dick and Cheryl.

That day we stopped to talk. His name is Victoriano Méndez, and he said that he picks a spot every few months to paint and then moves on. He had studied art in Michoacán and had settled on the Pacific Coast some years ago. He happened to be here in Sayulita for the foreseeable future. We looked over the paintings he had leaning against the easel and did not see exactly what we were looking for.

I asked, "Do you take commissions?"

"*Cómo no,*" he says. (Of course.)

After a little artistic conference, we decided to ask him if he could paint the Sayulita coastline from the perspective of the fishing boats that were pulled up on the beach. He held up his paintbrush, closed one eye, and said, "*Cómo no.*" (Why not.) I asked him if he could include a

103

few pelicans, and he said, *"Cómo no."* (Oh, all right.) We walked off, not certain if we were a couple of philistine Americans who had asked an indigenous artist to paint by numbers, or, more likely, Lorenzo and Clarice de' Medici, now embarked on a new life of patronage of the arts. The agreed-upon price was four hundred dollars, and the delivery date was two weeks later.

Today, Three Kings Day, the painting is due to be finished, and we walk down to see about our commission. Victoriano Méndez looks up from his easel and smiles.

"Ah, so *many* tourists stopped and asked to buy this," he says. He stands up and locates a large canvas he has stashed behind the tree. He holds it up, and we are delighted: the coastal scene is bright and vivid, the reds and yellows he sees in the sky reflected in the water below, and the pelicans are there in midflight. We carry the seascape home and put it away until we can frame it properly.

A call from Harvey. In not a few words, he tells us that he has someone who has bid our asking price for half our hilltop lot. The buyer is Scott Bretschneider, a young executive recruiter from California with a yen for a beautiful view. He arrived in Sayulita a few days ago, got the fever, and asked Harvey to find him something to buy. When he saw our lot, he spent a whole day up there from sunrise to sunset, transfixed by the vista, and decided it was the spot for him. We tell Harvey to tell Scott that he has a deal.

"Well, there's one thing," says Harvey. "I gotta tell you, I don't see a problem here, but I do think in order to wrap this up, we ought to have a firm idea of what you're selling him, eh?" By that Harvey means that we may have decided more or less what portion of the lot we are selling, but we have not done anything so detailed as actually to measure it or section it off.

"Good thinking," I say.

Blair and I meet Harvey and Scott, whose excitement about his purchase is palpable, at our lot on the top of Heart Attack Hill. I have my surveying instrument with us—the same ball of twine that served so capably atop the mango tree—and we set about dividing the property approximately in half. Blair and I hold the string at each end and pace off a logical dividing line along the hillside. Scott joins in, and we decide together what would make the most sense for each lot—a little more room for Scott's parking area here, a little more room for the unsold lot's driveway there. It is remarkably cooperative and very Mexican, this roll-your-own division of property, but I see no reason not to make our buyer happy. After all, I am left with six thousand square feet of a desirable lot that I can sell at some future date, and the sale to Scott will finance some of the construction on our walled property—and just in time. Without this return on our investment, as they say on the financial cable shows, our plans for diversification would be negatively affected. We'd be plumb out of cash.

Back at Harvey's office, Scott is being coached on how he must complete the closing on the property in order to obtain a bank trust. I never completed the requirements to get the trust papers, so he must fill out a slew of documents stating that the bank holds the property in trust for him for fifty years, renewable automatically. I see in his eyes the familiar half-glazed-over, half-terrified look I know so well—the look of a man pretending he is following the tortuous points of Mexican real estate law while at the same time he realizes he is falling into a terrifyingly foreign all-cash hole from which there is no climbing back. I give him a comradely pat on the shoulder and get out of Harvey's office before Scott gets hit with buyer's remorse.

I come home and see that Gaby is still in a holiday mood. I ask him if he would like me to take a family picture with my digital camera. His face lights up, and when I tell him I can do it right away, he points to his well-worn T-shirt and says he will come back when he is dressed properly.

Later, he knocks at the door. His wife, Ofelia, his five-year-old, Fabiola, and two young nieces are with him, in their Sunday best. Gaby is in a crisp, new T-shirt with a Las Vegas logo on it. I pose them, and get the feeling this may be the first family photograph for the Ponce Muñoz family. I get them to smile, snap a good one, and after they have gone, I crop it on the computer before making several prints.

A day later, I am about to go over and present Gaby with his photos, when he shows up at the door with a bottle of wine. It is a village varietal, Los Sabores de Sayulita, bottled by a friend of his here in the village. Thia and I are touched. It doesn't seem as if Gaby can easily afford gestures like this. In any case, we give him his photos, which we have had framed.

I tell him that I am available for birthday parties and such. Gaby mentions that his birthday is in February. "Ah," I say, "big fiesta then, eh?" No, says Gaby. He explains that one year ago his brother, sister-in-law, and a nephew were killed in a car accident nearby. It seems as if everyone we have met has had a friend or relative killed in a traffic accident. Gaby has a photograph of his brother and his family, the only photograph ever taken of them, and says he is not in much of a mood to celebrate when his birthday comes around. His soft smile never leaves his face as he tells us the story.

Blair has shown a knack for cooking and prepares a number of family meals, including a serious breakfast of *chilaquiles*—fried strips of tacos and a fresh tomato salsa. He has become interested in health food and tries hard not to disapprove of our eating habits, particularly my shameful fondness for Bimbo brand white toast, but it comes out anyway. He has embarked on a quiet campaign to improve the nutritional health of his parental roommates, volunteering to do the shopping and increasing our consumption of fruits and vegetables (which must be soaked in Microdyne, an iodine solution that removes impurities). Stealthily, the groceries that I had stocked are replaced by Blair's healthier choices until there is nothing left in our pantry of unwholesome cookies, unwise canned sodas, or totally unacceptable Rice Krispies Treats.

More acceptable are the tortas I buy almost daily for lunch from Doña Lety. One noonday I line up behind two young Huichol girls, dressed in long embroidered dresses and kerchiefs. I ask them if they agree that these are the best tortas in town. "Yes," one of them says shyly in Spanish, "we love them." As they take their torta, they speak to each other in a tongue I cannot understand. They leave, and I ask Doña Lety, "Was that the Huichol language they were speaking?"

She looks past me and calls out, "My daughter, what were you speaking?" Doña Lety's graceful way with the Spanish language includes referring to younger women as "my daughter."

The girl looks back and says, *"Huichola."*

Dona Lety says, "They are authentic, originals."

"What do you mean, authentic?"

"There are fake Huicholes here—they just want to get free peyote and resell it."

Huichol Indians are among the few tribes whose religious use of peyote is legally permitted.

"How can you tell who's fake?"

"Their physiognomy is different from the real Huichol," Doña Lety says, using her remarkable vocabulary with precision as she gestures at her face. "And their shoes. You can spot them."

"Doña Lety, I learn something every time I come here to buy lunch. You're my professor here."

A big, delighted laugh. "Don't exaggerate."

I do not exaggerate.

We now have the final architectural sketches in hand, and, as we thought, our decision is to go with Aurelio. I call up the remaining contender and thank him for his time and tell him a check will be waiting at Lloyd's for him. I then call Aurelio and ask him to meet with us. When he shows up, his straw hat in hand, we sit down, and I say to him formally, "It gives me pleasure to say that we'd like you to be our architect." Aurelio throws back his head, laughs, and says, "Ah, but the pleasure will be mine!" It has been agreed that although Aurelio is also a builder, he is not anxious to spend the better part of a year on yet another construction project. So we will be looking elsewhere for a contractor, with Aurelio's blessing.

We talk a bit about the sketches so far but decide to put off a serious discussion until the next day. Thia and I stay up late talking about the plans. Should we keep it strictly Mexican villa-hacienda? Or should we mix and match, perhaps with one of the immensely popular palapa roofs? Except for a handful of rarely enforced zoning regulations, we are free to be as creative as we wish.

The next morning, at our table, we dig in with Aurelio. We tell him that we want to keep it to Mexican style, not beach style, and so there will be no palapa roof on the house, just a small one by the pool. The house will be a hip roof and tiles. Aurelio patiently explains about weight-bearing walls, where the plumbing pipes would go, how the electrical lines might be laid in. Aurelio's courtliness is cut somewhat by his excitability—he can get dramatic and animated in pursuit of a point. Thia tells him she would like to have the sink positioned so that when people are doing dishes, they are facing the living room. Aurelio smiles, reaches over to pat Thia's arm and says in a Spanish I rapidly translate, "Sometimes it's the job of an architect to tell you what you really *do* in a kitchen." He gets up and does an entire pantomime of bringing food into the house, putting the bag on the counter, bending over the sink to wash the fruits and veggies, saying, "Here you do your tortillas, here you do your dishes . . ." all the while darting from hypothetical refrigerator to stove to sink to show the disaster an inward-facing sink would be. Thia, impressed by the performance, can only agree—the sink must face the wall.

What we have more serious questions about is whether Aurelio has designed or built enough in the Mexican style. Most of what he has shown us of his work is the modern, curved-concrete, beach design. He says there may be a house or two among the dozens he has designed or built that will match what we want, and he would like to take us on one more short tour to look at a couple of his homes—for ideas, if nothing else. We had it in our minds to show *him* a pair of brick houses next to each other done in hacienda style that we had noticed since our arrival. I ask Thia if we should have him swing by that place now, but she says that it might seem rude, that it was his turn to show us something, and we can follow up with our choice later.

Aurelio overhears us and says he would be happy to include a home of *our* choice on this short tour—where would we like to go? We can go look at his houses afterward. We are in Aurelio's truck, and we tell him where to turn. As we approach the houses we have admired—a pair of rambling brick homes set against a hill overlooking the beach—I motion to Aurelio to slow down.

"Why just slow down?" Aurelio says. "Why don't we just go into the driveway there and you can show me?"

We stop, he gets out, and opens up the gate to the driveway.

"What if someone's home?"

He shrugs. "Let's walk up the path there and you can show me,"

We begin to walk up the path to the brick buildings and he breaks into a grin. It finally dawns on me. "This is where you were bringing us, right, Aurelio?"

He continues to smile.

"You designed and built this?"

He bows, sweeps off his hat, and says, *"Su servidor."*

CHAPTER 14

A Golf Round . . .
Sandals and Swords . . . A Departure

Though Blair is here for the long haul, Tyler is staying only ten days, and I want to spend as much time with him as I can. Golf for us has always been a bond, and for years he and I hacked our determined way around public golf courses in the New York City area. We would never talk about anything important; we concentrated on our game, the natural surroundings, and the intrinsic unfairness of the sport. Once a few years back, we went to golf school, at the end of which Tyler had the beaming pleasure of watching me get a middling report card on my athletic progress. "Maybe you'll do better next semester, Pop," Tyler said.

Here in Mexico, he has been dropping hints that if we could afford any of the fancy resorts, it would be way cool if we could hit the links together. We are, after all, living in a vacation area, and I am trying out retirement—both strong indicators to Tyler that golf should be imminent. But in fact, golf courses for those without country club assets are a disappointment in this part of Mexico; it is difficult to find a course that costs less than $150 a round. It is not a sport for the commoner, at least this part of Mexico, so public (affordable) courses are rare. More frustrating, there is a Four Seasons Resort course in nearby Punta Mita that is reputed to be among the best in Mexico, but unaffordable for me.

Punta Mita is the most moneyed neighborhood in the region, where spectacular homes on pristine beaches sell for three to six million dollars. Suites at the Four Seasons range from five hundred to four thousand dollars a night. There is a direct road from Punta Mita to Sayulita, not yet finished, and the talk around our village is that soon Sayulita will be a day trip for millionaires who want to cruise through a quaint village before going back to their immaculate paradise. (Sayuleños are already grumbling: Quaint we ain't.) There is also some loose talk about the way the land was originally acquired that catches my attention. So, in part because I knew Tyler would be coming, I solicited an assignment from a sports magazine to play at the Four Seasons—expense account!—and look into the loose talk.

Several days after Christmas, he and I drive over to Punta Mita and present ourselves at the guard gate. Security precautions—walkie-talkies, uniformed patrols—are elaborate. The property and its buildings, with refined casitas perched along the coast, are of course extravagant, if a bit antiseptic for my cobblestone taste. The hotel is designed to give its fabulous guests privacy with a lot of lebensraum; we see only a few fabulous guests wandering about.

The course is designed by Jack Nicklaus and it's a par-72 set on 195 acres of Bermuda grass, with eight oceanside holes. It is a knockout. Once, several years earlier, when times were still flush, I was in Monterey, California, and unexpectedly got a reservation on a weekday morning at Pebble Beach. Pebble is, of course, the once-in-a-lifetime dream round for every duffer, usually requiring a year-long reservation. So there I was, about to tee off on the famous seventh hole. I used my cell phone to call Ty, who was back home in New York, and told him to wait. I placed the cell phone down on the grass next to the tee and hit a decent shot. I picked up the phone said to my still-sleepy son, "Hear that?" Yes, he said groggily. "That was my tee shot on the seventh hole at Pebble Beach." "No *way*!" he exclaimed, wide awake. I promised I would treat him to a great course some day.

The Four Seasons course is in the Pebble Beach class. We play our usual game, rich with whiffs and balls caroming off rocks into the sea. There is one stunning hole on a natural island that must be reached by amphibious vehicle when the tide is high. It is close to the outer point, the Mita Point, a gorgeous finger of pine and palm and sand and rock. The golf pro, Juan Muñoz, is waiting for us in the vehicle to escort us out to the island green. Once there, we take in the view along the coast: the brown, craggy, tumbled rocks, the frigate birds dive-bombing the surf.

Later in the clubhouse, Muñoz talks about the island hole, also known by its shape as the Tail of the Whale ("Nicklaus said it was the most exciting hole he ever designed"), and how the golf course was developed. Muñoz, lanky and affable, is good-looking in a Lee Trevino sort of way. He says the hotel was opened in September 1999; it is part of a huge resort development on a point of land long known as one of the most beautiful settings on Mexico's Pacific Coast. The Four Seasons was the first hotel to go up; at least two more super-luxury resort hotels are planned, as well as a new golf course.

It is this setting that I ask about. I have heard a curious tale: that a fishing village on this most picturesque part of the coast was made to disappear to make room for the golf course. I ask Muñoz about it. Is it true, I ask, that the village was demolished and the inhabitants transported away? And is it true, as I'd heard in whispered conversations back in Sayulita, that some villagers had to be forcibly removed?

Muñoz, who seems well prepped to speak about the hotel's development, explains that there had indeed been a fishing village on the land. The villagers did not own the property but had been living legally as squatters, which the law allows, in their modest huts. After a majority vote, the villagers accepted the offer to relocate. "They were given three things: new homes, money, and employment opportunities," Muñoz says. "This was a positive move for them." Muñoz says a good number of villagers are now employed by the Four Seasons and that it is his impression that although there had been some "resistance," everyone was now content.

I decide to investigate further. One thing driving me is the eerie idea that an entire village could simply vanish, with all of its life and its people, so that a few players like my son and me can enjoy the undeniably great golf and spectacular scenery. Very few players. Tyler and I saw just one other group out in carts the entire day, and it was high season.

The Punta Mita property was originally part of a communal ejido. For at least a generation, on the land where the golf course now lies, a small, thatched-hut seaside village known as Corral de Riscos was home to about three hundred people, mostly fishermen and their families. After a series of legal moves and expropriation decrees beginning in the seventies, the land passed from the ejido to federal ownership, then to state ownership, and from there, in the nineties, into private hands. In 1995, after a vote endorsed by the leaders of the ejido group, a majority of residents decided to disband their village, and all were moved a few kilometers across the point.

A couple of days after our game, I go to the new village, now known as Nuevo Corral, and find a cluster of about a hundred neatly maintained, identical concrete houses. I ask around, both in the village and in the outlying area. Though I speak to them in Spanish, I encounter wariness and even suspicion. That is, until quite by chance, I meet Richard Trainor, a colorful gringo who turns out to be my not-so-Deep Throat. Richard, sixty-two, an expatriate who's lived in the area for nineteen years, is a cheerful and outspoken eccentric who lives with his wife, Deborah, on a high bluff close to the Four Seasons property. The exterior of his house is painted with a primitive jungle-themed mural; there is usually an RV camper or two in the driveway, and yapping dogs and old-hippie friends wander freely about.

Richard, who sports a ponytail on the back of his curly head and wears yellow-lensed glasses with gold geckos on the rims, knows everyone. And yes, he knows all about the relocation, and strongly opposed it, in solidarity with his Mexican friends who lived in the village. In fact, he was so angry that he videotaped the demolition.

"Looked like a goddamn war zone," he says in his native Brooklynese. "It was *great* before the bulldozers came. There were nice huts, and boats and nets drying in the sun, and they had a good life. Little restaurants, palapas with palm roofs, and tents for the families who came to camp out on holidays and enjoy nature. There was even a monument to the fishermen made out of coral—it came down, too." He says the Four Seasons was not involved in the initial arrangements for the land; a consortium of Mexican and American interests was responsible.

I mention that the official Four Seasons story is that the new location is just as good as the old one. "Crap," says Richard. "It was a true seaside village in a great fishing location. They used to have a natural wave break. They'd see fish, and—boink!—they were out there with the nets. Where the fishermen are located now, they have to take their boats and dog-paddle way around a bend."

I ask him to introduce me to some of the villagers. I am not yet convinced that my new friend isn't just being excitable. As Muñoz says, all the townspeople got better homes, and the extras—money, jobs— sound pretty good. So how much bitterness remains? Perhaps the Four Seasons's story of widespread contentment is true.

We arrive at the Nuevo Corral home of Aurelio Solís Verde. He is eighty-eight, with a white mustache, white cotton pants and shirt, and enormous dignity. Richard says to him, "Aurelio, this man would like to talk to you about the land you used to live on." The old gentleman looks at me and says in Spanish, "Oh, the property they stole from me?"

Solís, who was a shark fisherman for nearly seventy years, does not tack into the wind as his son and daughter gather around him in the backyard to hear him speak his mind. "Crooks!" he says. In this, he shortly explains, he includes former presidents of Mexico who allegedly had financial interests in the properties, the land developers; the hotel builders; the federal and state authorities; and the leaders of the ejido.

He talks about how the ejido referendum was held, how a bare majority voted for relocation, and how seven residents refused to leave their homes. Armed state police carrying Uzis arrived at dawn, he said, and dragged the protesting men away in handcuffs. "They took one of the young men away in his underwear and hit him over the head," he said. *"Cabrones."* I ask Solís about the other offers made to the villagers— money and jobs. "Some of the *chiefs* got money," he says. "I never got a peso. I was too old for a job, and who was going to hire fishermen to work at a fancy hotel?"

Richard introduces me to another dissident, Florencio Ramos Virgen, a burly cantina owner in his forties, who meets us at his home in nearby Higuera Blanca. He too lived in the village and voted against the relocation.

"People used to come from all around to see what was natural, what was beautiful at Punta Mita," he says. "Now, despite the fact that Mexican beaches are supposed to be public property, the only way people can reach the beach where we used to live is to go by boat." Ramos reserves his strongest scorn for some select ejido leaders. "They were the ones offered new homes in the best locations, they were the ones who received money—all to persuade other villagers to vote their way."

As I drive home to Sayulita, I reflect that it is hard to know how widespread the resentment is. It is clear to me that the new homes are a material improvement over the huts where the villagers once lived. When I attempt to find other former villagers who might be pleased with the relocation, I get mostly palms-up shrugs. But later Juan Pelaya, a restaurant owner and a lay preacher at the local Seventh-Day Adventist church, contacts me. He tells me that he and "most others," with the exception of a "handful" of villagers, are happy with the relocation. They appreciate the electricity, the running water, the paved streets— all nonexistent in the original village. As it happens, Pelaya was one of four men who made up the "enterprise committee," the village group that favored the move and lobbied for it. When I ask if he received money for his work on the committee, he says it was "the ejido" that received payment, of which he was a leader.

Back at Richard's mural-bedecked palapa home, we watch a little television together, a rarity for me, and during commercials we ponder the ways of governments, bureaucracies, and little people the world over. I suggest that land grabs have happened throughout history and none of us lives on property that wasn't muscled from someone else at one time.

"Yeh," says Richard, "but for boinkin' *golf*?"

Thia and I have been television-free since our arrival and do not yet miss it, but among most resident Americans, the search for the perfect television service is a sport pursued with enterprise. Though Mexican satellite service is available, gringos miss their own programming. American satellite signals can be captured, but not legally. For a number of years, the preferred technique was the purchase of a bootleg card inserted into the television set. The U.S. satellite service, however, was onto them, and every few months would send signals that would fry the card—at which point someone would make a run into Puerto Vallarta to buy a newly programmed card. Sometimes the service would zap reception of the channels one by one. "I'd begin losing the networks, then HBO, then the Discovery Channel," Barbara tells us one night. "Then I'd be down to CNN and Larry King—which I'd have to watch three times a night." Eventually the service became more proficient at the game than the gringos, and the cards became useless.

Today the preferred service is another satellite system, which I shall not name out of discretion. Enterprising locals run thriving little businesses bringing set-top boxes and satellite dishes into Mexico and selling them to customers here. The customers are instructed to sign up for service giving a non-Mexican address and telephone number. To be available to the television service when it calls to spot-check, the entrepreneurs employ a team of at-home operators to answer phones and pretend to be customers who "are out right now." Local gringos share the cost of the service with two or three other locals by claiming each box is located in a separate room in their house. No one seems to consider it theft of signal, since the service is properly paid for—it's just a necessary international work-around any Mexican would appreciate.

We may do without television, but our sons are unwilling to forgo movies. A visit to a local video store provides a welcome, if not very legal, surprise: sitting on the shelves are DVDs of current movies still playing in theaters. When Blair and Tyler bring home a couple of first-run movies, we set aside our scruples and prop my laptop on a table in front of the couch. As the credits roll, we notice an odd shadow along the bottom of the screen; right in front of an ancient Greek city under siege, the silhouette of a man holding something shaped like a popcorn box moves across from left to right and seems to find a seat. In a country where foreign checks take a month to clear and where a package from the States can take a week to be delivered, bootleg copies of new movies arrive on video-store shelves within days of opening in New York. On other nights, instead of videotaped silhouettes, we see a stern notice that this DVD is intended for the sole use of Academy members for Oscar consideration. It is encouraging to know that those who toil in the motion-picture industry are so willing to share. I never find out how the distribution system works, just that it works.

Tyler devotes the rest of his time with us to a serious sunning regimen that starts when he gets up at the crack of one. On a couple of evenings, he elaborates on his Mexican-Syrian comparative research: the truck-and-loudspeaker brigade is the same in Damascus as in Sayulita, the markets sell similar bric-a-brac, the buses drive at the same reckless speeds. He reels off more Spanish words he has learned that derive from Arabic: cotton—*algodón,* from *al-qutun;* olive oil—*aceite,* from *al-zeitun;* sugar—*azúcar,* from *assukar* . . . even *olé.* He tells us that Mexico's second-biggest city, Guadalajara, comes from waadii l-Hijaarah, a place in Moorish Spain meaning "stony creek." And I am surprised to hear that a phrase I used frequently as a child, *"Ojalá que . . ."* ("Here's hoping that . . .") is derived from *Inshallah* ("Allah willing").

The holiday break ends, and it is time for Tyler to return to Syria by way of the United States. His next stop after finishing his studies in

Damascus will be graduate school, and we know we are unlikely to see him back in Mexico for a long time. We are not yet reconciled—as we may never be—to this aspect of the expatriate life. The children will be a long way away. Unless, of course, one of them decides to surprise you.

We spend our last afternoon together at a nearby beach undiscovered by tourists. It is a certain distance from Sayulita, at the end of a long dirt road. It is about five miles of serenely isolated beach, and we are the only humans on it, despite the crowds elsewhere. We bring beer and cheese, and lay down our towels in a circle and silently watch a huge sun go down in a wink of green. The next morning Thia, Blair, and I drive Tyler to the airport. We wipe our eyes and send him off, promising that wherever he may be studying, we will find a way, and the means, to fly him down again to spend another Christmas with us here in Mexico. *Ojalá.*

CHAPTER 15

Guns on the Table . . .
A Cautionary Tale . . . We've Got Guests

We have been feeling real-estate stress, yet again. The half-lot we sold to raise money for our construction has not closed. Paperwork problems. That's the way things happen, Harvey says. He doesn't have a problem with it—hey, he could use his commission too, he's not getting any younger, etc. Oddly enough, the walled lot we bought has had no such paperwork problem and has closed rather nicely, the proof of which is that our bank account is nicely depleted. Thia and I have been doing our construction-cost due diligence around Rollie's tables. Even though building costs have climbed above one hundred dollars a square foot with some of the more popular builders and architects in town, we have put our impulsive moments behind us and are doing our homework this time. We *know* we can find a reliable builder at about sixty dollars a square foot. Here, the square-foot price does not include windows and doors, which are contracted and installed separately, nor the tiles or appliances.

But even at that reasonable rate—for this part of Mexico—we can afford only a two-thousand-square-foot house, and we are aware that the costs will be higher for a vertical house: stronger foundations, more brick, more wood. A three-story family home with a partial view begins to look like it's more than we can afford. We tell Aurelio to scrap the sketches so far and use the ground-floor plan as the basis for a more modest single-level home with three bedrooms. He sighs and agrees, though he clamps his hat onto his head with a slight snap as he walks out our door, leather hat thong bouncing.

We are also increasingly aware that despite our fondness for the amiable people in the village, we are not living in some Mexican version of a Norman Rockwell setting. Sayulita, and its neighboring villages, have a rough-and-tumble past not much different from the Wild West. There is one story about the early days—perhaps some ten years past—when land, which was all once part of the greater Sayulita ejido, began to be sold and resold in earnest. (Parcels were originally distributed by the ejido to local Mexicans on the condition that they work on them and make them productive.) As visitors from Guadalajara, Mexico City, and the United States, attracted by the beauty of the region, began to express interest in "buying" land through prestanombres, the incentive for local leaders to "persuade" people to sell went up sharply. At the end of one particularly frenetic selling season, a group of about a half dozen of the most active ejido leaders called for a meeting to divide up the cash that had been collected from legitimate "sales," as well as by various kinds of extortion.

They met, the story goes, at a restaurant in nearby Bucerias on a summer evening. The chieftains arrived packing pistols, accompanied by bodyguards. As each sat down at a round table, he laid his gun on the table and emptied out a sack of cash. When there was a mountain of peso bills in the center, each chieftain began to count out the portion he felt was deserved. When the counting was done, a shot of tequila was poured, and each man pushed the mound of cash he had amassed to the man on his left. They picked up the swag that had been pushed in front of them and they were gone into the night.

Colorful though the story may be, we are assured by old-timers that it is not a reflection of what is happening today. With a few notable exceptions, as near as we can tell, the vast majority of land sales, even those with prestanombres, have been honest and legitimate—if highly profit-oriented. But it is instructive to hear about the bad old days, if only to avoid being too naive about what *could* happen. As was the recent case with an American couple in Lo de Marcos, the next village north of San Pancho.

Barbara and Bill decide to introduce us to the couple not to discourage us but simply to hear their story—a cautionary tale. We drive over, about a twenty-minute ride north of San Pancho, and meet with Mike and Jocelyn in their half-completed house perched directly above a lovely beach. Lo de Marcos, unlike Sayulita or San Pancho, has not yet been discovered by hordes of tourists or gringos. It is a plain, quiet town with not much going on in its streets. Its main claims are a picturesque beach and good fishing off shore.

Mike has a worn, weathered face, and he sits down with us in the part of his house that is finished, on the terrace. He seems tired. His wife, Jocelyn, sits nearby with a religious book in front of her on the table. He begins by telling us of his unusual occupation before moving down to Mexico.

"I was a major pot grower. That's all I ever did, nothing more. I loved growing plants, and I started growing pot, and yes, I liked the money. I'm not proud of what I did. I'm not pro-marijuana, never smoked myself. But I had the bad luck to be picked up by federal agents. They confiscated everything: my houses, my land, my CDs. I served my time. I began painting. I met Jocelyn. She was incredibly straight, a religious person, worked for the government doing real-estate contracts for thirty years.

"When we decided to come down here to live, we stopped in Lake Chapala—all gringos. We checked out Sayulita—quite a few gringos. We wanted to be part of a little Mexican community; we didn't want to be around a bunch of gringos. Nevertheless, the first people we hooked up with in this little burg were gringos. They were very friendly, seemed very trustworthy. But they turned out to be con artists and took us for a lot of money on an early land deal. We didn't get onto them for a while, and when we found the piece of land we wanted to build on, they introduced me to a Mexican partner who would technically own the land—be my prestanombre. He introduced me to a relative as a potential contractor, and we checked him out, too.

"The contractor had good recommendations from other gringos, and I drew up plans for our dream house here. He said he'd do it for one hundred and ten thousand dollars. I was proud that I got him down to seventy thousand. Well, what happened was that I was haggling with him, and like a lot of Mexicans, he didn't want to say no. So he said sure, knowing he couldn't do it. We even went to the trouble of getting a written contract—did it with a *notario público,* a government-appointed lawyer—and it was clear as could be. We could sue him if he didn't deliver.

"He laid some good foundations—a good first floor, about half-done—and by the time he got to the second floor, he announced he'd spent all the money that we thought we'd been carefully doling out. He started saying, 'For ten thousand dollars more, I can build this wall. For twenty thousand more I can do this second floor. . . .' When I refused, and he stopped building, I fired him. So he started spreading stories that I wasn't paying workers. Plus, when you employ someone in Mexico and fire him, you owe him three months' pay. A nightmare.

"Also, we thought we'd paid his workers' government health insurance—they call it social security here—which you have to do in Mexico, very important. We gave our prestanombre money to do that every month. A few months after we fired the contractor, some government agents show up at our door demanding past health-insurance payments and huge fines of twenty-two thousand dollars. There was no record of our having paid. We were told if we didn't pay immediately, they could confiscate the house. They go after the house, not the person. We were able to resolve it by appealing to the authorities, and we ended up paying twelve hundred dollars.

"Y'know, all the trouble I got into in the States, all the torment of prison—*nothing* compared to being ripped off down here, feeling helpless and cheated. Finally we found some decent people in local government to help us out. My experience now is that I no longer believe Mexicans are just these smiling, helpful people. I have some good Mexican friends, but I no longer want to know the Mexican people. As a pot grower, all my criminal activity was with honest people. And I came down here innocent as an eight-year-old, straight as can be, and I got fleeced."

Mike's bitterness is softened by Jocelyn, who says, "Now, Mike, things are probably a lot different in Sayulita or San Pancho."

"There's no future for us here," snaps Mike. "It's never going to change. The people were slaves since the Aztecs, and they're slaves now. The first person to distrust is the smiling guy who comes up to you and says, 'Eh, amigo, can I help you get something?'"

Jocelyn agrees with him on this. "Even if we got everything cleared up, I wouldn't want to live here. I just don't trust that I won't wake up to another knock on our door demanding more money."

Before we leave, I ask Mike why he thinks all this happened to him.

"We ran into the wrong crowd, who introduced us to a worse crowd, who introduced us to an even worse crowd. You have to start out with decent, trustworthy people, and maybe it can turn out all right. But it didn't for us."

The next day, feeling chastened and wary, I stop for my lunch torta at Doña Lety's. It is on my mind, so I decide to ask her what she thinks of the land speculation around the village. As she heats a bun, I ask her about her place,

"Are you tempted to sell your house, Doña Lety? You must have been offered a fair price for such a good location."

I cannot see into the back rooms of her very plain kitchen and sandwich shop, which fronts onto the street just off the plaza, but I could just imagine what an American wanting to open up a sleek sandal shop would pay her for it.

"Ah," she says, "but what would I do if I got the money? Give it to my children, let them spend it on cars and *cerveza* and pretty things. Soon, the money would be gone, and my heirs would be without a home, a business. Here, our family gathers, and here I have a business to pass on to them. *Eso es lo que vale.* That is what is worthwhile."

I walk away holding the torta, which she has wrapped in aluminum foil. It is warm to the touch.

It is not too early to be looking for someone to build our house, so we are talking to people about every contractor-builder we hear about—at Rollie's field headquarters and elsewhere. A Canadian couple of our age, Bruce and Maggie Nesbitt, who have recently moved here from San Miguel, speak particularly highly of their builder, Humberto "Beto" Ramos Balcazar. Because they have owned, lived in, and sold a house in San Miguel, they know the ropes by now. They like and feel they understand Mexico, and Maggie, in particular, is the kind of person who spends months comparison shopping, looking up materials and building techniques online, interviewing customers of tradesmen they are thinking of employing. Maggie says her friends call her the Ferret. They are building a small two-bedroom house in San Pancho. Beto is their construction chief, and they rave about him. Given what we can tell about Maggie the Ferret's thoroughness, we promise ourselves we will meet with him when we are closer to breaking ground. But we will not jump to any early conclusions. And we mean it.

When we go to visit Barb and Bill in San Pancho, we use their bathroom scales to weigh ourselves. Something interesting has been happening: I have dropped ten pounds, Thia has dropped twenty. The activity at night has been good for her, and my regular schedule of walking and swimming has had an effect. Thia's hair, when not hanging ecstatically in a sink, has begun to be a pain; she has to pin it up when she swims, and in the humidity it does not dry as quickly. When a couple of friends from Massachusetts, Serge and Lina Paccaud, show up in Puerto Vallarta for a few days with her parents, we drive the four of them out to Sayulita for the day. Lina's father, Nino, is a hairdresser. He travels with his professional tools the way a doctor carries around a black bag. Nino never goes anywhere without his clippers—the better to assist in some roadside fashion emergency, I suspect—and recently cut his daughter's hair on the run. This leads Thia to a momentous, life-altering decision: her own long hair has to go.

Nino agrees to do the deed. Thia sits down in a plastic chair on the terrace, wraps a towel around her neck, and Nino sets to work. The hair flies, and my wife, who has kept her hair shoulder length for thirty years, is down to not much more than an artichoke cut. She gets up, pirouettes around the terrace, and everyone goes *ooh*. In truth, the weight loss plus the hair shearing have transformed her.

In *A Year in Provence,* Peter Mayle's enormously popular book about following his dream to live in the south of France, he describes an acquaintance who comes from England to visit as the Guest from Hell—demanding, arrogant, woefully clueless. The main threat he presents to Mayle and his wife is that he may just buy a place nearby, a plot thread they manage to pinch off in the nick of time. It is funny and true that when you live in an exotic locale, your friends may tend to think that you too are on vacation, but with the added benefit that you happen to live there, and have nothing better to do than entertain them and show them around.

It turns out that we, too, have a number of visitors planned for the end of January and early February, and we wonder briefly if we will have our own encounters with infernal guests. But Sayulita is not Provence, and our emails to friends about the raffish nature of our Mexican paradise have the effect of making our roster of visitors self-selecting. Those who generally take their winter vacations in a Caribbean luxury hotel are not the ones who will show up here first. Those who do decide to take the cobblestone pledge are a hardy bunch, and sensitive to the fact that we are living here, not merely taking the waters. Thia must honor her commitment to Rollie's at Night, and I am busy with my freelance work and, of course, my time-consuming qualms about the house. Our guests are welcome in the second bedroom—Blair can sleep on a mattress out on the terrace—but, with all respect and friendship, we are busy making a life here.

So we are visited first by my sister, Michele, who is taking a break without her husband, Tom. They both love Mexico, but Tom could not get away, so Michele flies in one bright January day and stays for a week. When I drive her into the village, she gets out, coughs up a bit of dust, looks around, and says, "Hey, Lupe, this is *great!*" She is the kind of guest we adore, a hardy explorer who has beaten back breast cancer, a survivor. When the lights go off the first evening that she arrives, she is the one to find a candle stuck in a tequila bottle, and when I cannot find a match, Michele improvises: "Hmmm . . . gas stove . . . there must be a pilot light." When Thia has to work, she and I go off to fish dinners. The fact that we are here, in this transforming period, leads to long brother-sister conversations about topics we haven't generally gotten around stateside.

"Hey, big brother," she says to me one afternoon at our secret beach. "It's beautiful down here, but not everyone in the family understands why you two chose to do this. This is a lot more basic, and there are *lots* more hassles than the New York crowd would tolerate at this age."

I say that is true; life is in many ways less easy. But, I tell her, I think often about my general state of mind in the States. "I would take it all for granted," I say, "and complain about the little stuff. A long line at the deli, and I'd stomp off irritated. No taxis in the rain, and I'd get nuts. Here, there are *so* many inefficiencies, you're grateful when something goes right—as it usually does, by another route. Things always have a way of eventually working out in Mexico. So on average you end up happy more of the time."

"Pretty deep," she says, but she knows what I mean.

Our friends Paul and Cindy Prewitt are also fans of Mexico and stay for four days. Paul, my roommate at college, is an internist in Laguna Beach, California, whose second calling is to keep his friends looped into the latest email jokes. Cindy has some kind of boondoggle to check out a time-share opportunity and gets us a free round of golf at the El Tigre course in Nuevo Vallarta. Thia and Cindy drive a cart together, enjoying each other's exceedingly casual game, while Paul and I spray the surrounding jungle with a variety of well-intentioned shots. We've known each other a thousand years. We end our day trolling though Puerto Vallarta's tourist art galleries.

My brother, Chris, and sister-in-law, Kit, are the last of our February visitors. Kit is the one who expressed sweet terror about Mexico's crime before we left. Chris, a successful Silicon Valley exec, and Kit, his soft-spoken Southern-born wife, have never gone on a vacation anywhere in the world without asking a real-estate agent to show them around and becoming enthusiastic about buying something. They invariably decide this is *it*—in Italy, in France, wherever—and boldly make a bid on a house, a decision they rescind as soon as they return home to California.

We show them the best restaurants in the area, introduce them to our Mexican and American friends, and take them to an outdoor carnival fiesta. One of the concessions is a knock-over-the-bottles stand, but of the Sayulita no-liability variety: You toss rocks at a row of sand-filled bottles, which merrily shatter and spray the spectators with shards of glass. Chris and Kit get into it. It is satisfying to watch Kit relax into Sayulita's tempo; the first couple of days, she is all glances and wary looks around her. Late one night, at the approach of a couple of tough-looking Mexican teenagers who turn out to want nothing more than directions to a disco, I can see the tension drain away. Toward the end of their stay, Chris and Kit ask if they can look at real estate, and earnestly discuss with us the prospect of investing in a small lot down here. This may be *it*. On the day before they leave, they decide they will, in fact, make a bid on a place in the north of town. We are not hugely surprised to get an email from them shortly after they get home saying they have changed their minds. But not about Mexico—they like it fine, and will be back.

*   *   *

Around the time that our last winter guests leave, Blair, who has inherited and gone through Thia's Spanish tapes with the discipline he learned at his Jesuit high school, announces he wants to go to Guanajuato for a three-week immersion language course recommended to him by Barb. This may be related to his long-distance breakup with his stateside girlfriend. He has checked out the local female talent, but has found it lacking. It does not surprise us to learn that Blair might want to find social companionship other than two roommates who once diapered him.

Guanajuato, a colorful Colonial university town set amid a series of hills about ten hours' drive away, offers inexpensive courses at two hundred dollars a week that include living with a Mexican family—quite a bit less than the better-known language institute in San Miguel de Allende. He wants to spend his slender savings on it, and I ask him to be sure and email us. He is a reporter and he writes well, and I am interested in how Spanish is taught to motivated foreigners. We drop him off at the bus terminal and head back, our nest again empty for a while, looking forward to the solitude and the prospect of a renewed struggle with our house plans. I stop off at a grocery store and pick up some Rice Krispies Treats.

CHAPTER 16

A Change in Plans . . . An Email Home . . . The Amazing Staircase

One bright morning in early February, I awake to the certainty we are going to go broke. Last night, I went over our bank accounts and budget. Our hilltop half-sale has not closed, but even when it does, it will go only part of the way toward our construction costs. We have been living on savings and freelance writing income for almost two years. Neither of us has quite faced the crucial rite of passage for those of us who reach semiretirement age without pension or adequate savings: the realization, finally, that *there are no more paychecks coming our way.*

So it is all the more puzzling that Thia and I have been talking to friends in the village, most quite a bit better off than we, about their plans to build one, two, even three apartments and casitas on their property to rent out while they live here. All these well-set people are looking to create income for themselves by renting to tourists, while we well-stretched city mice have concentrated on just getting our own home built. What we've been avoiding is how to plan our future—will we have to choose between living here without income or living somewhere else to make the house pay its way? Since we are determined to put down a stake in Mexico, something has to change.

The puzzle is why it's taken this long for us to take it in fully. We understood from the outset that we had to tackle this little problem of creating some kind of income down here, but in dealing with all that was new and unfamiliar, we lost sight of our intention. Like a walk through Sayulita's plaza, we set off on an errand of practical importance but were waylaid by our new life.

It comes to us in our pajamas: We have to build in such a way that we can both live down here *and* secure a modest income. Renting out a place, as longs you pay taxes, is permissible; it does not take away a Mexican's job. This morning, we are a few hours away from giving Aurelio the final OK on the single-level three-bedroom sketch that is supposed to lead directly to final blueprints. If we are going to change something, it will have to be now.

So: scale down the ground floor to an affordable two-bedroom layout, but go back to the three-story plan, with a small one-bedroom unit on each upper floor. And the crucial leap forward: We can live in the top unit while we rent out both floors below for as long as the tourist season allows. We will be part-time innkeepers. There!

It is a satisfying breakthrough, but as we sit back to reflect on it, Thia tears up. "My beautiful little house," she says, "the courtyard, the garden—it's going to be for *renters*." I tell her it's only for part of the year, that it may not rent out during the hot and rainy summer season, so we'll have plenty of chance to sit in our courtyard. (I don't say "hot and rainy courtyard.") Besides, our finances are such that somewhere down the line, we would have to find other sources of income, so we were never just going to sit in our courtyard. She thinks about it, and we give each other a resigned look, knowing we've passed another milestone. Then we launch into another frenzy of sketching, which we just finish when Aurelio knocks at the door. It is nine in the morning.

Aurelio has already spent plenty of time on the shape and dimensions of the single-level plan, and has every right to expect that all we will have for him are minor adjustments. I can see as well that he is still battling a flu. "Sorry, Maestro," I say, "we have a big change for you." Theatrically, he leans back in his chair and clutches his chest. We explain that to make this thing work for us, we have to find a way of renting out the main floor while we live above, and that means back to the old three-story plan: two units above, one less bedroom below. He listens, nods, seems to understand.

"I see," he says, "you want to change your lives, not just the blueprint."

He's a good sport, Aurelio, and gets to work sketching with us. He has his original three-story plans to fall back on. Two hours later, we have agreed on how to make the ground floor smaller (in Spanish, the interesting verb is *castigar,* to punish) and how the upper floors will lay out. I remind him that he needs to include a shed roof over our ground-floor living area, a must in this tropical sun. He nods impatiently. Considerably weakened from the flu, and possibly from his indecisive clients, he looks haggard as he gathers his papers.

"If you please, Señor Barry and Señora Thia," he says. "I said I would make all the changes you wished while at the sketch stage. But I, Aurelio Carrillo, implore you to be—" he searches for the word in Spanish, then says it in English—"*mature* in your commitment to these changes."

Fair enough, we deserve it. He staggers out, promising to be back in two or three days with a "final-final" sketch. Thia and I are psyched. Finally, it is coming together. We will not have the personal dream house, the one we'd be able to invite friends and family down to visit at any time. We will have to give up our courtyard for half a year or more. But we finally have a way to make the adventure work over time. And on the bright side, we will get another chance at the vista pequeña, that tiny partial view.

Email from Blair:

> Hello Mudda . . . Hello Fadda . . . Here I am in . . . Guanajuadda!
>   I arrived near midnight at my host family's place, an unassuming house wedged into a pencil-thin cobblestone alley. Meeting me at the gate was my host father, Señor Enrique Santebanes. He's a city architect, now semiretired in his early sixties. The house is spread over three levels—as are most in this city, which is built into the hills. From the third-floor terrace, the view blows me away: unlike Manhattan, where almost all the stalagmites rise in dull, weary shades of gray, the hill town of Guanajuato is a rippling sea of homes and churches in pastel; peaches and aquamarines blend in with the burnt oranges and banana yellows. It's an architectural gelateria from up here!
>   A shuttle bus took me to the school the next day. The Instituto Miguel de Cervantes is perched atop a steep set of hills overlooking Guanajuato. Cacti, stone walls and shrubbery

surround each of the semi-outdoor classrooms. It feels more like a holistic spa in Arizona than a language school. The day is split up into two ninety-minute classes.

There are maybe fifteen students here of all ages and backgrounds; I've been matched up with Michele, a late-middle-aged French Canadian with a good command of Spanish grammar, but who speaks with an outraaahjis Fraahnch accent; and a white-haired gentleman named Paul; he's in his mid-sixties, and speaks his brand of Spanish, as nearly as I can tell, with a Klingon accent. All, in fact, have more grammatical knowledge than do I, but being honest, I don't think anyone has my CD-inspired pronunciation skills.

Apparently the classes are just sort of rolling enrollment, because there wasn't any obvious rhyme to where we started—sort of midway through an explanation of a few basic verb tenses. It's all done in immersion Spanish, of course, and I'm finding that I can follow the lessons without a problem. No textbooks or anything, so I'm basically copying lessons into my notebooks and hoping I can read my wretched handwriting—your fault, Dad, for bringing me up on a keyboard. If anything, I was sort of hoping for more structure. We got about thirty seconds of homework, whereas I would have happily done an hour or more.

As luck would have it, a foxy classmate named Britt lives around the corner, and we've taken to hiking up the hills to school every day. But major frustration: she's got a boyfriend back home. Ah well. At least there was a party last night at a house perched atop a hill so steep it made the inclines of San Francisco seem like the plains of Nebraska. The highlight of the night for me was talking to a Spanish teacher at another language school. Even more so than my maestros, this guy was very used to speaking with excellent diction. He was giving me a fairly nuanced account of the problems experienced by the Catalonians and the Basques in Spain, or something like that, but the cool thing was that I *was holding a conversation*. To top things off, so to speak, the maestro showed me how to use one beer bottle to open another. I *knew* this was going to be an enriching educational experience.

Okay. The Internet café is closing. My plans for the weekend
include a day trip to San Miguel de Allende; and I'm looking into
the possibility of renting mountain bikes for a bunch of friends
and hitting the hills outside of town. I love school!

It is not working. The house we have been designing and redesigning
has a pitched tile roof that ceases abruptly about two-thirds of the way
across, giving way to space for a palapa. We are confident that a roof
that ceases being a roof just past its midpoint is a bold design departure,
but we are insecure about *how* bold a departure it is. We are, in fact,
afraid it may look ridiculous. In any case, Aurelio's newest draft incor-
porates our semiroof, so the house now resembles a Monopoly hotel
with the top corner snipped off.

Aurelio has also come up with a twist of his own. On the elevation
plan, he has solved an alignment problem between the first and second
floors by making the side of the house take off at a right angle before
rising again. Rather than go back and fix the original problem, Aurelio
has created a work-around that would be charming if it were not so . . .
weird. But even more significantly, he has been wrestling with the stairway concept.

I originally suggested that there should just be a set of steps up the
back of the building with a roof over them; Aurelio, however, appears
to have immersed himself in the stairway design as a major metaphys-
ical challenge—which is the true way up? how many landings are one
too many?—and emerged with a structure that towers over the house
by a dozen feet. It is like a battlement gone mad, with huge arched open
windows, a roof with a turreted ledge at the top, and a cost in cement
that, for all I knew, could overtake that of the house. The horses are not
just galloping, they are out of control.

I am not at home when Aurelio drops off the sketches, and Thia tells
me later that she looked them over and tried politely to tell him that
there was something wrong with the *planes*. Aurelio nodded and
smiled, and, as near as Thia could tell, reassured her that the garden will
be big enough for all manner of *plantas*. He took off in his truck, cheerfully charading to her that he would be in his office tomorrow if we
want to call. When I come home to see the sketch of his Gothic basilica of a staircase, I am aghast. With its flying buttresses, our stairway

will be the tallest single structure in Sayulita, aside from a six-story blight on the shoreline known as the Eyesore. I nearly lose heart.

"You let him get away without telling him?" I ask.

"I don't know *what* he thought I was critiquing," Thia says. "Besides, how do you say politely, 'Oh my *God*, Aurelio, what on earth *is* this?'"

We sit down with the sketches. We pencil and erase, tearing up new sketches, unrolling and tearing off scads of tracing paper. What do I know about stair construction? I try to reduce Aurelio's mega–Stairway to Heaven into a modest flight of steps. But our truncated roof is still there, as it has been all along, and may be on its way to becoming Sayulita's *second* gringo eyesore. The problem is what it's always been: this hacienda-colonial look we are trying for, with its pitched tile roofs and wooden beams, is integral to our vow to "build Mexican." But we also would like to get up *on* the roof to get a glimpse, just a glimpse, of the sea. Short of perching on the roof's transverse, we were not going to get our wish in any aesthetic or harmonious way.

We go to bed glum, get up at the morning's first jackhammer, and after our morning swim at Playa de los Muertos, go at it again. We take our tracing paper and our coffee and our sharpened pencils and huge erasers out to the patio table and begin to sketch once more. Soon I get exasperated and throw my pencil down and begin to curse.

"Don't blow your top," says Thia.

"Why not? There are houses here that look like misbegotten Moorish beach mosques, but we can't get a simple hacienda designed. It's a *great* reason to blow my top. Plus . . ."

But I don't get to the plus; I stay with the earlier thought. Haciendas, in their pure form, don't *have* tiled tops. They have flat roofs, upon which can be placed *tinacos,* water cisterns, and sometimes terraces. What they do *not* have is the two-sided pointed tile roofs, the kind we've included in every preliminary and every follow-up sketch since we began this hacienda-colonial extravaganza.

I lick my pencil stub, which I waggle purposefully in the air like Art Carney in *The Honeymooners,* and set to work. In a few inspired minutes, I have sketched out a rectangular edifice and a flat roof with a thin railing around the top edge, which I hope looks vaguely wrought iron. No more pitched tile roof. Behind the railing I draw the outline of a viewing pavilion. I sketch the underlying windows and terraces, making the railings below echo the grillwork above. There. We have *harmony*, damn it.

I push the sketch across the table to Thia. She looks at it without expression for a moment, then lets a smile play across her lips. We've got it. At last. Now we just have to convince the third member of our working couple.

Aurelio rolls by the apartment about two and a half hours late. Thia and I have decided I will meet with him alone, because if he is going to have his staircase multiplex taken apart, it might be well if only one of us were to confront him. I have been practicing what I am going to say, consulting the dictionary for diplomatic translations of "overblown" and "wildly extravagant" and "I implore you to tell me, what were you *thinking*?" The longer I wait, and the later he is, the more nervous and irritated I become. Why should *I* be nervous? Who was working for whom?

Aurelio arrives at the door with a smile, no explanation, and a slight bow.

"*A sus órdenes,*" he says. At your orders. Sure.

I am grim faced, and Aurelio, still smiling, picks up on it as he sits down at the table.

"You look less than felicitous, Señor Barry. I can tell."

This is ticklish. In the States, you tell someone with whom you are doing business why you are dissatisfied . . . and get on with it. If I say what I feel now, I am liable to trip over history. In Mexico, we are learning, the concept of *dignidad,* hard-won after four hundred years of Spanish rule, is crucial. Under the viceroys, mestizos and Indian serfs suffered cruelties and discrimination that they had to stoically endure. It has produced in today's proud Mexican an elaborate *paso doble* of respect-seeking and face-saving, especially when dealing with foreigners, that trumps other considerations. No less than the Japanese, the Mexican demands that courtesies be observed and bluntness softened.

Yet sometimes hard truths must be told.

Mincing no words, I tell him that his stairway has many, many fine features, and that both Thia and I were very impressed by it. Then I get really tough. I tell him Sayulita may not be ready for something as extraordinary as this stairway, and that my wife and I feel, alas, that we must do without this particular creative fruit, though who knows if some other building, in the not-too-distant future, might require a stairway of such sweep and ambition.

Aurelio takes it all with a rueful smile, shaking his head more in sorrow than in anger.

"Ah, Señor Barry," he says, when I wind down. "Apologies are not necessary between people who have respect for each other. Nor is there any shame in trying something that may not work. It is only important that we move ahead and learn from our errors."

If Aurelio is acknowledging his mistakes in the plans—the pageboy flip along the side of the house, or his Tower of Tenochtitlán staircase—I certainly can't tell. It sounds as if he is acknowledging *my* mistaken notion for a roof, while finessing his own moves. I don't even know how he has done it, but I end up feeling defensive, even apologetic. I tell him about our ideas for the flat roof and for straight vertical walls.

So it is, literally, back to the drawing board for our plans. When he returns next, he has done what we asked, though he is a trifle impatient. When I point out to him that in this almost-final plan he has not included the shed roof over the main open living area, he frowns, knowing he will have to return yet again. When he comes back with the new roof sketched in the next day, I get the impression it was done hastily, but at least we are finally done. We agree to meet the next day for our drive to Valle de Banderas, the municipal seat. We don't want to lose any more time; we must get our building permits. Aurelio says it will be good for me to see how typical Mexican bureaucracy works, and he, Aurelio Carrillo, will be my guide.

CHAPTER 17

Dogs and Visas . . . Bob and Vicky . . . A Mountain Trip

It is now early February, and the nights are cool enough to wear a long-sleeved shirt or windbreaker. Thia "La Luz" continues to serve food at night and drop pounds during the day. She's looking as trim and attractive as I can remember. Even I am beginning to feel fit from my walks to Playa de los Muertos every day. Not that the walking is aerobic; too many stops along the way for *chisme*, gossip.

Sayulita is a small town, and like small towns everywhere, gossip is conducted more swiftly than electricity. One day the rumor spreads that the Mexican authorities are cracking down on foreign-plated cars, stopping them on the road to Puerto Vallarta and confiscating them. Americans tell each other to stock up on food at Wal-Mart and stay off the road for the duration. It takes weeks for the rumor to be tracked down as a case of mild mass hysteria resulting from a couple of Americans being pulled in for having no visas—an experience Mexicans could certainly testify to in the States.

Another story that crops up every few months is that the dog population is kept in check by regular poisonings. Supposedly someone spikes slabs of meat with poison and drops them off on the beach. Any dog running loose is vulnerable, so dog owners tell each other to keep their pooches at home. A couple of friends tell me they know someone who has lost a dog. Dick Dobbeck says he has actually seen a dog convulsing before his eyes. Whether it is true or an urban legend, the talk fades, and then renews itself every half year or so. In fact, over in San Pancho, Barb and some other Americans and Mexicans have arranged to fly in a pair of U.S. veterinarians for a weekend spaying clinic. The vets do it pro bono and get to stay at Casa Obelisco. But here in Sayulita, dog care can be both sweet and appalling: Many run free and serve as fine watchdogs; just as many are mangy and ill treated.

The latest rumor, one that is hardest to shake, is that the municipal government is now requiring an environmental-impact study for all new construction in and around the villages. This is fine, a good thing. However, nobody has any idea how to go about obtaining such a study, or whether construction within the village proper falls under the new regulations. On the face of it, it is encouraging that some kind of environmental awareness is beginning to be felt. In both villages, water resources are strained, sewage treatment is antiquated at best, and some builders—mostly foreign, as it happens—are ignoring existing guidelines as they clear jungle growth for development. It is illegal to cut down an oil-coconut palm, for instance, and even in this free-wheeling part of the country there are zoning regulations that are supposed to be enforced. They rarely are.

The town association whose meetings I have begun to attend is attempting to move against the most flagrant offenders, especially the deep-pocketed developer of the six-story Eyesore. The entire coastline has been included in a government-sponsored strategy to bring massive tourism south of here, beginning with the Four Seasons property down the shore. The sitting president, Vicente Fox, supposedly has property interests in the region, a fact that raises the usual cynicism. But it is difficult to find out what you can, or must, do here. Don't necessarily expect the authorities to help you, both our gringo and Mexican friends tell us.

It is time for us to convert our tourist visa into a retiree's immigrant visa. This is the famous FM3, the one most expats obtain. If you can show enough income—about $1,500 a month for a couple—it will allow you, your dependents, and your car to reside in Mexico, and will let you import your household goods once. There are actually fifteen different kinds of visas offered by the Mexican government, and we decide this is not something we want to blunder into on our own. I ask around, and

call Vilma Habelloecker of Puerto Vallarta. She charges a modest fee for
legally facilitating the paperwork, and it seems well worth it.

Since we do not have either Social Security or a pension, I spend
some time online transferring funds from one account to another, then
printing out the figures, to establish some kind of income stream.
When I show these to Vilma, a cheery can-do woman working out of
an office by the Vallarta Marina, she waves me off. She knows how the
system works and can help us show that we have enough in savings to
yield $1,500 a month, even if the income is not regular. It takes about
a week, including a wait in line with one of Vilma's assistants, and the
deed is done. We are immigrants, so to speak; we have new green pass-
ports to prove it. And it has been done properly.

For the past few months, we have mostly talked about real estate. It is
embarrassing to say, but I have even taken part in conversations about
how hard it is getting to get good help in a tight labor market. Little of
this has been ennobling, despite our modest involvement in some local
volunteer work. It is true that we came down here primarily to live in
this village and build a home. But we feel a need to look beyond the
small concerns of our little boomtown.

I have been corresponding by email with bed-and-breakfast opera-
tor Bob Howell, whose online accounts of his trips into the mountains
have a special poignancy. He and his partner, Vicky Flores, a registered
nurse, offer Jeep trips to remote Indian villages for adventurous travelers. On many trips, Bob and Vicky distribute food, medicine, and
clothes to poor Indians in the mountains, primarily Huichol migrant
workers. Although this kind of charitable work is common among gringos, it is often limited to occasional visits and fund-raisers. With Bob
and Vicky, it is a way of life.

I arrange for Thia and me to accompany them. We agree to meet
at Bob's bed-and-breakfast in Rincón de Guayabitos, another coastal
town about a half hour away. When we arrive at a large stone house
at the edge of an ecological preserve, we are greeted by Bob, slim with
thinning white hair, blue-eyed and energetic. We are shown around
the B and B and out onto their small walled garden. A small flock of
wild parrots swoops in and settles on the branches of a tree in the
garden.

Inside, we meet Vicky Flores, a lively, compact woman with Indian features and sharp dark eyes. She is filling bags with clothes from a stack in the middle of the table, loading bags of toothbrushes, shoes, and food (rice, beans, oil, sugar, tuna) into a basket. She says that Bob's B-and-B guests donate most of the clothing—they come to vacation at the house, get caught up in the spirit of their enterprise, and the next time they fly in from the States or Canada for a repeat stay at the B-and-B, they bring an extra suitcase filled with old clothes to donate.

We set off in Bob's ancient Jeep and in less than an hour from our prosperous little village, we encounter our first Indian settlement. It is eight or ten wooden shacks with tin roofs, debris strewn about, and from inside the huts emerge a dozen shyly smiling Indian men and woman. The children are less shy than the adults and run up to Vicky as she gets out of the Jeep. She goes around to the back to pull out some packages of toothbrushes.

"Do you use these?"

Nods all around, and Vicky hands them out. As she gives a toothbrush to a boy, she demonstrates how to use it. She has a disarming way of talking to them, not patronizing, but frank and direct, like the nurse she is. She looks at a man who is wearing just an old leather sole tied with string as his sandals, shakes her head, and hands him a pair of shoes. There is a little boy with a large wound across his nose, from one side to the other, and big, protruding stitches. I ask about him, and the boy's mother explains that a tool fell on his nose, and she had to stitch it herself with string.

"Did you have anesthetic?"

The mother shakes her head. Not no, she didn't have any, but no, she does not understand the word *anesthetic*.

Aboard the Jeep once more, Vicky tells us that many of the Huicholes subsist as seasonal coffee-bean pickers for three months a year. It is the best work around—a strong picker can make $13 a day—but they must keep their children out of school, if they send them there at all, to help out during the three-month coffee-picking season.

Vicky says she gave a class in latrine digging because the men all defecated out in the open where they worked. "They all go po-po in fields, and make dirty the water supply!" says Vicky in her idiomatic English. (She is a Totonac Indian and speaks Spanish in a cultured, sophisticated manner. But her spin on English is distinctive, and I think it gives a flavor of her no-nonsense approach.) "I tell them also, no smoke or I no bring them food any more! Very bad for you, I say."

Bob points to a large, already old-fashioned satellite dish behind a shack with a rickety tile roof. "Sometimes, it seems they'd rather have television than food."

In the jeep, I ask Vicky about her background. She says she was expected to become a nun. She was sent from her home city of Puebla to a convent in Mexico City, where she was well educated in nursing. She led a secluded life. But at graduation, she and a group of novices were allowed a spring trip to the Pacific Coast. Vicky says that she took one look around and said, "I no go back!" She has been a nurse and a guide in Guayabitos ever since.

At yet another village, Vicky gives out clothes, shoes, food bags, more toothbrushes. Thia gives a tiny pig-tailed Huichol girl a Barbie doll whose hair she has arranged to look like the little girl's. The little girl squeals when she sees it and takes the doll so it straddles her side, like a mother with a toddler. A couple of men come up and ask Vicky if she has brought any coloring books. Vicky says no, not this time, and says, "For your children?" *"No, para nosotros,"* he says. For us.

As we drive away, a middle-aged woman with a shawl and scowl glares at us from her door. Vicky says, speaking in Spanish, "Not everyone likes us. These store owners bring up food and jack up the prices terribly. The Indians have no choice if they do not want to walk twenty kilometers. Some of them do." I translate for Thia, and Vicky is staring out the window, her lips set.

We pass a padlocked church. I ask if the church is able to do much good up here. Vicky says, "I once asked one of the women here, 'Does the priest come here once a week?' She said, 'Once a year.' Then I asked her, 'Does the priest help the people?' The woman said, 'No, the people help the *priest*—to buy a car.'

We are on our way back, and as the Jeep rattles down the mountain road, I ask her what, of everything she has witnessed on these trips, has moved her the most. She is somewhat taken aback by the question and thinks for a moment. Then, leaning over the seat to let it all pour out, she says, in a spontaneous monologue in Spanish I think worthy of Tom Joad:

"When I see the children without shoes, when they have no clothes, when their faces are dirty, it hurts—it hurts me so bad. I feel a great pain for the children of Mexico, for the Indians who are rejected and neglected, who are not being helped, for the Indian men who, because of their own innocent ignorance, have to search for food for their families—for their women, for their children . . ."

She clenches both her fists. "Hunger, suffering, that's what moves me . . . and that there are people *of our Mexican race* who sell food at such high prices . . . that they *have no humanity, no sympathy for their fellow human beings* . . . that is what hurts me." Tears are running down her face, and we drive on in silence.

CHAPTER 18

Meeting Beto . . . A Visit to Valle . . . Another Fateful Choice

Humberto "Beto" Ramos Balcazar is a short, compact bulldog of a man, dressed functionally in shorts and dark T-shirt, direct in gaze and manner. He has cropped black hair, a leathery, mottled face, and dark bright eyes that miss nothing, absolutely nothing. He could pass for a day laborer, so spare and plain is his look, but it is what he says that immediately makes you take notice. And how he says it: succinctly, with a fierce conviction.

"If we work together," he is saying as Thia and I sit across from him on the couch, "I would like it to be on the following basis: that I give you one price and stick to it. That I understand that you will make changes, and that I allow for them. That I take care of both the labor and the materials, and that you understand I have high standards for both. I do not believe in talk, talk, talk. I believe in getting the job done for someone who has confidence in me and will let me do that job."

I am surprised, and do not know what to make of this. We are performing our due diligence, and Beto is the last of our four scheduled interviews with prospective contractors. We know that finding the right contractor not only can make up for a multitude of impulsive sins, it is *the* critical decision in house building, here as in the States. Beto could not meet with us earlier because of his schedule in finishing the house construction for our friends Bruce and Maggie in San Pancho—he could not get away from the site. That impresses us right off.

We have had hour-long interviews with the other three builders and asked for bids from two of them. With these men, there was a great deal of talk, a certain fuzziness about who would be responsible for what, as well as unmistakable warning signals that anything that departed from the blueprints or went beyond them might have to be negotiated later. As to duration, the estimates for completion were both on the long side and imprecise: "eight months, maybe more," "seven to ten months."

Even as first-timers, we understand that disasters in home building come from cost overruns, innocent or otherwise. It is typical of home construction anywhere, of course, but it is especially so here in Mexico, where it is impolite to disappoint. There is a tendency to promise lavishly at the outset, and to conclude regretfully about halfway through that it may take just this *bit* more than estimated to finish the work. We have been advised to be meticulous from the outset about what is included in the estimate, to be even more meticulous about what is *not* included, and to make certain that we adhere to a strict interpretation of the cost-per-square-foot calculation. Everything, from a terrace to an exterior corridor to a palapa roof, undergoes the square-foot calculation. For that reason, as we have begun interviewing for our builder, we are simultaneously urging Aurelio to diminish the size in his latest sketches, to "punish" this bedroom, that hallway, to find ways to keep our square footage within our budget range. (Aurelio responds to this by saying in exasperation, "Americans save pesos and waste dollars.")

And here is Beto, telling us—without a lot of talk, talk, talk—that he understands amateur home builders, that he disdains the kind of nickel-and-diming endemic to the local trade, that there would be no arguments over the costs of materials or labor, because they would be his responsibility, that he is looking to do a job, not to enter into a state of constant discussion and renegotiation. I ask him how long it would take him and his crew to finish the house.

He does not hesitate. "Five and a half months."

I am now not just surprised, I am stunned.

"What about the square footage," I ask. "Can you give us your rate based on what you've seen of our plans?"

Beto is leaning forward on the couch. He is not a relaxed man, as Bruce and Maggie have warned us. "I will give you an overall price and *stick* to it. I am not even sure what the square-foot price is, but I will give you enough room to make changes because I know changes are part of—" he searches for the words "—human nature."

We have studied Bruce and Maggie's house, a sleek, modern structure in stuccoed brick built close to the ocean in San Pancho. Its workmanship, as nearly as we can tell, is solid, and Maggie the Ferret, who researches everything, was more than merely satisfied; she was joyous. So we have no fears on that account. Beto's choices of materials obviously met Maggie's exacting standards. He promised them he would finish their ground-floor two-bedroom house in four months; Beto finished it, to our certain knowledge, in four months and three days.

One problem: Beto does not speak English. I am getting better at simultaneous translation, but I know I am passing along only about 75 percent of it to Thia, and less than that from her to Beto. One fear I have for the future is that as we begin to use more and more construction jargon, for which I have no aptitude in English, it will get tougher, especially for Thia. I mention my concern to Beto, who gives a little grin, waves a hand, and says, "I have built for many, many Americans. They spoke no Spanish. There are always ways of communicating. It will not be a problem." He speaks slowly, simply, with none of Aurelio's florid prose.

I begin to translate for Thia, and she stops me.

"I got it."

I need not have worried. Although my semifluency has been a help, in truth I have not heard any non-Spanish-speaking gringo complain about language problems since arriving here. Mexicans who have worked with Americans are adept at a combination of gestures, sign language, English phrases, and a gift for pantomime that allows them to communicate well with us. They are used to us, after all.

The word *gringo* is often said to have originated with invading American soldiers who sang the lyrics from "Green Grow the Rushes, O" in marching cadence, which the Mexicans are supposed to have adapted phonetically. But, in fact, the word was in Spanish dictionaries a century before the 1846 war and is thought to refer to any foreign unintelligible gibberish. In Spanish, as in English, there is a saying, *hablar en griego,* as in Shakespeare's "It's all Greek to me." *Griego* became *gringo,* and the marching Americans may or may not have added something to the mix on their cheery way to Chapultepec. The point being, Mexicans have a lot of experience deciphering us and have even defined us by our language. (Everywhere else, we're Yankees. And not once I have seen a sign saying, Gringos Go Home.)

At the same time, gringos who at least try to stumble through broken Spanish are rewarded by Mexicans, who appreciate the effort and zero in on their key phrases to get the drift. Thia, who remembers French gendarmes in Paris staring at her with haughty miscomprehension at her pronunciation of a French word, has been delighted by how well Mexicans understand her—even when the Spanish she is speaking is pure college Italian.

When Beto leaves, as the door closes behind him, I prepare to go over some of his responses in more detail for Thia. I am deeply impressed, but I am still doubtful that she could have picked up on the man's evident integrity and dignity; you need to follow the subtleties of spoken language, I think, to make this kind of judgment.

"Really, I got it," she says. "Everything about him—his attitude, his body language—tells me he's our guy."

In the next several days, we call around and talk to other people Beto has built for, and the recommendations are unanimous: this is a remarkable man—reliable, honest, skilled, resourceful. No complaints; not one. Still, we're so wary of making any premature moves on this, we put Beto off when he calls to say he has an estimate for us. We want to continue to investigate his background.

In this part of Mexico, unless one builds in a development, house construction is far more do-it-yourself than most Americans are accustomed to. Some, if not many, of the gringos are comfortable building here precisely because they have had experience in construction or real estate in the States. That must give them the confidence to run projects where the customs, standards, techniques, tools, accessories, and language are unfamiliar. Mike Scannell, for example, has built two homes here, one of which he sold. He is a developer in the Seattle area, so the prospect of supervising a crew, choosing his own materials, hiring individual craftsmen, and having to decide on everything from cement to plumbing was not overly daunting, even though he speaks Spanish haltingly. Bill Glaysher, in the apartment below us, has experience building several homes in the States, so he has decided to be his own contractor down here. He and his wife, Kathy, are planning an ambitious art-gecko home, designed by Estela; he is already comparing the qualities of various kinds of concrete, wood, and bricks as well as the costs of local labor. Since neither Bill nor Kathy speaks Spanish, they are working with an American friend who has already built here and has promised them advice and translation. It sounds impossibly daring to us.

If we have acquired some humility since moving down here, it is that we are getting to know how much we don't know. We have a vision of what we want our home to be, and we know we want to build in the Mexican style, the Mexican manner. From the talk we hear around town, we know there are more modern, more up-to-date American ways of building that owners try to get their Mexican contractors to adopt. We are going another way. We want to find someone we trust and learn from him and his workers how things are done *here*.

Our interviews done, Beto finally arrives a week later with his estimate, handwritten on notebook paper, which he tears out to hand us. In his rough cursive script, he has separated the phases of construction and given each a cost, give or take 10 percent: ground floor, second floor, third floor, pool. We are now satisfied as to his bona fides, and his estimate is extremely competitive, coming in just under another contender's, and 25 percent under someone else, the one who estimated the time at eight to ten months.

We go over the figures in some detail. I will learn later that he dropped out of school in the fifth grade, but he is quicker than I with the figures. It turns out that Beto has a splendid way to decide what will be his responsibility and what will be ours. With his hands, he traces the shape of a house. "Besides the structure itself," he says, "I propose that anything *not* visible will be my concern: the foundation, the structure, the materials, the pipes, the wires. But anything that you can see will be your concern. That way, you can choose appliances, hardware, toilets, sinks, tiles, flooring, and paint according to your own taste. I will, of course, install everything you decide on for the agreed-upon cost."

As I have been coached, I ask what else, beyond the visible-invisible line, is not covered in his estimate. He reminds us that in this part of Mexico, doors and windows are commissioned separately, to be installed by the carpenter and crew. We have to find a carpenter, order the doors and windows, and make certain they are delivered at the right point in the contractor's schedule. And carpenters are, Beto points out, notoriously unreliable about delivery dates. He says he cannot tell from our plans what sort of driveway, pathways, and ground surface we will want. Other than that, he says, the estimate will cover everything.

We have decided that we will not dicker. Not only are we generally against the gringo custom of haggling for everything, but we see no point in it with Beto. He has said he will not nickel-and-dime us; why should we? I tell him that I have every confidence that he will build a great house, and that we accept with pleasure.

Beto nods with a small smile. No flourishes, unlike Aurelio. Thia is the one who reaches over to pump his hand, telling him in English how delighted we are to be working with him. He flushes a bit and grins. I add that we have been unable to get an environmental-impact study because nobody seems to know how to get one; we have Aurelio on the case for the normal permits, but we cannot be certain when or how we will get the study. At this, Beto frowns. "I have to keep my crew working. It would be difficult not to know when we can start." He explains that most of his crew, including two sons and two brothers, have been working with him for five to fifteen years. This crew loyalty is a wonderful thing, of course, but I get worried. I now know that we do *not* want to miss working with Beto.

I tell him we are hard on the trail for our permits, and we hope to have a resolution on the impact-study soon. He shrugs a little and says, "Then God will decide."

It is rare to have a conversation with an American or a Mexican about local government without a mention of payoffs. Like traffic cops, municipal workers are woefully underpaid, and those who are elected to office are often of humble origin, with just this one chance to put a little extra aside. As Eagle George says, when I tell him about a more troublesome piece of red tape—getting an environmental permit— "Everything is possible in Mexico," as he rubs his thumb and two fingers together. The old-timers here all say that.

But for better or worse, we've decided we're going to live in Mexico without paying anyone off, without mordidas, if we possibly can. We appreciate the attitude of the play-it-as-it-lays people, but we came down determined to try to put cynicism aside and assume that there *is* a way of playing it by the book here. This not-entirely-naive New York City couple is going to take it on faith that most people want to do their jobs honestly, no matter what the current wisdom says, and we intend to rely on the better angels of human nature. And on Aurelio, whose job as our designer is to help us legally obtain the necessary permits.

Aurelio has drilled me in what we will need beyond the troublesome environmental study: a more mundane urban-compatibility study, a soil-use permit, a structural permit, and, finally a construction license. Several friends have paid go-betweens a fee to secure this paperwork for them without personal involvement, but I decide I want to experience at least some of the steps we need to take, with Aurelio's help. I tell him only that I want us to make this happen without mordidas.

Early one morning, Aurelio comes by in his truck. He is wearing, as always, his flat-brimmed straw hat, the cord behind his head. Thia says good-bye to us with her usual cheer. He opens the truck door for me, and I get in. He mentions Thia's enthusiasm and says, "What a wonderful thing to have, to wake up in the morning and say, 'Here we go— another day!'" I am struck by the contrast between the two principal Mexican professionals now in our life: Beto (if we can keep him) blunt, terse, focused, to the point; and Aurelio, sly, effusive, talkative, gracious.

We take off for Valle de Banderas, the county seat about forty minutes away, where the building permissions and licenses are handled. I have a passport, the legal papers attesting to my bank trust, and a copy of the capital-gains taxes paid by the previous owner. As we tool along toward Valle, I ask Aurelio how certain he is that we can get the necessary permits without cravenness. He says, "With the previous director of public works, who just stepped down, I would have been able to say, 'Hey, how are you? How is the family? Let's go out for a drink afterwards.' With the new director, *quién sabe*? It will depend on how he and I get along."

On the way, we talk about Sayulita's growing pains, and how both foreigners and Mexicans are scrambling for financial advantage—rising prices, land disputes, and so on. "Well," says Aurelio, "there is a saying here: 'When the river is churning, the fishermen do well.'"

The Department of Urban Development and Ecology, as the wooden sign says, is a single office with two casually dressed women sharing a desk, while behind a room divider sits the official to whom I must apply with most of our papers. He is Sergio Barajas, in short sleeves and khakis, and he waves us to a couple of aluminum chairs in front of his desk. Aurelio immediately begins to glad-hand, asking him about his family and where he grew up. I cannot quite follow it, but there is apparently a cousin who is good friends with Aurelio's nephew. Sergio stamps a couple of documents, and then Aurelio and I walk across the street to a photocopy office to make the necessary copies. On the way back, he says, "The girls looked like they were perspiring. Let's bring them a couple of soft drinks." Back at the office, he hands them to the women, who accept the drinks graciously, and he asks them about their families, where they grew up. There is a girlfriend who married Aurelio's second cousin.

We are supposed to return at another, unspecified time to pick up the validated documents, or so Aurelio hopes. "We made a good beginning here," he says. "*Ojalá* it will all work out." On the way home in his truck, he says, "We Mexicans often hear about American efficiency. But here we have two kinds of efficiency—one based on gratuities, and the other based on relationships and friendship. Aurelio Carrillo has been around, he knows about both, but one kind works best." I ask him which he means. "We'll see, won't we?" he says, and laughs.

CHAPTER 19

A Romance Buds...
A Girl Blooms... A Frijol Floats

Blair is back in the fold, and the level of cuisine in our apartment has once again climbed to acceptable levels. His stories about thwarted courtship in Guanajuato indicate the sap is rising, so we are happy when he comes home one night from Puerto Vallarta to tell us of a new acquaintance. He has met a young Mexican woman, Pilar, from Puerto Vallarta. (I've given her a pseudonym, the only one in this narrative.) She is going to be a graduate student in business administration, and, hey, wait till we see her. He brings her over one afternoon.

Pilar is indeed a stunner, sloe-eyed, slim, and curved, with the midriff-baring blouse and shorts that her counterpart in the States would be wearing. She is shy and a bit awkward with us, but Thia immediately sets her at ease. We talk, and she tells us about her family: her father is a waiter in Puerto Vallarta, her mother is a homemaker, and her brothers are also college graduates. It is clear from her conversation, however, that she has been the one in the family with the steepest climb—she works full-time while attending classes—and I am struck anew by how often it is the woman in the modern Mexican family who seems to work the hardest at overcoming obstacles.

After a few visits, it becomes clear that they are having a romance. The fact that we give them plenty of privacy while she is visiting sets Pilar at ease. She will later tell Blair that she appreciates being treated as an adult, and that that has not been the case with her parents or those of her previous boyfriend. Mexican young people, she says, are as free—or as conservative—as their American counterparts, but at no time have parents permitted any but the most old-fashioned rules of dating behavior. She thinks we're way *padre*. (Padre, or *padrísimo,* means way cool, while *madre,* literally a word of utmost respect, is colloquially a term of harsh derision. *Figúrate.* Go figure.)

In another world, a village away, Barb and Bill ask me to join them at a celebration hosted by their maid, Irma. It will be a *quinceañera,* the commemoration of a girl's fifteenth birthday, traditionally the passage to womanhood in Latin countries. Though fading from popularity among the middle classes, it is still one of the signal events in a poorer family's life; among the upper classes, it can still be an extravagant, expensive affair complete with ballrooms and trips to Europe. Irma, whose only family income is her domestic wages and her laborer husband's earnings, has held two quinceañeras in the past twenty-four months. The impact on her exceedingly modest means is hard to imagine.

Thia has had a passing encounter with an earlier quinceañera in Sayulita when she ran into Mayela, the daughter of the woman who takes in our laundry, and walked with her to the home where a fifteen-year-old friend was holding her celebration. Before Mayela walked in, Thia noticed an older couple dressed in groom's clothing and a bridal gown. She asked Mayela who the couple was.

"Oh, they're her mother and father. They're taking advantage of their daughter's quinceañera to get married. This happens often."

Tonight, Thia is visiting another friend, and I am the one attending. A reason we admire Barb and Bill, with whom we have become fast friends, is their commendable attitude toward what they see as their responsibilities as Mexican residents. Triny Palomero Gil has told me how respected they are by their Mexican neighbors in San Pancho, and we see it as well. They buy presents, take town children to the water park in Vallarta, organize and reward trash pickups, and make loans they know are gifts. Most of all, they make it a point to attend every wedding or funeral they hear about. "We don't want to be known as just easy touches," says Bill. "They need to know we're a part of the community."

On this occasion, they are both. Irma has asked Barbara to be *ma-*

drina, the godmother, for a second time, this time to a girl who is not even Irma's daughter. Irma, a soft-hearted woman who picks up strays, heard that a local prostitute who worked in the San Pancho cantina had deserted her three daughters. One of the daughters is Sara, whom Irma took into her home when she was fourteen. "Irma couldn't bear for Sara to be deprived of her birthright, a quinceañera," Barb says. "She was determined she'd have one even if it broke her. And it could."

Pragmatically, it has become a custom for Mexicans in this village to persuade their American employers to act as padrinos and madrinas of the girls—and, indeed, all manner of casual foreign visitors are regularly invited to act as godparents as well. Renting a hall, buying food and drinks for virtually the entire town, and in particular purchasing a traditional party dress, can be ruinously expensive unless the cost is spread out and subsidized. So Barbara, as a number of American residents regularly do, agreed to buy Sara's dress for the occasion. "It's more than a little poignant," she says. "A dress will typically cost four or five hundred dollars—it's as important as a wedding dress and is also just worn once—and may add up to a huge part of a family's annual income. We really have no choice but to help."

But it's not all about the financial help. Mexican children get padrinos and madrinas at every important stage of their life, beginning at birth, at First Communion, at important birthdays along the way. Often, the honor is offered to a friend from a neighboring village, as a way of widening the child's arc of relationships. In a country where neither church nor government is seen historically as a reliable source of support, family is all, so it is important to expand the range of family. Having a padrino gives a child a greater range of possibilities in the next village, the next town, a richer country. Ideally, the parents and the padrinos become compadre and comadre for life, a level above friendship. "He's not just my pal," a Mexican said to me, "he's my *compa.*" A *padrino* becomes an honorary relative who might someday offer advice, an introduction, a job, a leg up.

We hover in the back of San Pancho's church during the service. Sara, an ordinary-looking young woman transformed by a radiant smile, is sitting in front of the altar. The priest is swinging his incense pot, two guitar players on the side strum a hymn, there is a rustle in the congregation, and a drunk ninety-year-old man in a back pew is throwing his hands up in the air in time to the music. The ceremony is briefly interrupted when a chicken wanders down the aisle and flies up into the air, squawking as a village woman tries to shoo her out.

Three young men in powder-blue tuxedos, "chamberlains," are her attendants, and they stand respectfully by. I expected that there might be snickering, or at least some attitude, considering the poor young woman's provenance, but the boys seem to know they are players in a singular day of a woman's life. Besides, there seems to be relatively little opprobrium aimed at prostitutes (relative to the States, I would say), and none that I can see aimed at the child.

Afterward, the congregation repairs to one of the town's largest covered marketplaces, where tables and candles have been laid out. The crowd is now bigger—there is markedly more interest in fiestas than in masses—and taped music comes out of large loudspeakers. As we wait for the main ceremony to begin, Barb talks about her last quinceañera, for Irma's daughter, held earlier in the year.

"Her daughter is a bright girl," Barb says, "and we'd been paying for English lessons for her. But I heard she was going to be dropping out of school right after the party. Well, I was her crowning madrina, and there was a moment when I was supposed to go up and crown her. I did, but I whispered in her ear, 'If you feel like a princess now, just think: if you go back to school, you can be a princess *every day of your life.*' I thought, 'She'll probably never go back to school; she'll look for someone to marry, get pregnant, and this party will probably be the personal high point of her life.' Two weeks later, I heard that the girl had returned to school and passed her equivalency exam. She's now studying to be a nurse—once a week, on Saturdays, the world's slowest nursing course—but at least she's on her way."

The rituals of the quinceañera are variously attributed to the Spanish and the Aztecs, coming-of-age celebrations for daughters of the nobility. It seems to me as I watch Sara, who has been escorted to a chair placed in the middle of the cement floor, that it may be the only time in a girl's life—wedding day included—that she will be this solely the focus of her family and community.

With a light shining on her, the theme song from *Titanic* is heard, the Spanish lyrics crooned by a Mexican Céline Dion. Irma's husband, Sara's unofficial foster father, has bowed to her and stepped aside, and the three tuxedoed boys, each with a hand over his heart, march to a choreographed step around one another, and the celebrant.

The stepfather then asks her to dance, the music changes to an English (and Disney) version of "Someday My Prince Will Come," and each of her padrinos and madrinas takes a turn dancing with her. Sara is holding the hem of her dress with one hand as she twirls around, beaming. She sits back down, and her "stepparents" walk over and help her out of her flats, replacing them with high heels. They give her a cellophane-wrapped doll, which she stands and tosses over her shoulder at waiting girlfriends, symbolically discarding her childhood. A cake is wheeled out, and, still alone, she puts her face into the frosting, and comes up with a big, still-childlike grin.

I return to the apartment later that night—Thia is not home yet—and come upon Blair and Pilar, spending a domestic evening together. She is in an easy chair writing in a notebook—her graduate exams are coming up—while he is curled up on the equipale couch, iPod wires dangling, reading a book on Greek mythology. I recall Pilar telling us she never had a quinceañera; her parents preferred to save for college. I watch their bronzed young faces gleaming beneath the lamplight, their futures limitless, at peace with privilege.

Aurelio has called to say that we have to make another trip to Valle. He has been told that one of the documents I signed was not done in duplicate. We drive back to the dilapidated municipal building, and Sergio Barajas receives us cordially. His two assistants are particularly friendly, no doubt the result of Aurelio's thoughtful cold sodas. When Sergio Barajas finds our folder, he stamps it a couple of times, gets me to sign it, then the first assistant stamps it, and the second assistant also stamps it. It goes back to Señor Barajas for a final stamping. There has been no hint, no suggestion, of a gratuity.

It looks as if we are through with this phase, and I take the opportunity to ask Señor Barajas if he has any suggestions for obtaining the environmental-impact report, which remains as big a mystery as ever. He tells us that the best thing to do would be to drive to the state capital, Tepic, about sixty miles away, and apply for an exemption, since it seems my property is clearly in the urban zone and has no environmental issues. One common mango tree will come down, but we're keeping all the other plants and trees intact. We thank him, Aurelio asks about everyone's family, and we leave.

We stop for lunch at a family restaurant under a tent outside Valle, where they have fresh fish and shrimp sizzling on a grill. Aurelio speaks for the first time about his wife, who he says stayed home with the kids: "I told her when we married it was better if she brought up the kids, took care of the house, and helped me with our personal finances, while I found work as a builder." He went to architecture school but had to drop out when his father died. Aurelio talked about his twenty-year-old son, who just shaved his head in solidarity with a classmate who had leukemia and had lost his hair. The friend later died. The boy, like Aurelio's son, was studying to be an architect.

I congratulate Aurelio on getting us past this first bureaucratic hurdle and ask him if he expected it would go this way. He shrugs and says that paying someone off is part of the world he lives in, and he tells me a story about his son getting into an accident and having to pay off authorities to get him proper care. But, he says, "I was glad you were able to see how we Mexicans have a second currency—besides bribes, I mean—and that courtesy and friendship can be just as effective. I, Aurelio Carrillo, know how to use both, but I sleep better with the currency we just used." I pay for lunch, happily.

At poker later this week, I am staring at my cards and trying to decide if Mike is bluffing—he is clacking his chips less and his tell is not as obvious—and I notice a blemish on my forearm. I start to scratch it, and one of the guys says, "That doesn't look good." Rollie peers across the table to inspect it, and he, too, shakes his head. It is dark, raised, and irregular. Thia likes it even less when I show it to her at home.

The next day, Dr. Mauro doesn't say whether he likes or doesn't like it, but he says I should have a biopsy. It is a hot day, and there is quite a crowd of Mexicans and Americans outside in his waiting room. "It could be skin cancer, right?" I ask. "It could be," he says. "I see a lot of it." I'd been on the Internet the night before, and of course became conversant with every deadly kind of dermatological malignancy that exists. The Internet is catnip for hypochondriacs.

With Dr. Mauro's office so busy, I expect that he will send me to a fancy lab somewhere in Puerto Vallarta for a biopsy. But he motions me to his curtained alcove, where he tells me to lie down. Donning gloves, he gives me a shot and slices off a piece of the lesion. He reaches over, takes an empty medicine bottle from the sterilizer, fills it with alcohol, and drops the frijol-shaped piece of skin into the bottle from his tweezers. He says, "We aren't formal around here. You can take this over to the lab yourself. " He motions out the window toward the highway a half block away. "Try to get across the highway—you may have to run— and deliver the bottle to that white storefront you can see from here." He walks me out and points at a one-room structure next to a tool store.

I am not entirely surprised. I remember Barb talking about a family member who was told by this doctor that he needed to submit a stool specimen. The doctor told him to purchase a specimen kit at the drug store. He went into the village pharmacy and made his request. He was given an empty Gerber baby-food jar and a popsicle stick.

I pay Dr. Mauro his fee, this time thirty dollars, I am happy to say, and cross the highway. As it turns out, the storefront is just a receiving station for Guadalajara's leading medical laboratory. The biopsy comes back positive, however—basal-cell carcinoma—and I notice another lesion on my back several days later. Same run across the highway, same result. In both cases, as Dr. Mauro is quick to reassure me, the lab confirmed that all traces of the carcinoma had been cut away, and he expects no further problem. I admit I called my old college roomie, Dr. Paul, in Laguna Beach to verify the prognosis. And I admit to having some mortal thoughts. But I have no reason to doubt I was given proper treatment.

It is not the only unsettling moment of the week. I hear from a number of people, including Harvey, and the lawyer I hired for our hilltop sale, José Luis Barrios, that the enforcement arm of the state environmental agency has been on a rampage. A dozen gringos in town who are in the middle of construction have been served with notices that they are being shut down, since they had not applied for or received the proper environmental study, or an exemption from it. Nearly all involved had cleared lots within the urban zone, meaning that there was very little likelihood any environmental issues were involved. When the owners asked the enforcers how they might obtain either document, they replied that that was not their department. The owners were on notice, however, that fines could be as high as $10,000 and that it could take as long as three months for an approval—or denial—to be issued.

The word around town is that this is either payback for some of the antidevelopment stands taken by the gringo-dominated town environmental association, or, just as likely, some say, the final year in the electoral terms of officials eager to pocket the fines. Some gringos are so discouraged that they have packed up and gone back to the States. Our friends Bill and Kathy Glaysher have other reasons, too, but when they tell us they are giving up for this year and will come back to try to build again next winter, we are sorry to see them go.

It is disheartening. We are here to do things as legally as we know how, not to push our weight around, and to abide by all known regulations. And now it is possible we are going to lose our contractor Beto to another job, and our chance to build anytime soon, because of politics, graft, or bureaucracy. No one, however, has any idea which of the three is involved. Like Bill Kirkwood's dogged attempts to investigate how to pay his taxes, it's sometimes difficult to learn how to do the right thing in Mexico. That, and the capricious swing between rigorous law enforcement and no enforcement at all, can keep a person in paradise on edge.

I meet Aurelio as he is driving his truck through town, and he sees that I am down. He stops, gets the latest update on the problem, and says, "*Felicidades*. You have me on your side. I, Aurelio Carrillo, will resolve this dilemma."

CHAPTER 20

A Perfect Day

While we wait out the impact-study problem, Thia and I have decided to find a frame for our Victoriano painting. We hear of a carpenter in nearby La Peñita. It would be simple enough to drive into Puerto Vallarta and buy a frame off the shelf, but we feel the painting deserves a more natural setting. We drive down a side road in La Peñita and find a dilapidated lumberyard dotted with old woodworking machinery. There is a man of about sixty wearing an old T-shirt and long shorts, examining a two-by-four, with a gray bang flopping forward like a kid's. We introduce ourselves. He is Armando Vázquez, nickname of El Surdo, Lefty. I ask him if this is where we can get a painting framed.

"Yes," he says, "we are custom makers, we do what *you* want." His voice is gravelly, and he coughs. The man has been around sawdust a long time. He asks what kind of painting the frame would be for. I go back to the car, where I have stashed the painting, and bring it out. I notice again that there is still a bit of real beach sand among the paint strokes, which both Thia and I agree adds to its authenticity.

"Ah, *mi amigo* Victoriano," Armando says, appraising the painting, nodding. All the older guys in these towns seem to know one another. He says, "This should be framed by a natural wood, nothing too *caprichoso,* but strong, resistant." So he picks up a piece of wood, tells us it is teak, and puts it through an ancient buzz saw to get us a cut so that he can show us the grain. He paints it with a light varnish. What do we think?

We like it, and Thia sits down to sketch a robust but simple frame, indicating concave cuts. Armando's son, a young man with the start of a mustache, comes out to watch. He introduces himself as Eumir, named after a Brazilian musician Armando likes. Armando gravely nods at the sketch—he approves. As we watch him shape a sample, he says, "You know, this kind of wood really *lives*, it has character."

We ask him how much it will cost. In the States, a teak frame this large could run $1,000. He gives us a price of $110 and says it will be done in three days. We accept. We ask him if we should leave the painting with him. He says no, his everyday trade is a little rough for that. Eumir adds, "Not everyone coming through here appreciates art."

As I am putting the rolled-up painting back in the car, Armando asks, "Where are you living?" We tell him, and he says, "Well, I know Aurelio the architect. We're in the same political group, and he's coming here tonight for a meeting." So we give him a note to give to Aurelio, writing, "From your secret gringo admirers." Apparently our knowing Aurelio means we've passed some test with Armando, because he takes me aside and says, "Look, I know everyone in this region, everyone. If you ever have any official problems with anyone, you can call me." He takes out his card to show me he's a member of the regional council.

We chat a bit more. He seems in no hurry, and neither are we. I go down the street and bring back a six-pack of Corona. All four of us open a bottle. Armando tells us his father was a carpenter here, as are two of his sons, of whom he has six: Eumir, Ulises, Sócrates, Aristóteles, Diego, and Jesús. I ask him about his sons' names, and he says he has many interests—Brazilian music, Greek mythology, biblical characters—and he has taught all his sons that learning is what is most positive in life. "We are never too young or too old to learn something worthwhile."

It is not the first or last time I will find Mexican working-class people with a passion for culture and learning that I might not have expected. Armando calls himself a fatalist and says he believes people benefit more from errors than from success. "Mistakes are my teacher," he says. The conversation meanders, from the difficulty of finding oysters on restaurant menus, to his enjoyment of the nearby petroglyph reserve of Alta Vista, where he says fascinating pre-Columbian rock carvings can be seen.

"Look, I have an idea," says Armando. "I have a good friend who is a guide. Why don't I ask him to come over here when I've finished with the frame on Friday? The four of us can go visit Alta Vista."

I translate for Thia, and she is eager to do it. "That sounds great, Armando. But can you just take the day off that way?"

He looks at me through his bang of shaggy gray hair. "Life is short, my friend."

On Friday, we arrive at noon, and Armando is at his workplace, along with Eumir and his second son, Ulises, looking over four pieces of diagonally cut teak. A buzz saw is whining, and Armando is coughing sawdust. In one corner of the shop is another man, dressed in long pants—a rarity—and a collar shirt. Armando introduces him as Manuel Villareal, friend, owner of a local ostrich farm, and guide extraordinaire. I bring out the painting, and we watch as they stretch it on a frame.

We chat with Manuel, who speaks passable English, which is a relief to Thia and to my translating reserves. He tells us that although he raises ostriches for cash, he is a certified personal guide and likes to take friends and a few customers on cultural and historical tours to nearby locations. He says he disdains the big tours and knows quite a bit about local Indian customs. Although he has read the histories, he says most of his knowledge comes from growing up here and spending years listening to local Indians tell their stories. He is pleased to take this afternoon off from ostriches for a friend of Armando's.

We agree that we will pick up the frame on our way back later in the afternoon, and Armando shuts down the machinery. His sons politely wish us a good day, and Thia and I and Manuel and Armando get into our car. We drive about a half hour away, to a turnoff onto a very rough unpaved road that goes deep into the jungle forest. Manuel points out a smooth tree with peeling red bark, and says, "copal—the tourist tree." We bite. "First the bark turns red in the sun, then it peels off."

The SUV gets a full workout; the road becomes almost impassable at one point, and we tank-crawl over huge rocks. Manuel says the government keeps the road that way so as to discourage visitors. Why? Because the site is thought to have so many artifacts—only about 10 percent are thought to have been found thus far—a flood of visitors would lead to looting. And they'd have to pay for greatly increased security. Better just to make it near-impossible to get to. Just as we get to our destination, we look over, and there is a lone eagle sitting majestically atop a copal tree. "Good omen," says Manuel.

At a clearing, we park. Thia, Armando, and I get out, and Manuel goes into guide mode. He picks up a large staff and stands there like Moses, addressing his followers. Rock carvings, Manuel says, along with cave paintings, are humanity's oldest artifacts—they predate the pyramids. A sagging strand of barbed wire is the only indication that we're entering an important archaeological area. There is a rock by the entrance, and it is a petroglyph. There are two carvings on it: a sunlike whorl and a starlike cross. They look ancient. "Sun and Venus," says Manuel. "Night and day. This is what you will see here this afternoon: duality. The ancients in this region believed that life was defined by the symmetry of opposites—male and female, light and dark, spirit and flesh." Manuel tell us that although the glyphs have been interpreted, archaeologists do not know their age or the precise tribes, but the local Huichol visit this site, and since they are among the pure Indian strains in Mexico, it is thought they might be descendants.

The Huichol are unique in the Mexican culture, he says, poking his staff into the ground. They are the only tribe that remained unconquered by either the Mexica or the Spaniards. While other tribes were being sacrificed, enslaved, or wiped out by European disease, they took to the mountains and survived largely intact. intermarrying among themselves, for three hundred years. Unlike the American Indians, who were thrown off their lands and then concentrated in reservations, in Mexico the federal government honored the independence of the Huichol by declaring that there were no boundaries to their territory. They are allowed to wander freely; they may practice their rites, which include peyote ingestion, without harassment and enjoy a measure of self-rule unique in Mexico. I cannot help recalling that their isolation also causes them wretched poverty, as our Jeep guide Vicky showed us earlier.

Manuel leads us down a path to the side of a dry river bed. There are holes bored into rocks that look as if they could be natural, but they are evenly spaced. They are like footlights, marking the trail. We stop at one mossy rock. There are a series of connected 8s—representing infinity, says Manuel, with the same symbol used by the Greeks and, by extension, modern mathematicians. On another, the symbols for the three levels of existence—the underworld, the physical world, the spiritual world—identical to those found at Stonehenge, he claims.

On another rock, there is a stick figure with a head made of a corn stalk—the god of maize. "This is the god," says Manuel, "that told the wandering nomadic tribes, 'You can settle down.'" On one altarlike rock, there are offerings left by the Huicholes, who leave personal effects the way other Mexicans leave them in cemeteries: jewelry, a piece of corn, coins, a cigarette. "This is an important sacred place for the Huichol," says Manuel.

About twenty minutes on, rounding a turn in the dry river bed, we come upon a remarkable sight: beneath a canopy of trees, the light streams down on a large open area of tumbled rock and pebbles, like the ruins of a palace. It is enshrined by cliffs made of a profusion of smooth, squared-off rocks—it is difficult to know if they are man-made or natural—and a couple of pools filled with water. Above the largest pool, there is a large throne made of flat rocks that looks sculpted, but is in fact a natural formation. This is the River of the Font, Manuel says, the most sacred location of this sanctuary. Armando borrows Manuel's staff and climbs up onto the throne. When he sits down in it, his legs dangle like a kid in an oversized chair.

We climb up on the hill above the main pool, where we see more petroglyphs. Standing by the pools, with the light pouring down through the flat-rocked canyons, we become quiet. I, who am not given to mystical moments, have one.

On our walk back through the riverbed, Manuel says that an hour north, the island of Mexcaltitlán is thought to be the legendary Aztlán, birthplace of the Aztecs, or Mexica. "The legend says the early Mexica worshipped the god of snakes, so when they migrated to the Valley of Mexico, there were other tribes already there. They were given the worst land, an island full of snakes and scorpions. They thrived on them, became strong, and turned it into the greatest Indian city, Tenochtitlán, now the biggest city in the world."

When we come out of the reserve, there is a truckload of American "adventure tour" visitors, wearing backward caps and thin-strap T-shirts, shouting and joking and drinking beer. They are about to make their own noisy visit to the sacred site. I have a flash of proprietary spite and think, Maybe the government is right not to make this more accessible.

We drive back toward La Peñita, and Armando takes over as our little group's director. He says he has a surprise for us. He has remembered our earlier conversation about oysters. He has friends in a small village nearby who are diving fishermen; they make their living plunging down to collect lobster, octopus, and oysters. He says that it is legal for these fishermen to harvest a limited number of oysters for their personal use—and their friends' use too.

We drive down a couple of dirt lanes and stop along the street outside one modest two-room home. Armando gets out, disappears for a few minutes, and comes back out, saying, "They have oysters!" He is followed by a man with a dark, weathered face and striking blue eyes, and a thin, pretty woman. Armando introduces us to El Güero ("the Fair One") and his wife, Alfonsa. They are carrying a folding card table, which they set up in the street, by their driveway. Four plastic chairs are dragged up.

"Can we have four dozen?" asks Armando. El Güero and his wife disappear down the driveway. While Thia and Manuel make themselves comfortable on the chairs, Armando and I drive a couple of blocks to pick up four double-size bottles of Pacifíco beer and bring them back to the card table. Ten minutes later, El Güero comes out carrying a platter of forty-eight shucked oysters in their shells, some lime halves, and a couple of bright-red bottles of Huichol chile sauce. Alfonsa brings out a large plate of sliced cucumbers, still warm from the field where they were picked, also with limes and hot sauce.

The oysters are no more than a half hour out of the ocean. With each oyster, I squeeze in the lime, shake in some hot sauce, and put the shell to my mouth and swallow it down, tasting the sea water. Best ever.

Thia leans over to Armando, squeezes his arm, and says, with a quick translation by me, "This is why we came to Mexico. I cannot remember an afternoon like this. It is a gift."

Armando grins. "I don't ask God to give me something," he says. "I just ask him to put me where I can reach it."

By the time the last of the oysters are consumed, the cucumbers disposed of, and the beer finished off, we are slumped back in our plastic chairs, licking our fingers. Armando, rubbing his belly, is beaming, as happy to have brought us this special, improvised moment as to have enjoyed it himself. "¿Esto es la vida pura, no?" he asks. "Is this not pure life?"

When we drop off the two men at Armando's shop and pick up our painting, the four of us exchange *abrazos*. As we drive back to Sayulita, there is a brilliant burgundy sunset spread across the sky.

CHAPTER 21

A Breakthrough . . . A Confrontation . . . A Mad Holiday

Aurelio has made three visits to Tepic, where he has finally tracked down somebody he knows at the environmental office. A *"familiar,"* he says. A relative, though he is coy about how close a one. He feels we are making progress. The official relative, he says, wants a complete description of the property, including its trees and plants, and the blueprints. He also wishes to see photographs. I ask Aurelio if this is the undiscovered official procedure we have been seeking, but he says no, the man appears to be creating it on the spot. But at least it is something.

After I take digital pictures and print them out, and deliver the other documents, Aurelio drives again to Tepic, and comes back that afternoon with requests for further documents, duly stamped. I deliver those. Aurelio says the official also did not like the fact that we were planning a pool. I say, "Didn't *like*? What does that mean?" Aurelio shrugs. "I believe he does not like swimming pools. It is meaningless, because he has no authority over what you actually build, just whether you need the impact study. We just erase the pool from the plans, and later you build what you want." I have no idea where this is leading, but I know I cannot put Beto off any longer.

Aurelio sets off on yet another trip. That evening there is a knock at our door. Aurelio is standing there, his smile stretched nearly to his earlobes. He is holding a letter.

"Did I not say that I, Aurelio Carrillo, would solve this?" He reads aloud from a letter whose official language says that our property is exempt from an environmental-impact study. This will be proof against any rogue enforcers, since the sin other gringos committed was in not obtaining *something*, preferably with a stamp on it. Aurelio says, "Persistence and patience, the two Mexican virtues!" He is beaming. Thia jumps up, kisses him on the cheek, and says, "Bravo, Aurelio, you are a miracle worker!" He understands all her English, and his smile is beatific.

We had never agreed on a fee, but it has taken Aurelio three long trips, so I suggest that I pay him three hundred dollars and a monthly honorarium. Though his role is drawing to an end, I suggest he drop in on our construction once or twice a month when we finally get under way and offer architectural advice. He is pleased, and we shake hands. The miracle worker departs, his circular hat cord bobbing on his neck like a rawhide halo.

As soon as he is gone, I jump to the telephone and call Beto with the news. Characteristically, he betrays little emotion, but says he is pleased, and that now it is time for us to sit down with the blueprints and make definitive plans. In fact, he tells me, he has one or two items on the blueprints he wants to discuss with me. Beto is a warm enough person, I think, but seems to be exceedingly focused on the project, not on its niceties. I suggest a sit-down for the following day with architect Aurelio in our apartment.

That night, after La Luz has hung up her Mexican apron, we join Jeanne and Rollie for a late dinner out at a taco stand and tell them the news about our exemption. They are happy for us. They have cut back on their supervision of Rollie's at Night, delegating it to their longtime Mexican partners, Ismael and Adriana, and his staff, including, of course, La Luz. This is a victory for Jeanne, who constantly urges Rollie to cut back on work. "As an entrepreneur, he's a big success," Jeanne says. "As a retiree, not so much." In fact, Jeanne works just as hard, though she clearly enjoys having Rollie as a foil. They are refreshingly public about their spousal bickering, and breakfast diners have long become accustomed to hearing Rollie call out, "*Jeanne!* Plate's getting cold!" To which, Jeanne, across the room, will shout, "Hold your *horses*, Rollie!"

Like Bill and Barb, Rollie and Jeanne have roots that go deep into the

Mexican community, attending birthday parties, sponsoring children (Jeanne will often informally "adopt" a young woman who needs help), and listening to long, convoluted tales of mishap and woe. When they were still working as educators in Salinas, where most of their students were poor Chicanos, their house was a haven for all manner of wandering pilgrims. Their daughter, Jodi, describes walking into their living room at night to find actors from their community troupe asleep under their grand piano. They are also people of intense feelings. Months later, Rollie will tell me the story of a white stray Sayulita dog that used to sleep inside their restaurant. Since spaying is uncommon, when the dog would go into heat, packs of males would swarm around her; that is, until a small, scrappy male with brown fur fought off their advances, and the two became an item. One night, a truck struck and killed the white dog. Rollie, out for a walk with their own Sayulita stray, Stretch, happened upon the body on the side of the road. There, he recalls, he saw the brown dog, his paws upon his dead mate's, howling at the sky. Rollie sat on a nearby stair with Stretch and cried. "It was the story of all Mexican dogs right there in front of me," he will tell me. "It was the story of Mexico, maybe even of the Mexican people." As he tells me the story, his eyes fill.

We have also become closer to a number of other gringo residents. There are Chuck and Teke, of course, and Ian and Kerry, and prominent among the creative folk who have settled at least part time in Sayulita are screenwriter and novelist Patrick Hasburgh, his wife Cheri, and their daughter. Patrick, the creator of the TV series *21 Jump Street,* made serious Hollywood money. He and Cheri moved here about five years ago; in addition, they split their time between Aspen and a country manse in British Columbia. Patrick is outspoken and witty, with rich, salacious Tinseltown stories; Cheri is warm, bright, and something of a girl jock. They are quiet contributors to the community here, donating money to the park and the softball team, of which Cheri is the shortstop. The fact that she is pregnant slows her down not at all.

Patrick also directed the cult ski movie *Aspen Extreme,* which it turns out Blair has seen six times, so he is starstruck. The two of them have become sports buddies, since Patrick, unlike the other writer in town, is a fit and enthusiastic surfer. Like many gringos here, Patrick's politics are progressive, and a lot of dinner conversations around town are about That Man in the White House.

We have found, in a word, community. Between our American friends and our growing closeness to the Mexicans we are working with and have come to know, our life is filling up. We had, and still have, many friends back in New York and Connecticut. But in our old life, when we made arrangements to see one another, with all the advance planning, mutual consulting of day planners, intricate transportation schemes, and table-reservation hassles, we often felt as if we were making grown-up playdates. Here, with the expatriate bond between us so quickly made, and the common topic of our gringo adventures such a natural conversation stoker, it is easy and natural. The fact that we meet almost everyone we know almost every day, strolling around the plaza, makes it easier yet.

Some gringo purists do not like it that, so often, in high season, it looks like there are as many gringos as Mexicans. It's getting overrun, they say. The truth is, these villages remain overwhelmingly Mexican, as is evident when there is a fiesta or a political event, and the plaza brims with its native people and we few gringos recede to the sidelines. I think the reason that on ordinary sunny winter mornings there appear to be so many gringos out and about reflects a hunger for an ideal 1950s small town in America, where everyone meets and greets his neighbors in the town square. It's not that, of course; it's *their* town. But I think our delight in having this plaza life, a given for Mexicans, is what makes us so visible and so mobile.

Rollie has stayed out tonight later than usual, so Jeanne nudges her yawning husband toward home. We, too, need to get a night's sleep. Tomorrow Aurelio meets Beto for the first time. I wonder, given their widely divergent personalities, how they will get along.

Beto arrives first, a half hour early. I am so nonplussed that I walk out with my bed hair sticking up on my scalp, while Thia rushes to offer him orange juice, coffee, some fruit. *"Sólo agua, por favor,"* says Beto. He is dressed again in a dark T-shirt and familiar knee-length work shorts. We make small talk, and I am relieved to see Beto soften up a bit, with a quick, authentic grin that briefly lights up his craggy face. We chat until Aurelio arrives, a half hour late.

Aurelio is still riding high, very high. He enters like a grandee, all smiles and murmurs, shaking my hand, Thia's hand, seeking out Blair, who is back from an early morning surf and is in a far corner on the couch, reading the wireless morning news on his laptop. Then Aurelio comes over to shake hands with Beto, who rises to greet him.

"Let's begin, shall we?" Aurelio says, and he rolls his copy of the blueprints out on the equipale table. The three of us are gathered around him, and Aurelio begins his walk-through of the plans. He is clearly in his element, speaking in Spanish, and I am keeping up a low murmur of translation to Thia. He begins by saying that this is the blueprint for a three-story house and pool of "relatively modest proportions" and that he, Aurelio Carrillo, has at all times sought to accommodate the desires and alterations of his clients, of whom he is, it hardly needs to be said, su servidor. He points to the ground-floor plans and explains the scale and dimensions he has used. He traces along the contours he has drawn, emphasizing the flat nature of the property and the relative lack of challenges it will present to a builder. Pretty basic stuff, even to amateurs like Thia and me, but Aurelio deserves his day.

As Aurelio goes on, I glance at Beto, whose face is impassive, hard to read. Aurelio then turns over the first blueprint, setting it aside with a crisp, exaggerated elegance. He smooths out the elevation blueprint and begins to talk about the roof line, which extends from here, he says, to there, his finger describing its circumference. About five minutes have passed, and Beto has not said a word. As Aurelio is explaining how the roof will slope from the terrace, I hear a rumble coming from Beto's throat. His fingers begin to tap on the leather tabletop, and then something startling happens.

"Look," he interrupts in a steely voice, gazing directly at Aurelio. "You are treating me like a novice, and I do not appreciate it. You are wasting my time." It is as if Thia and I are not in the room; for the moment, I do not have the presence of mind to translate. Aurelio's head has snapped back. He has slumped in his chair. In all the months we have been in Mexico, we have not seen an impolite confrontation. Whatever a Mexican may be thinking, at least in this part of the country, it is simply not done to manifestly show direct displeasure, certainly not in front of a gringo. I wait for the next *zapato* to drop.

Aurelio finds his voice and says, coolly but shakily, "What seems to be the problem?"

"I have built more than fifty houses," says Beto, "as I'm sure you have. I am completely familiar with plans like these. Everything you are saying is evident, and I would not think to bother *you* with it. In fact, I suggest we skip to an area that I do find troubling."

Grim faced, Aurelio leans forward again. I murmur a summary to Thia, whose eyebrows rise belatedly.

"Where this roof slopes down and meets the other," Beto is saying, gesturing at the print, "I foresee a problem. You have brought together two planes at variance with each other, and both the fitting of the wooden beams and the juncture of the roof edges will suffer."

Aurelio, his composure regained, smiles thinly and begins to defend himself in a patient, and, I have to say, patronizing voice. They continue to debate, civilly, it seems to me, but I am no longer listening. I am recalling something: the shed roof. The one Aurelio put in at the last moment. I felt a small stab of concern that a roof had been added so nonchalantly. I recall now that I wondered how, small task though it was, the roof could just be added without engineering it carefully.

Beto is holding to his point, saying that the roof was not thought through, while Aurelio smiles and says there will be no problem. It is a tense situation, almost as tense as the verbal confrontation, because now I know that Beto has homed in on the blueprint's major vulnerability, the one spot only another experienced architect could have been expected to recognize. And Beto, the builder, spotted it at once.

The discussion ends unresolved, and the two men shake hands stiffly. Aurelio leaves first, and I am saddened, because he came in on such a cloud. I sit and chat with Beto, and determine to ask him why he decided to confront Aurelio so directly. It is difficult to bring up such delicate topics with a Mexican maestro when my Spanish is so imperfect, but I manage to make the sense of my question understood.

Beto says, "I felt he was being condescending, and that is not how two professionals should treat each other. Added to that, I saw a real problem that Señor Carrillo had avoided, and for your sake, I felt I needed to bring that to his attention." He stops and looks me in the eye. "That is how I am. I will tell you what I think."

I realize then that a torch has been passed, if truculently. Ever since we arrived, I have talked to Mexican professionals in various fields and have gotten used to the polite, amiable, often circuitous routes they take to the destination of a discussion. I have become used to the slight tension we gringos feel when making an agreement, or exacting a

promise from a Mexican national—a tension that both sides aren't
really equally firm as to date, hour, price, or clarity of purpose. But here
with Beto, in another moment that belies easy generalization, I am
dealing with a Mexican professional who is, if anything, more direct
and prompt and committed than most gringos. We will forever be in
Aurelio's debt. He has been patient with us, humored us, and did what
no one else in town was able to do with the impact study. But now we
will be in Beto's rough hands, and they are no less natively Mexican.

If Sayulita has a gringo grande dame, it is Evelyne Boren, a celebrated
artist of beach and jungle landscapes whose work is exhibited around
the world. She and her husband, Michael Sandler, live in the house
Aurelio Carrillo built for them, 120 steps above the main Sayulita
beach. It has one of the singular views of the region. She gives art classes
when she is in residence, and many Sayulita gringos, if they can afford
it, have her work on their walls.

We spend a couple of spring afternoons with the couple, sipping
iced tea on their sweeping terra-cotta terrace. Evelyne is tall and leggy,
with the kind of looks that might have kept her in the movies—which
is what she did for several years as a younger woman. She was an action
double for the girl Sean Connery chased around in an early James Bond
movie, *Thunderball*.

She discovered her talent for oils and watercolors, began exhibiting
and selling her work, and arranged her life to be in Santa Fe, New
Mexico, four months of the year, Europe four months, and Puerto Vallarta four months. "I began coming down with Michael in 1972, when
Puerto Vallarta was still a small town," she recalls. "We used to play
backgammon with John Huston, with his bottle of Russian vodka."

Michael, who had spent time in Puerto Vallarta a decade earlier
building condos, remembers the town in its youthful heyday. "John
Huston loved the place," Michael says. "He told me he talked Jack
Warner into letting him make *The Night of the Iguana* down here. It was
a stage play that could have been filmed on the back lot, but John loved
it down here, and of course it turned into a logistical nightmare. They
had to take their equipment on barges from Vallarta to location on Mis-
maloya Beach. Ava Gardner used to water-ski back."

Evelyne and Michael, who were part of the party scene in Puerto

Vallarta, wanted someplace remote they could drive to, and discovered Sayulita in the mid-seventies. "There were no cars, everyone got around on horseback, everything was one floor and just dirt roads—not unlike what we have now, come to think of it," Evelyne laughs. "There were no real-estate brokers, but we heard about a piece of land on this wonderful location."

"We spent eight thousand dollars," says Michael, "and we overpaid by two thousand because we were gringos. It was a beach house, and we added to it through the years." Like Eagle George, Evelyne remembers the days before television. "Every other Saturday a truck would come into town, and they'd string a sheet from one building to the other, and show these wild Westerns, old American and Mexican films. Everyone would carry their chair on their head to go to the movies. There would be dances on the plaza afterward."

And like other expats, she says the trials of living here are a tonic. "It takes a certain kind of person to want to do things the hard way," she says. "It isn't always presented to you on a platter. You have to get out there and get your hands dirty and get it done. That's what makes it interesting and brings interesting people down here to live. I worry that once it gets too modern and slick, you get a different crowd. I see it in Vallarta: they want to stay in a bubble and not explore. Here, they still want a challenge. People ask me, 'What do you do in Mexico?' They don't realize that it's a full-time job just to survive—it takes a lot of time to do the few things you do—and that's *fun*."

Easter in Mexico, especially here on the Pacific Coast, is not the mild holiday it is in the States, all bonnets and bunnies and egg hunts. *Semana Santa*, Holy Week, as it is known, may have an overt religious significance, but it is more Mexico's mad spring break, a traffic-snarling, sidewalk-clogging, one-hundred-million-strong catapult toward the beaches and other sunny locations. Though most towns pause respectfully as their more observant congregants make the stations of the cross on Good Friday, usually with one burly volunteer carting a huge, rugged cross to its various stops, it is a fact that here the beaches are more crowded than the church pews.

Holy Week is neither entirely holy nor just one week. The village old-timers tell us that every hotel and spare room along the coast is

booked, as Mexican families cram themselves into their cars, sometimes a dozen at a time, and disgorge themselves to frolic and feed and
fiesta. On the week before Easter Sunday, by largely unspoken agreement, the working class takes its vacation, and the streets are filled with
older cars and huge family groups taking their *cervezas* and *ceviche* to
the beaches. On the week after Easter Sunday, when the working folk
are gone, the middle- and upper-class Mexicans, many from Mexico
City and Guadalajara, invade in their BMWs and Tevas, and put up chic
sun tents and spread out their blankets with cheese and wine.

Many gringos get out of town. If they do not, they stock up early on
food staples in Puerto Vallarta and do not attempt to drive around the
village, much less the highway. Holy Week is no time to be brave. We
take the cocoon strategy, sticking close to home—and end up enjoying
it. It is common among the gringos to grouse, because petty thievery
and public drunkenness goes up, but Rollie, for one, always relishes
Semana Santa. He says he genuinely gets a thrill out of watching Mexican families on holiday. Rollie, the former principal, who has written
a booklet on humane child raising, has a special view of Mexican families and their children.

"I look around this town," Rollie says, "and I know kids only go to
school a half day, and I know parents only make ten or fifteen dollars a
day. But I see children in the dirt playing with bottle caps in their front
yards, and I see their parents always nearby, and, I don't know, but
those kids look happy to *me*."

Indeed, one of the pleasures of this kind of retirement is the constant presence of children—underfoot, in plastic wagons, running in
packs, spinning wooden tops on the cobblestones. They have the run
of the village, and there is no fear, as there seems to be in the States, that
a stranger will harm a child. Almost everyone seems to be related, anyway. Kids are picked up for a hug, their faces wiped off, and set down
again to run with the pack. I understand the impulse of so many older
Americans to live strictly among their own age group, but I cannot help
thinking that life without kids about must hasten what they are so anxious to put off: their marginalization from life's vitality. At least it seems
so here.

In our apartment, our own child decides to brave the highways to
go visit Pilar in Vallarta. Blair is too old and too experienced a driver for
us to put our foot down, so instead we tap ours in nervous rhythm until

he returns the next day. "Piece of cake, Ma," he says. He has news: he is the first in our family to pay a mordida.

At a speed trap near the airport, where the police are known to favor foreign-plated cars in a game Dick calls Bingo Gringo, Blair was stopped for going a few kilometers over the limit. The cop said he could pay his fine at the municipal office, but he would have to give up his driver's license. He then awaited Blair's response expectantly. Blair, like everyone else here, has had conversations about what to do in this situation. He knew our views, but he also knew that if he handed over his license—an illegal demand in the State of Jalisco, I believe, but one commonly made—he might have trouble getting it back. Besides, he says, he remembered from talking to Barb how poorly Mexico's police are paid, how they have to buy their own guns and uniforms. Better that *they* get a little bonus than the municipal office. A mordida seemed like the Christian thing to do, so he offered the cop a two-hundred-peso note, which was accepted. The officer wished Blair a happy Easter.

CHAPTER 22

Ground Breaking . . .
Roof Slithering . . . Leave Taking

On the first of May, Beto comes by the apartment to say that his crew is ready. We lay out his handwritten estimate in front of us, do some calculations, and agree that Beto will draw 50,000 pesos—$5,000—a week to pay for materials and wages. It is standard procedure by gringos to dole out the money week by week, to retain some control over the spending. There are a number of stories about contractors getting all their money up front, then suddenly changing their domicile to another part of Mexico. One charming pair of local Mexican contractors we know about juggled too many work advances, got behind, and by the time they had paid off their back debts, owed seven gringos $400,000 they no longer had. When I heard about it, I recalled a friend recommending the pair when we first arrived. We never interviewed them, and so, quite by chance, dodged a bullet that could have put us away.

We have no such concerns with Beto, and in any case, he is fine with the weekly pay schedule. He does say, however, that he will need a large initial payment of $20,000 to get started. Although he can cash the weekly checks at the bank, he would appreciate the initial outlay in cash, since his start-up costs will involve a lot of vendors. I drive into Puerto Vallarta and set up a payment schedule with Rosie Rubio at Lloyd's. They are used to American home builders and are accustomed to large weekly disbursements in cash. I withdraw 220,000 pesos, stuff the three-inch-thick wad of bills in the bottom pocket of my cargo shorts, button the pocket, and drive back. At the military checkpoint, I pat the money in my pocket, hoping this won't be the time I get pulled over.

Beto and I meet again, and I hand him the cash. There is no contract. Bruce and Maggie did not have a written contract, and neither will we. Some argue that even in Mexico, where pursuing a lawsuit is rare and tortuous, a written contract is prudent. We made a decision with our gut that more good would come of a genuine show of trust in Beto than requiring that he sign a contract. In any case, he did not expect one, and we did not bring it up. I hand him the cash, tell him the weekly disbursements are set up, and we shake hands. I say, "I know you'll build us a beautiful house, Maestro." Beto says seriously, "Together, *we* will build a beautiful house."

Because Beto is not a glad-hander and so focused on work, we have had relatively few chances to get to know each other better. But I now find time. Beto has five children—three daughters and two sons. The youngest, Govany, eighteen, will be helping him, as will Hugo, twenty-three. I am struck by how often we have seen fathers and their apprentice sons working together in the family trade. This sort of apprenticeship may limit a child's choices, but it guarantees work, and the family stays together. On the other hand, one of Beto's brothers has gone to El Norte, just like all his wife's brothers. What they want in the states, he says, is a nice car and—well, it's almost always a car. Plus all the amenities and conveniences that are up there. Beto prefers to stay. He has a full life in Bucerias—family, friends, the soccer field a block away, the baseball field a few blocks away, the outdoor fiestas.

He tells me he was educated only up to the fifth grade, and that everything he learned he got from books and from living. He started out tending cattle and did some fishing. When he married, he realized he had to better himself, so he joined construction teams and rose through the ranks. "I found I was the one who could figure out answers to problems. I was on a big job, and an expert was hired. He gave the bosses an estimate of twenty-one days to finish the job. I offered to do it in five and did it."

He once spent several months in San Diego, but preferred his life back here. He says he admires Mayan architecture and is constantly reading about how the Mayans constructed their cities and temples, trying to figure out how they did it. He wants someday to visit Chichén Itzá in the Yucatán, but his greatest dream is to visit Machu Picchu in Peru.

We have contracted with an accountant recommended by Aurelio, a young woman named Sonia Pintor Pérez from La Peñita, to pay employer's so-called social security on our behalf. It is what Mexico calls its health-insurance system, a compulsory safety net for workers paid by employers, as well as a retirement fund. It is well named for gringos as it plays the same role as employers' Social Security contributions in the States: you can skip them, but you can also land in trouble. Old-timers here scoff and say *they* built without paying social security, but times have changed. As we heard from Mike and Jocelyn, the ill-starred Lo de Marcos couple, Hacienda, Mexico's IRS, can come knocking on your door years after you have finished building. If you don't have proof that you paid, they have the right to put a lien on—or even seize—your house. For a fee, Sonia will see that Hacienda gets our monthly payments. In cash, please.

Rollie, Jeanne, Thia, and I have begun playing bridge together in the afternoon and on Thia's evenings off. It is another dip back into our younger days; all of us were taught bridge by our parents, played it a bit in our youth, but dropped it in the intervening years. One evening, as we are playing, Jeanne recalls a card game shortly after moving down here, when things were more primitive. She and several woman friends were playing hearts in their living room—Rollie and Jeanne's home is a three-story brick building, with the restaurant on the bottom floor—whose roof was rather casually attached to the house. She and two friends were waiting for their fourth to show up. Jeanne looked up to see that a boa constrictor had slid through an opening in the roof and slithered around the ceiling beams. It spotted an iguana on the wall and moved in for the squeeze.

"Our friend joined us," Jeanne says, "but she never looked up to see the boa constrictor wrapped around a dead iguana hanging over us. We started playing and cracking up and kept saying things like, 'These cards are *strangling* me . . .' and 'You're really *constricting* my hand!' Our friend thought we had lost our minds. We never told her."

A Mexican neighbor woman came in to dispatch the boa with her machete, slicing the boa in half and throwing it in the stream beside the house.

In May, the weather begins to get considerably warmer. For most resident gringos, these villages are not their year-round home. Between June and September, it gets so hot and humid that they take off for the interior, or for second homes in the States. Some of our friends stay, like Bill and Barbara and Dick and Cheryl. Others, like Rollie and Jeanne, begin to wind down their life in paradise, avoid the summer inferno, and head for their stateside limbo.

Needless to say, we will be among the stayers. Though we bought the lot the second night after arriving in November, the paperwork, the interviews, the research, our own changes, and the red-tape delays have made six months pass before we could begin construction. It will be different, building and supervising in the summer. The winter months are mild and dry; the summer months, our friends warn us, are hot beyond anything we have experienced, and the afternoon rains are torrential downpours. When I ask Beto how he and his men will be able to work in the heat and the rain, he shrugs his shoulders. "It won't bother us," he says. "We live here."

So do we, and as some of our friends pull up stakes, we make our summer plans. Our Niños Héroes apartment is spoken for after May, so we line up another two-bedroom apartment a few blocks away. It is again courtesy of Rollie and Jeanne, who have offered us their house for free, but have ordered construction work on their place—something about a roof that needs replacing. Their close friend Flip Baldwin, a former advertising exec who moonlights as a waiter at Rollie's when he lives in Sayulita, is generous enough to offer us his place just across from the plaza church. It is, again, ideal. It has, again, a telephone. Most of all, it has air conditioning in the bedrooms. There will be enough room for Blair and for us.

On the fourth of May, we break ground on our property. I have considered a ceremony—Rollie has a lay-preacher certificate that lets him marry couples and bless sundry enterprises—but we agree to wait until the house is finished instead. Indeed, there is so much activity, nobody pauses much to mark the day. That morning, we go watch Beto and his crew of about eight men begin their work. The mango tree in the center of the lot, where our living room will be, is taken down, and the lot is cleared. They take care not to touch the small palms around the side of the lot and the tall mango that will shade the back of our house. The lot is already flat, so the bulldozer's work is simple, leveling some mounds of dirt. One of Beto's men pours chalk lines to define the outline of the house, including its interior, and we all step back in the afternoon to admire the handiwork. There it is, in chalk dust, our first house from the ground up.

I mix a bit with the crew, introducing myself and Thia. They are a truly motley crew, wearing a variety of colored T-shirts, short work pants, and a hat shop's worth of assorted headwear, from baseball caps to battered sombreros. They range in age from eighteen (Govany) to about sixty (Pablo, a dignified gentleman wearing a straw boater). They are a little shy at first around the *dueños,* the owners, but when I ask them how they enjoy being part of Beto's team, they are enthusiastic. They are proud to tell me how long they have worked with him—none of the older men has worked less than five years for Beto—and they tell me that they are there because Beto trusts them to do their work well. "Often, he does not even have to supervise us," says Roberto, a tall, thin man wearing an L.A. Dodgers cap. "We know what to do." I look over and see Beto, who is giving soft-spoken directions, but also stoops down to carry away tree limbs with his workers.

Late that afternoon, we are stepping around the chalk periphery with Beto. We complete the circumference and stop, looking up. He seems to know we are imagining what will rise from the white lines; we need to survey our domain in our mind's eye before the digging starts. He stands back and lets the dueños have their moment.

The next day, the bulldozer digs in, and ground is broken. The foundation holes, about five feet deep, appear in what seems like hours. The heavy front gates have been removed from their hinges to allow a dump truck to drive in, and the lot is alive with land crabs scurrying off to the sides, as their holes disappear in the crush of the bulldozer's scoop. There's always a land grab somewhere. The men take a siesta from one to two thirty, when the sun is hottest, but are otherwise productive the entire day.

Several days later, the cement foundations are poured. Bricks for the outer walls are beginning to go up, breathtakingly fast, it seems to me. We confer with Beto nearly every day. He understands that it is our interest in the process, not our need to check up on him, that brings us to the site every day, and he is generous with his explanations. I am not familiar with U.S. construction beyond what I have read or observed casually, but I can tell that things are different here. Once the bulldozer is gone, an old rusted cement mixer appears to be the only motored device on the premises. Everything else is picks and shovels and hammers.

On Saturday, the crew, now about twelve men, works a half day. I have been tipped off by Bruce, veteran of house construction in San Miguel, that Saturdays are an owner's chance to celebrate the week's work with a little ritual. I drive to the nearby grocery store and pick up two dozen beers and some big plastic bottles of soda. I lug them back to the site. At half past noon, the men begin putting away their tools, and we break out the refreshments. I have forgotten to bring disposable cups, but no matter. The men would rather slice older empty plastic bottles in half and use the bottoms as cups. (They will later be reused to hold paint and thinner and grout.) There is a lot of joking about plans for the weekend; they seem to be a bunch of guys who know one another well and get along. Beto then pulls out his notebook—I have just now noticed that it has a Daffy Duck logo—and has each man sign his name, after which he counts out his weekly pay. They earn between ten and fifteen dollars a day, depending on their experience.

By mid-May, many of the gringos have gone. We have a good-bye dinner with Jeanne and Rollie, and promise to email. They will be gone until October 1. We spend a last night in the Niños Héroes apartment and feel a little sentimental. We have come to know Gaby and his family, and are happy that prosperous times are coming to them as well. He has recently tiled his dirt floor and has a load of bricks to build an addition to his house in the rear. We fall asleep listening to Gaby's ranchera music and get up on our last morning to the now-familiar squawking of *"puto, puto, puto"* from the parrot. We begin to pack up. We'll miss this place, including Iggy Mom and Iggy Pop, especially as they have produced a new family member, a gray-green iguana infant we have naturally called Iggy Tot. Gaby's little girl, Fabiola, is on school vacation, and we give her a hug, telling her we will be a few streets over.

With Blair pulling the heavy weight, we move our stuff to Flip's new, smaller apartment and settle in. We string the satellite antenna onto the roof. Most of the town's traffic rumbles by our front door, so it doesn't have quite the neighborhood feel that our first apartment did, but it will be fine until we finish the house. When we go for our plaza walk that night, there are almost no Americans around, there are parking spaces around the square again, and all the faces around are Mexican. It's a nice feeling, knowing what the village must have been like in the old days, oh, five years ago.

On our construction site, the brick walls of the two bedrooms on the ground floor are now up to chest level, and when we walk inside them, we have a good idea of their size for the first time. And that is when the crisis occurs.

Mindful of Maggie's warning that a room always seems smaller until it is fully built, we begin to measure the distance between the walls. We are hopeful that we are just overreacting, but it is soon clear something is wrong. By Thia's calculations, we will not have even enough room to put bedside tables next to the queen-size beds we have planned. We had never wanted big bedrooms; everyone's advice was to create a large living and dining space, because visitors, including renters, did not. come down here to spend a lot of time in their bedrooms. Sure, but when we approved Aurelio's plans, from the earliest versions, we had planned for more than enough space for a normal bedroom set. What has happened?

We go off to talk about it at a nearby lunch shop. We retrace our steps through each new sketch brought to us by Aurelio. And we realize what must have happened. The measurements on the last set of plans were in meters, and though Thia and I have become pretty good at conversion—one meter multiplied by 3.28 feet—we apparently did not realize that the last meter and a half Aurelio had taken off the house was at the expense of the bedrooms. In our constant refrain to Aurelio to "punish" the design to stay within our square-foot budget, he must have diminished the bedrooms, and the new sizes snuck in unnoticed by us. Perhaps Aurelio should have alerted us, but, really, this was our doing. The gradual downsizing was occurring constantly throughout the design of the house, and we just weren't careful enough to recheck at every stage.

We are despondent when we walk back to the plaza. But the foundations are poured, the bedroom bricks are a quarter of the way up. To gain an extra yard and a half, bricks would have to come down, the foundation at this end destroyed, a new ditch dug, and there would have to be new foundation and bricks. What sort of added expense were we letting ourselves in for just a week into major construction? And what kinds of dopes were we?

We are walking forlornly past the plaza, talking about our options, when we meet Chuck and Teke, our friends with the infinity pool on a cliff. They are among the few gringos left.

"You look like your donkey died," says Chuck.

I tell them about shortened bedrooms, and about the time and expense it would take to rectify.

"Look," says Teke. "The easy thing here would be to let it go, to save yourself the extra charges. You want to tell yourself a few feet aren't worth the trouble of going back and getting it right. But a year from now, when you're squeezing past the bed, you'll regret it. And every year after. Change it."

"It's only cement," says Chuck. "Gravel and water."

We go home, talk about it some more, and decide that we are going to have to tell Beto we have to make the change. The next morning we walk to the site, and I tell him diffidently that a mistake was made and that the bedrooms will have to be lengthened by one meter and a half—about five feet. He rubs his chin, looks at the foundations, and shrugs.

"*Bueno,*" he says. "I thought the bedrooms were a little small when I first saw them on Aurelio's plans."

"I'm sorry, Beto, and I know this is going to cause delays and extra costs."

He shoots me a slightly pained grin and says, "We can probably get it done in two, three days. As for costs . . ."

I wait for it.

"As for costs, why don't we just say I will absorb them?" I am surprised and show it. "If something else comes up," he says, "we can discuss it, and I will have to adjust. Is that all right?"

"Of course," I say.

Later, walking home, Thia says, "I *love* this man." And she has not yet begun to call him *San* Beto. That comes a day or two later.

CHAPTER 23

Cars and Metaphors . . . Trucks and Drivers . . . Holidays and Mother's Day

There is a classic book about home building in Baja California in the eighties written by Jack Smith, the popular columnist for the *Los Angeles Times,* now deceased. In *God and Mr. Gomez,* he describes the relationship between an American writer and a highly idiosyncratic Mexican builder who sold him a lot but moved its boundaries each time he visited. In a series of misadventures and loopy architectural innovations, Mr. Gomez ends up placing an orange toilet in the middle of Jack Smith's living room. I have wondered more than once since moving down here if I will have a Mr. Gomez, if our house building will be amusing in the retelling but painful in the living.

Certainly there is still fodder for Mr. Gomez stories, even in these times. One American woman, living alone, has fired eleven contractors and their crews since she began construction on her small house, and cannot fathom why she has failed to find another contractor. A monumentally picky supervisor, she tells of gringo-Mexican warfare on her site where each tale is more excruciating than the next. Over in San Pancho, a friend of Barbara's contracted to have an enormous hot tub built, made of marble with bronze faucets and porcelain fixtures. He was inordinately proud of it and asked Barbara over to look at it. "What do you think of it?" he asked. "I think it doesn't have a drain," said Barb.

We hear another story: a contractor was told to add three light sock-

ets to a room that was mistakenly built without any, and the contractor put in three—in a row. And another: a contractor who badly mis-
aligned some holes in a weight-bearing wall was phlegmatic when it
was brought to his attention. "Only God can do something perfect," he
explained. "It would be an insult to him to do something perfectly, so
we always leave a small imperfection." I recall Tyler telling us of the
Muslims' firm belief that only Allah is perfect, which is why Arabs
always leave a small thread imperfectly undone in their cloth and tapestries. In Mexico, it seems to be less deep religious conviction than deft
religious improvisation.

The safest way to enjoy these stories for what they are, I think, is to
put away the broad brush, to avoid generalizing. My actual experience,
as opposed to the café chatter, is that I have met far more competence
than fecklessness, more honesty than venality, and more thoughtful, cultured civility than small-town provincialism. This small town, as any the
world over, offers a fine parade of humorous characters. But there are no
stereotypes. Real life, now that I have the time to savor it, always offers
a twist.

My car begins stalling on me. On Dick's recommendation, I go to see
Ramiro in his auto mechanic shop in Puerto Vallarta. A heavily built man
who wears dark glasses even in his dark shop, he has my car put up on
the lift and directs his men on how to find the cause of the stalls. When
he finds out I am a writer, he is excited. He belongs to a Vallarta literary
society himself. He is holding a corded safety lamp over the hood to help
his assistants, and in between giving them directions, he addresses me.

"The object of poetry is to find the right metaphor!" he shouts above
the garage noise. He speaks English just a smidgen short of full fluency.
"It comes to my mind that one of the persons I most identify with is
Ernest Hemingway. You have to read his prose to find the poetry! There
is a huge problem in translation today"—(the screech of an automatic
wrench is heard)—"and you have two powerful languages: Castilian on
the one side and English on the other! But what is lacking is the proper
conviction to truly propel an idea from one language to the other!"
(More screeches.)

He pauses, peers into the open hood of my car, and points somewhere. "The belt needs tightening, boys," he says in Spanish. "Start
with that."

Back in English, the din lowered, he resumes his seminar. "A long time ago, I met a man who became my friend, and his name was James Michener. He came to Mexico and said, 'I'm going to make a novel about Mexico.' He said, 'Can you help me to start this novel? Can you help me meet people who I can write about?' I said, 'Eduardo, come here.' Eduardo was a mestizo with gray eyes, and I said, 'This is Mr. Jim, tell him about the Indians with the gray eyes.' Eduardo told Michener all he knew about the Indians, and Michener turned him into a character in his excellent novel about Mexico!"

Now the electric jacks are hammering off a wheel rim. Ramiro is projecting at me as he glances sideways, to make certain his mechanics are performing. "People from the United States are convinced Mexico is a simple country!" he shouts. "They do not realize that Mexico is a *di-cho-to-mee*! On the one side, the Spaniards; on the other, the Indians. On one side, the pyramid; on the other, the church. On one side is red wine, on the other is pulque. Two countries that merged but never bonded. Yet now it is the new Indian writers who give back the language to the Spanish! The di-cho-to-mee of Mexico!"

He turns back to his team. "The alternator," he says in Spanish. "It may be the alternator."

It would be fitting, it would be a better story, if I were to say that he proved himself as good a mechanic as he was a literary commentator. But it didn't unfold that way. Ramiro tells me I should order eight hundred dollars' worth of parts from an American distributor, ship them down here, and he will able to fix it. I get the parts, he installs them, and his bill is over two hundred dollars. But the stalling continues. I make another trip into Vallarta. He spends time with the car, charges me again, and the stalling continues. I call him up again. This time Ramiro loses it. "I have no more time to give this car! I am *im-po-tent*!" he shouts. "I am like that Hemingway character, I declare myself *im-po-tent* to fix this car. I will put up a sign that says I cannot fix your make of car. Sorry. Good-*bye*."

I ask around the village some more. I make an appointment with a mechanic named Manuel Selvas, not from Puerto Vallarta, as Ramiro is. He owns a run-down mechanic's shop hard by one of the poorer villages north of San Pancho. He is soft spoken and appears focused solely on the job at hand. He has placed illustrated romance comics in a rack for his customers to read while they wait for their repairs. He diagnoses the car's trouble in a couple of minutes, does something to fix it, and sends me on my way with nary a literary allusion. His bill is thirty-five dollars.

One morning just a day or two after the Affair of the Shrunken Bedrooms, I am talking to Beto on the site. I say to him, "You know, Beto, when you talked the other day about how small some of our rooms were, I wondered later if you felt that way about other parts of the house." He looks at me without saying anything. I go on. "If you felt there was something we could still do now about spaces that are too small—a corner, or a closet—I would like to hear it before any more walls go up."

Beto goes over to Aurelio's blueprints which he has lying on the lid of our cistern. He takes out a pencil, wets the point with his tongue, and begins to sketch.

Our house, with its two bedrooms forming the courtyard, is designed so that the upper level, narrower than the ground-floor footprint, rises up on a line with the peaks of the bedroom roofs. I look to see what Beto is sketching. He has moved the walls of the upper level out on each side so that they now rise from the outer edges of the house. He has added a full ten feet of horizontal space to each of the second and third floors, perhaps two hundred square feet.

"Thia, come over here!" I call. By the time she arrives and has taken in Beto's penciled lines, I have come to realize what this could mean. The second floor would become a far more spacious rental unit, but on the third floor we could have what we did not dare hope for: a small second bedroom. We had resigned ourselves to not being able to put up our kids or close family when they came to town if we were renting the ground floor. Now, by squeezing the main bedroom a bit, we could have a whole new room, a working office for me that could be converted into a small bedroom, with a sink.

I tell Thia in a low voice what I am thinking, and she is already there.

"Beto," she says, "this would be amazing. But we can't afford it."

Beto does not need a translation. He pauses for a moment, in thought. He says, "Look. I saw the plans. Right away I knew you were punishing your house to keep within the square meters. But I look at it like this: I will already have my muchachos at work. I am buying the materials in bulk. It will not be *much* more expensive to put walls up like this than the way they were designed, straddling the roof peaks. I can do it at cost, which should work out to half of the square-meter price we have been working with."

Something has happened here that goes beyond generosity. In offering us a choice he sensed we wanted but had not articulated, he could have taken credit for the gesture. Having dazzled us with the unexpected prospect, he could have suggested a straight extension of the square-meter cost of his original reasonable estimate and seen if we'd bite. But he volunteered what we could not possibly know: that the actual costs of building something larger were obviously greater but not *that* much greater, than building straight up from the rooftop lines. He could make it happen at half price. That is not just generous, it is fair-minded.

I do the calculations, realize that we can afford it, and tell Beto that we are grateful. I see that Thia is about to lunge forward to kiss his cheek, but she checks herself. Beto projects too much dignity. I say to him that I assume we should now go back and get the blueprints professionally altered. This would mean Aurelio, of course.

"No need," he says airily, rolling up the blueprints. "I have enough here to follow the changes on my own." He points at his head. "I have it right in here."

As we go home, I am bouncing my heels off the cobblestones. We are as happy as kids with an extra dessert. Beto has not just changed a cramped, small apartment into a well-proportioned home, he has given us the gift of a new, small bedroom at half the cost we would have imagined. That is when Thia decides who Beto really is.

"San Beto," she says. "Canonize the man."

On the Cinco de Mayo, which celebrates a Mexican victory against the French invaders (the French overcame their defeat, and went on to take Mexico City and install their Austrian emperor, Maximilian), there is yet another parade. They are always worth watching here in the villages. The rickety nature of so many of the floats always adds a little tension to the enterprise. The little girls riding on the roof of a truck, and the abuelitas, little grandmothers, swaying on plastic chairs in the back, make each and every parade a nail-biter.

Mexico, in the countryside, is a culture of pickup trucks. I have seen pickup trucks used as police vehicles, as sleeping lofts, as school buses, as wedding limos, as rolling sports vans with rows of teenage buttocks aligned over the edges. I have seen mariachis standing—*standing*—in the back playing their instruments as a truck bumps along from one party to another. I have seen a parked truck loaded in back with a huge mound of ice, beers stuck in it to cool, the radio blasting music, as men drink and chat, with their boots on the running board—a bar, fridge, jukebox, and bar stool all at the same time. There are, of course, the trucks of the loudspeaker economy, piled high with fish and gas cylinders and radiators and shrimp and mattresses. And there are the trucks on the highway full of tired, hollow-eyed, dusty workers, packed tight and swaying together like stacked palm leaves. But there are also trucks with whole families stretched out in back, homeward bound, hair whipping in the wind, the kids clapping along to songs they are mouthing. No expensive SUV or station wagon in my home country gets better use or embraces more humanity.

Yet these same pickup trucks, with their myriad cargoes of workers and children, add to Mexico's appalling highway bloodshed. In early May, Thia and I stand aside during one of our walks to the Muertos beach as much of the village gentry walk past in slow procession toward the cemetery. They are burying a promising young man of twenty-two, from one of the leading families. He was thrown from a pickup that hit a *tope* too fast. Not an unusual occurrence, and one unlikely to change, much less be prohibited; it is apparently accepted with the usual fatalism.

Our own close brush comes just a couple of days later, during a slow, backed-up drive to Puerto Vallarta with Blair to drop off Pilar. With the usual maniacs passing us in the oncoming lane, the slowing down and speeding up is intense. At one point, I have to brake sharply when the car ahead of me slows down, and I look into my rearview mirror to see a ramshackle little sedan hurtling toward us from behind. There is a loud *whump!* The three of us are shoved backward into our seats, then forward into our safety belts, and I am able to turn onto the shoulder. I look again and see that the little sedan, its front end crumpled, has also turned off.

I get out of the car, inspect our bumper, and see that it is battered enough that it will have to be replaced, but otherwise there is no further damage. The other car, however, is in bad shape. Blair and I walk over and see that a woman in the front seat is agitated and beginning to cry. The driver, a small, thin man in a soiled work shirt, is out walking around his car, and he is visibly shaken. I ask if he and his wife are all right. He says they are, but he is looking at his car in distress.

Another car pulls over ahead of us on the shoulder, and a dark, confident man in sunglasses walks over. He shows a badge and says he is a plainclothes police officer.

"What happened?" he asks. The other driver begins to say something, but at this point Pilar has joined us, and she interrupts him. I have not yet said anything, but Pilar, in rapid Spanish, says gently but firmly, for the benefit of the police officer, that it was the other driver's fault. The other driver begins to say that he braked as quickly as he could, there was no time. Pilar says, "That may be, but it is the responsibility of the car behind, not the car ahead." She has taken some law courses, I believe, and is anxious that the gringo family of her boyfriend not be victimized.

The officer, who plays the arbitrator without intimidating us, explains that we have three choices. We can exchange insurance information. We can agree between ourselves who will pay what. Or he could take us both to "the municipal offices" until it can be sorted out. At this last, he makes a face indicating that this is not the choice he would make if he were in our situation.

I look at the other driver, who is still shaking badly. I ask him if he has insurance. He says no. I take this in, then ask, "What do you do? What is your work?" He says, "I work in a factory near Mezcales." I look from him to his crumpled car to his distraught wife. I say, "OK. You pay for your damage, I will pay for mine." The officer gives me an approving look, Pilar gives me a quizzical glance, and Blair just nods. We drive away.

Though Beto remains focused on the work around him, we find time to talk. He tells me that he is strongly impatient with paperwork and bureaucracy. He wants only to concentrate on the job and its challenges, to shut out other concerns. He has a refuge at a house owned by his sister where he can sit with the drawings and plan his work. He plays soccer at a Bucerias park. I ask him about his crew, and he says his workers feel the same responsibility for the work that he does. He says that what is important is to set a goal—the deadline, the budget. It's not worth it to him to hire someone passing by, even if he can get him cheaply, because it would mean the reputation he has built over years could come crashing down with one person's irresponsibility.

He has worked mostly for Americans, but he got his early training not from Americans or Mexicans but from Japanese. "They demand that you be exact to the thousandth of an inch," he says. He has had Mexican clients, he says, and though they are more relaxed, they also appreciated his determination to arrive on time and to be exact in all things. I feel I am getting a small insight into Beto, who has combined traits from three cultures—Mexican, American, and Japanese—and blended them into his professional character. Historians have noted the similarities between Japanese and Mexican cultures: the reserve, the courtesy, the rituals, the dignity and face saving. It's enlightening for a gringo to learn that all out-side change down here does not come just from El Norte.

Beto seems familiar with American and Japanese techniques, but his tools are Mexican. No winch, but crossed two-by-fours and a rope lift the buckets to roof level. No modern level, but a string and a weight measure height and evenness. Sometimes the cement mixer seems superfluous; as his men mix the concrete on the ground, then add water from plastic half-bottle bottoms. Heavy sacks are lifted high not by con-veyor, but by being thrown from one worker to another. Why pay for contraptions when so many can be improvised?

The walls are up inside of two weeks. The first-floor roof goes up a week after that. So swift is the progress that friends—both Mexicans and the few gringos—stop to ask if this house on the corner has a special team working on it. I reply that it does. In the third week of May, Beto tells me that it is not too soon for us to begin planning for our doors and windows. I agree and say I want to start with his recommendations.

"Ah, carpenters!" he says. "I don't know if I can tell you any one for sure is dependable. They always promise, but they never deliver on time." Beto is right. Among both Mexicans and gringos, carpenters have a lamentable reputation. But they can be colorful rogues. One story is about a charming, likable San Pancho carpenter named Jaime. For more than six months, he had been postponing a big job he had agreed to do for a gringo home owner. After more weeks of pleading by the home owner, the carpenter announced that if he could use a certain expensive joiner available only in the States, he could jump-start the job and get it done sooner. Although the home owner had already paid for a num-ber of tools, he decided that one further blandishment might do the trick. He brought the joiner down from the States, and the overjoyed carpenter promised to finish the job. The home owner went back to the States and returned a month later. He found the job untouched, with a note left for him: "I am very sorry that I leave this town with all the tools and your joiner. I like you very much, and I hope you like me."

We may be on our own for this. I cannot use Armando of La Peñita; he does not do doors and windows, and it is a highly specialized craft. In this part of the jungle, because of the termites and the sea air, only a couple of types of wood are used, both expensive—parota and prima-vera. The choice in Jalisco and Nayarit is parota, also known as hua-nacaxtle, a beautiful dark wood that stains to a deep, ruddy brown.

We ask around, of both locals and remaining gringos, and we email departed friends. We get some names. I press Beto, and he finally con-cedes that he has worked with a carpenter who is more dependable than most. We bring each man over to the site so he can see, from the ground-floor walls and the apertures Beto's bricklayers have left, the measurements of our doors and windows. We have a price for our wood in mind, and we ask three of them to submit an estimate.

It's said that for every door that opens, a new opportunity walks in. They weren't talking about parota.

CHAPTER 24

A Radical Step . . . A Trip to the Mother Country . . . An Evil Auction

Any prospect of income from our new occupation as rental landlords is still a long way off, so the need to stanch the flow from our 401(k) is becoming more urgent. Fortunately, I get a writing assignment in June—to report on retirees in Panama, as it happens—so we decide to combine my business travel south of the Mexican border with a swing back up to the States. Not to spend money, but to save it. It's not just the house building and stuff buying here in paradise that is depleting us, it's the storage meter ticking back in the States.

Tony Cohan, in his elegiac memoir of life in San Miguel de Allende, *On Mexican Time,* writes about an expatriate ritual most of us down here go through: traveling back home to pay homage to our stuff in storage. Few of us make the decision to decamp the United States by completely striking our tents. Keeping at least some of our household goods in storage is a way of saying to ourselves, "If this fine new idea should not work out, why, we can *always* go back." It is also, in our age group, a sign of deep reluctance to part with our own history. When you first downsize, as we did, you swear you are happy to jettison a lot of the stuff you've accumulated. But throughout the United States, sitting in countless temperature-controlled storage lockers, packed tightly behind corrugated pull-up gates, are remnants of our past lives—what remain after the yard sales and before the letting-go of what is too painful to relinquish.

But we've made our decision. Thia is more reluctant to liquidate our storage than I am and wants to get back to tackle it before I do. That way, she can decide before the arrival of the heartless, marauding Hun—me—what can be salvaged for the kids, what can be stashed in our small Connecticut apartment attic, and what, alas (at long last!) should be auctioned off. So we decide that I will spend two to three weeks in Panama while she flies home to do most of the logistics work on the storage, and then I will fly from Panama City to New York and join her for the last few days of heavy lifting.

We long ago decided that we do not want to be absentee house builders, so the decision to be gone for three weeks is not taken lightly. We are grateful to have Blair here; our tanned surfing god has decided that he will stay at least as long as we are gone and have some real time to himself—and, not incidentally, Pilar. Although Blair's genuine interest in our obsession with floor space and brickwork is approximately the same as his interest in our music ("Dad, Mom, can you just turn *down* that Mel Tormé, please?"), he can at least keep us advised and send along word of any problems.

Beto is not the email type, although Aurelio is. So we arrange for Blair to drop in on the site every couple of days to ask Beto if there is anything we need to know, and we ask Aurelio to go by and take photos of the progress and email them to us. Aurelio likes his new digital camera, and it is a way of weaning ourselves from his care gracefully. He has been over to the site a few times to see the alterations Beto and the owners have come up with, and expressed his opinions on how they might be best achieved. Beto listened to him through narrowed eyes but did not bite back. Today we emphasize to Beto that Aurelio's drop-ins while we are gone will be for photographic reasons only.

We intended to get the estimates for our wood doors and windows well before we left, but we are so careful in our interviews, and so specific about what we want, that the deadline for the estimates begins to crowd our departure date. But all we need to do is choose our man and leave a deposit. If any follow-up is needed, Blair can do it.

We each pack lightly. Although I will be visiting a region as hot and rainy as this part of Mexico, I have read that Panama City is more urbane than Puerto Vallarta. So between that and the few days we plan to spend in New York City catching up with family, I will need city clothes for the first time in eight months. Over in San Pancho, Barb has long informed friends that Bill cannot accompany her back to the States—he no longer owns shoes.

The day our estimates are due is just two days before we are scheduled to leave. We have checked out their work and asked two local carpenters, as well as Beto's man, to submit bids. Our flights are booked, and we have made a megashopping trip for groceries at Gigante in Puerto Vallarta to provide for our surfer kin—lots of organic peanut butter and prewashed spinach. I sit down to make the calls to see what the estimates will be.

I call the two local men first, remain silent for a moment, ask them *both* to repeat their bids, and hang up the phone. I repeat the numbers to Thia, and she asks *me* to repeat their bids. I know I am being theatrical, but I ask Thia to pour me a shot of tequila, and she pours two.

Although we tried to do our homework, and knew that this phase of house construction is among the most expensive of outlays, we have not counted on the steep rise in the price of increasingly rare parota wood in the past few years. Add to that supply and demand of skilled carpentry in this town, and the bids for the doors and windows amount to nearly *20 percent of the total cost* of construction. We had budgeted half that amount. I down my shot and dial the last number, that of Victor Islas, Beto's candidate. This time I do not ask him to repeat the bid, and I hang up with my last hope shredded. It is for a lesser amount, at least, but it is not that much less.

Crisis. Despair. At least two more shots of tequila. We stay up late that night and spend the next day, our last day in town, discussing our remaining choices. A cheaper type of wood is out of the question—the sun and termites would do it in within a year. We could switch to aluminum doors and windows and get more reasonable estimates, but we have our heart set on the colonial-hacienda look of our home. Aluminum doors? The thought of someday sitting in our Spanish-style courtyard discussing the works of Carlos Fuentes as a seaborne gust slams our front door shut with a tinny metallic clatter makes the prospect hard to bear. Still, we walk over to the site after the workmen are gone to see how many aluminum windows we could install in the *back* of the house, to bring down the total cost. Not enough.

The morning of our departure, we bite the parota bullet. Our decision will be a Mexican one. We put our bags in the back of the car, and with Blair driving, we stop by the site. I go up to Beto and ask him if he can get away for a few minutes for a coffee around the corner. I tell him ahead of time, mercifully, that we have a "big change" we have to discuss. He looks up at me with one eyebrow cocked, and with a little shrug, motions me.to lead on.

A block away, Conny, a cheerful, no-nonsense woman, lives with her family in the back of a low concrete house, and cooks for both workers and residents in her plain, plastic-chair, Formica-table front room. A veteran cook in several restaurants here and in Vallarta, her café is our conference room and staging area. This is where we come not just for lunch, but when important discussions require us to spread blueprints on the table. I order a bottle of water for Beto and coffees for us.

Blair waits in the car, and Thia and I sit down with a wary Beto. In as concise Spanish as I can muster, I explain what has happened: the carpentry bids have ambushed us, and our bank account is just not ample enough to roll with it. When I tell Beto what the bids are, he whistles sympathetically. Even he had not realized how sharp the price increases for wood have been. I tell him the alternatives we have considered. Then I tell him what we have decided.

"Beto," I say, "it pains me to tell you, but the only option we feel we have—if we want to keep the character of the house we designed—is to cut off the top floor." Thia and I have gone over the numbers Beto gave us for each stage of the house. The foundations and ground floor were of course the most costly, followed by the second floor, followed by the third floor. By eliminating the top floor, we could pay for the doors and windows, and have a bit more to spare. No more second-floor rental, of course.

Beto takes it in and then shakes his head with a half-amused grimace. I get the feeling he's been here before. Visitors to Mexico are often surprised to see the large number of unfinished houses, both in cities and in the country. Throughout Mexico, a single-floor house with steel rebar rods swaying upright on the roof is a common sight. Without mortgages, Mexicans buy land and build what they can afford on it, putting off further construction until they earn enough to put up a second story. (Rollie says these rooftop rebars have a local name: "hope.") We have just done a very Mexican thing, and Beto knows it.

"I apologize, Beto," I say. "I know you scheduled your work and your team for three floors, and I know this will mean a smaller job for you."

"We do what we have to do," Beto says, "and God provides the rest."

I also tell him that I regret that this has happened on the very day we are leaving, and I ask him if he will need any architectural or engineering readjustments—which we would pay to provide.

"No," he says, tapping his head, "I have it up here."

We leave Conny's, and he accompanies us to our car. I have already called Victor to accept his bid. As we begin to drive away, Beto leans in and says, "You will not come back and ask for a *single*-story house, will you?"

It takes a moment for his grin to break through, and I am relieved.

"*Quién sabe*, Beto. We're getting more Mexican every day."

Panama is as beautiful as I have read, and I cover a lot of ground in twenty days. I meet Panamanians and American residents in sleek Panama City, in the mountainside retreats of Boquete and Volcán, in the laid-back island beach towns of Bocas del Toro. Though there are clear differences with Mexico—Panama is the size of one of Mexico's states, without the depth and range of Mexico's culture, with a currency and a history pegged to that of the United States—its growing corps of American retirees have many of the same pleasures and problems as Mexico's gringos. Panama is offering a package of retirement benefits that would make some of my expatriate pals in Mexico envious, including airline and hotel discounts, and tax abatements. I make some friends, watch the ships slide into their locks at the splendid canal, feed the howler monkeys from a skiff in the rain forest, and have an interview with the American ambassador in her well-fortified embassy in downtown Panama City. I take a plane for New York with a briefcase full of tapes and several pounds of fine plantation-grown coffee.

I spend my first night in New York City at the apartment of John and Laura Kaufman, Thia's sister. We get a lot of whoas! for our fitness and weight loss; Thia has lost a total of forty pounds, and I am a trimmer specimen myself. There is lots of good cheer and boisterous back-slapping, heightened by my joy at finding that Tyler, whose year in Damascus has come to a close, is returning to the States earlier than expected. He has been accepted at Georgetown University in its Arab Studies master's program, and there had been some question as to

whether his return would overlap with our visit home. My joy in seeing him on the day he arrives is adjusted in tone, if not timbre, when
the family ventures out to a restaurant that night. My scholarly son,
about to embark on a life of academia, decides to don a full Bedouin
headdress and robe he has brought back for the occasion. His cousins
think he's a riot.

Thia has been working on our storage, and except for her happiness
at Tyler's return, she is in an ugly mood. In two storage lockers in Connecticut are not only the contents of our two-bedroom New York City
apartment, but sizable relics from the earlier suburban home in which
we spent twenty years. She has called everyone in the family, and there
are no takers for even our more expensive furniture—the older generation is too set, the younger too rootless. A major yard or tag sale is out
of the question—we no longer have a venue for it, nor are we in a position to supervise it, or to dispose of what is unsold.

And the cruelest blow—the auction firm she has contacted says
there is a "glut" on boomer household goods, and the most we could
expect is a bulk purchase, for pennies on the dollar. Not even charities
seem particularly eager to take our stuff. Both the Salvation Army and
Goodwill say they are not taking clothes for the moment, and their
facilities are too full to take furniture. If we were willing to pay to ship
it to somewhere else, they might find a place for it . . . It is hard to avoid
the impression that we are back in a country that is too wealthy, too
willing to discard, too disdainful of anything secondhand. In my new
country, plastic bottles are treasured and reshaped and reused. (We
investigate the costs of shipping our stuff down for distribution to Mexican families there. It is prohibitive.)

So we make the trek up to Connecticut and spend three days sort-
ing though what we want to save: photographs, books, the "family silver" that Thia feels passionate about but I would gladly swap for half a
floor's construction in Sayulita. This is when we also make our final
decision about what we will take with us to Mexico. Our plan is to ship
a certain amount of stuff out to our friends the Prewitts in Laguna
Beach, and drive up from Mexico to collect it later in the summer. We
have our residential visas by now, so we are allowed a one-time permit
to bring an unlimited number of household goods into the country. But
in our jungle climate, most of our shoes and clothes will crumble; our
furniture will rot; our leather will crack; our metal will rust; and our

expensive electronics will clog. So we will not be bringing that much. Stuff that will be useful, but will either last or not be missed if it doesn't. We segregate five or six boxes and prepare to kiss the rest good-bye. It's not so terrible. Friends tell us that, when the time arrives, shopping to furnish a new house in Mexico is one of life's pleasures. We have that to look forward to. (More stuff!)

On the third day, the auction agent arrives at the storage facility, where we have spread out our stuff on what seems to be an acre of tarmac. In under an hour, he has walked through the open boxes, poking through our clothes, glancing at this armoire and that headboard, jotting what appear to be single digits into his notebook. At the end of his little jaunt, he approaches us with an expression I correctly interpret as profound shame for his profession, and for the insult he is about to inflict upon us. He tells us there have been so many downsizings of late that the glut has become a national surplus, and that in some cases he has had to tell clients that they will have to pay *him* to take away their goods. He explains all the expenses he will have in moving the stuff, keeping it in inventory, staffing the auction, and so forth. Then he shows us his notebook so we can see the figure he has arrived at: $1,305.

We are mortified. We had imagined a figure ten times that amount, and we do not feel particularly astute at having made two serious cost miscalculations in a single month. Downsizing your life can cut you down to size. We go off to talk together, and I make brave threats about turning down this agent of Lucifer and loading our stuff onto a truck and carting it to the poorer section of town. Thia reminds me there *is* no poorer section of town in this part of Connecticut, and I quit my huffing and puffing. In fact, the auction funds will pay for the trip we have just made, and these days, every miserable, fraudulent, swindled penny we are offered by a scheming auction house is a penny that will go further in Mexico.

Thia is in tears as we go back to the condo and close it up. We return to New York to spend a couple of final days with friends and family. She is cheered by being around them and by the prospect of going back to building our house in Mexico. The night before we leave, I watch several of the newest reality shows, conclude that the United States has gone insane, and go to bed. When I wake up on our last morning in New York City, I check my shoes for scorpions and go out to the kitchen to toast two bagels.

CHAPTER 25

A Stormy Night . . . A Departure . . . Mr. Blandings

When we step off the plane in Puerto Vallarta, we realize that our friends have not been truthful about the weather in early July—they have understated it. The sun scalds the pavement as Blair and I haul the bags out to our parked car, and it reflects back at us in waves of stifling, breath-catching heat thick with moisture. Blair is acclimatized, of course, and cheerily tells us the sparse village gossip on the drive back into the jungle.

Halfway home, it begins to rain. By the time we turn off to our village, it is a downpour, thick and slanted and relentless. Blair has been telling us that these afternoon storms have an eerie beauty, and gets an idea.

"Let's go up to our hilltop property and watch it from there."

Thia and I figure it is as good a way as any to welcome ourselves home, so we turn down the dirt road, now churning mud, that goes by our construction site toward Heart Attack Hill, the road to nowhere—except to our half-parcel of land. Our wheels begin to spin on the cobblestones, which causes Thia to ask Blair, "Sweetie, is this the *best* idea?" The SUV goes into vertical gear and somehow makes it. We dredge our way onto the promontory that so captivated us when we first came to this village, and Blair turns the car toward the edge.

We sit there together, looking down at the bay, now being lashed by sheets of long silver rain. From inside the dark car, we watch the sky light up every few seconds as the lightning flashes from cloud to cloud, and minutes later, we hear the deep bass rumble of thunder that explodes in overlapping claps. It is a magnificent thing to watch the heavens strobe and crackle over the illuminated sea. We three are alone and silent, observing our sound-and-light show, feeling the fierce authority of nature on this jungle coastline. At the same time, I feel faintly ridiculous: we have purposely perched ourselves on the edge of a slippery, muddy cliff in the midst of a tropical storm none of us has experienced before. But it is exhilarating, and we leave only when the lightning ebbs, and the mountainside becomes so dark that I become concerned. I switch places with Blair and take the wheel, soaking myself, and inch the car down the cobblestones as a river pours down the road surface in a rush. One slip, and the car will hydroplane straight down into the rock-strewn cow pasture at the bottom of the hill.

We make it.

The electricity is off in the village, an occurrence more frequent than usual during the summer. We get our travel bags back into the house, and Blair heats up tortillas on the gas stove and stir-fries some odd, healthy vegetables I am too hot and wet to recognize. The rain soon stops. We walk out onto the terrace holding candles; it feels fresh and crisp and—it *still* feels hot. We break out the Scrabble board and the three of us play a cutthroat game by candlelight, sweat running down our bare backs, sipping rum drinks. We have traveled across and down a continent since leaving New York this morning, but it feels much, much farther away than that.

The electricity comes back on sometime after we have gone to bed, just as it always, somehow does.

In the morning, before the sun has had a chance to bake away the night's rain, we slog our way through the muddy roads to our site. We have seen Aurelio's photos, so we expect no big surprises, and we get none. The heavy gate is open, meaning the men have arrived, and Beto's white pickup truck is parked on the side of the road. Thia walks up the driveway and does what she has been doing since the work began: She calls out, "Hola, casa!" and there is a staccato chorus of "Hola, señora" from various parts of the site.

The men have become fond of Thia, especially when she is wearing her less-than-Prada fashion statement: an oversized tool belt and a tiny umbrella wedged onto her head she got as a going-away present from my youngest brother, Geoff, and his wife, Laurie. Alejandro, who has a beard and a hat resembling van Gogh's (with a missing tooth rather than ear), comes up shyly and presents her with a ripe mango from our tree. Thia is delighted, as usual, and says, *"Para mi prima colazione!"* which is mostly Italian for "For my breakfast!" The guys have picked up a little Italian since they began this job and understand Thia just fine.

The ceiling above the ground floor has gone up since we left, and work is proceeding at its dizzying pace on the second floor, where walls have been raised. Behind the house, a broad stairway leads up, its columns framing the back entrance. Beto is on the second floor, orchestrating. He greets us—with a smile, but not effusively, not Beto—and we catch up. I have brought with me a picture book I bought at Barnes & Noble—a collection of aerial photographs of Machu Picchu. He expresses thanks and says he will look at it at home. Getting back to business: no problems to report, but he has a list of decisions (and purchases) he expects us to make in the coming weeks—the tile for the bathrooms, the floor tile, the height of the shelves. We hop to it. It's good to be back at work, keeping up with Beto.

On the Fourth of July, we make the trek over to see Bill and Barb. John and Judi have gone back to the States, and for this one day there are no guests staying at their Casa Obelisco bed-and-breakfast; it is now ranked the number one B-and-B in Mexico by an online travel site. They are having some friends over, and Bill is in an impish mood. He has bought some monster fireworks up the coast and paid for a couple of guys to come over and set them off. It may seem impudent to celebrate the Fourth of July with a spectacular public display, but Mexicans love fireworks for any reason.

On the roof, Barb has drinks and hot dogs served by Evy, their popular and well-tipped bartender, and then we repair to the beach across the street. There, the fireworks boys insert cardboard tubes into the sand and set fire to the fuses with their little lighters, scampering out of the way just in time for the skyrockets to shoot up and explode above thunderously. Amid the gaiety and fire bursts, it is hard not to think about our country at war in the Middle East, a few hundred miles away from where my younger son has been studying, a war no Mexican I have ever talked to can comprehend.

Thia's birthday passed while we were traveling, so it is agreed that we will celebrate it—along with Mother's Day—belatedly with a dinner in town. Blair brings along Pilar, and over dessert (yes, flan) the talk turns to women's issues. I ask her if she thinks women face obstacles pursuing their professions in Mexico.

"You mean at home, balancing family and career?" she asked, laughing. "Yes, I'd say so. Don't they in the United States?"

"What about becoming educated *for* a career?" I ask.

"No, women are beginning to outpace men in the colleges, and at grad schools. The problem isn't gender, but cost. Here, the free universities are the select ones, unlike the States. There is much competition to get in, and many do not. They cannot afford the private universities, where, if you *can* afford it, anyone can get in."

Pilar is leaving in a couple of days for Spain, to finish her business studies and get some work experience, and the air is bittersweet between them. We have become fond of her and know better than to ask about anything beyond the present. We are melancholy ourselves, not only because she is leaving but because within a short time we expect to break up our three-amigo family as well. Blair has been following leads in a new journalistic direction, and will be returning soon to the States for some interviews and serious job hunting.

The next morning, Blair and Pilar knock on our door at six-thirty in the morning. They stand in the doorway and, as Thia rubs her eyes, sing "*Las Mañanitas*," Mexico's traditional birthday song. This is an accomplishment for Blair, who has always been urged by his brother to stick to percussion during family sing-alongs. He has prepared a breakfast of chilaquiles, which he brings in on a tray. They present Thia with a card. On it, Blair has written, "Mom, this whole Mexican interlude has felt like a stolen moment in time for me. And though at times I pretend to chafe, I've relished my return to the fold, because it allows me to play again the role of son to a great *mamacita*. Happy Mother's Day." Pilar has inscribed it as well, in Spanish, telling Thia she admires her sense of joy and the way her family loves and respects her. Thia, of course, weeps like Moctezuma.

After Pilar leaves, Blair and I spend his remaining afternoons taking father-son walks to Muertos beach, chatting about his plans for the future. (Thia gets him in the evening, when, despite the cooking handicap she shares with me, she whips up natural-food dinners in a frenzy.) It strikes me during those walks that however much Blair relished his return to the fold, it is nothing compared to the rare parental privilege of having one's grown son as an everyday friend and companion. It's been very Mexican, having most of my family around me this way, full-time. It would not have happened back home in the States, not in the same way. Here in Mexico, we were at a time in our lives when we were not hastening daily to a job or running out every night to divert ourselves. He was not, for a while, swept along by the driving ambitions of a young American man on the rise. He was here to pick up Spanish and think about his young self; we were here to build a new life and consider our older selves. Nothing more. That has left plenty of time for us to live simply, and exceptionally, in each other's undemanding grace.

A week later, Blair is gone.

Another underestimated prediction is the summer invasion of land crabs. We have been told that in the rainy season, millions of crabs in the area seek higher ground and emerge skittering from the little bubble-holes you see everywhere. These are not just the cute little critters that scuttle along beaches, but hand-sized macho crabs that teem along roadways in such profusion that you can hear them crunching beneath your tires as you drive. They invade patios and gardens, and, most notably, have a fondness for crawling beneath door jambs and through drain pipes into your home.

The first time I encounter a couple of crabs in the living room, I hear them before I see them, making little scraping noises on the tile. It is fairly creepy. They try to get out of your way, but when you approach them with a broom, they raise their claws and clack them threateningly at you. I am not fond of crustacean visitors and let Blair take care of them while he was still here. Since his departure, I have found myself busy with various important affairs of state and have urged Thia to achieve fluency in crab eviction. But often I have no recourse and must take up arms myself. The preferred method of disposal is to corner them, sweep them into a long-handled dustpan, hold the wiggling bastards down, and toss them out into the street.

Dick Dobbeck disagrees. He says throwing them out will only encourage them. He chases them down on his marble floor and stomps on them in his sandals, making a nasty crunching sound, leaving a yellow gooey bisque on his white marble floor. He follows up by sending his two white Bichons Frisés to scout in their driveway, and he can often be seen out front in the evenings, his diminutive dogs yelping as he does a hat dance in his sandals while crabs splatter beneath him. This makes Dick the wearer of the least appealing footwear in the state of Nayarit.

I guess you get used to anything, and by mid-July, when I hear scuttling across our floor tile, I sigh and head for the broom. One night, I wake up at two in the morning, pulling at something in my hair, and jump out of bed with a shriek. A crab has somehow crawled up the cement bed platform (which are thought to deter scorpions and, yes, crabs) and sought a perch on my scalp. This night, I do the Dick stomp myself with a frying pan and go back to bed and have a nightmare about the Alien, from which my wife, looking like Sigourney Weaver, saves me.

I am proud of Thia for improvising a solution for the rest of the summer. She is at a department store in Vallarta and sees a clerk wielding one of those long-handled tongs used to reach items on high shelves. She offers the clerk a price for it on the spot and brings it home. The crabs may continue to wave their stubby claws all they want, but from now on I am *onto* them, clicking my own mechanical claws open and shut, chasing them into tactical retreat.

But between the rains, the heat, the humidity, and the diabolical crabs, it is clear that living in paradise year-round is not—as Bette Davis sort of said about getting old—for sissy gringos.

We see Barb and Bill a lot, including occasional evenings of television watching together. (We continue to resist buying a TV set ourselves, but during the spring, our guilty pleasure was hooting and hollering over *American Idol,* which we avoided admitting to our artier friends.) Other evenings we spend with Cheryl and Dick, watching difficult foreign videos that we dissect over ice cream and *cajeta,* the caramel-like all-purpose sweet sauce.

Like Bill and Barb, and Rollie and Jeanne, Dick and Cheryl are active in charitable activities, though Dick hides it beneath a cynical exterior, waiting for a gringo to tell a story of frustration and pronouncing, "There! You've been Mexecuted!" Dick, while immensely fond of his adopted country, believes that scamming is part of the Mexican culture, developed through centuries of playing the artful dodger to predatory governments and rapacious overlords. Barb would agree: There's no shame for many Mexicans in trying something, she says, just in getting caught. My argument, acknowledging that I've been here a shorter time, is that it's all anecdotal, and that nasty anecdotes travel the farthest, which in turn leads to stereotypes. Witness Eagle George's little gibe about why God made cows and gringos—to milk 'em. But he at least is quick to say that the vast majority of the Mexicans he has spent thirty years with are extraordinarily honest, more honest than some of the gringo "snakes" he has known.

I'm with the Eagle. I don't see Mexico through rose-colored sunglasses, but for every disappointment, I see something that astonishes me. One afternoon, Thia finds some peso bills missing from her purse. On investigation, it turns out that the daughter of a part-time maid she hired is the culprit. We know this could happen anywhere, especially where the prosperous live side by side with the poor. But it's still an unhappy incident.

The next day, Thia has to drive to Wal-Mart in Puerto Vallarta on a shopping trip. As she is parking, a young boy comes up to her and offers to wash the Sayulita grime off our car. She knows she may not see him when she comes out, so she says yes and gives him twenty pesos. When she comes back with the grocery cart, the car is unwashed. She looks around and cannot find the kid. She shrugs, writes off the twenty pesos as yet another unfortunate incident, and loads the car. As she prepares to drive away, an old lady is running—or rather, limping—toward the car. She raps on the car window.

"Señora," she says, out of breath. "I am Paco's abuelita, his grandmother. His father needed him, and he had to leave without washing your car. He asked me to be sure you got your twenty pesos."

When she tells me about it, I am reminded of the Pemex pump jockey on our drive down who tried to palm a note, followed minutes later by the old gentleman who drove his truck so far out of his way to help us. *No easy generalizations*. When we tell Dick about it, he acknowl-

edges the many kindnesses he has received as well. But he does not pull
back. "Someday, by the law of averages, you too will be Mexecuted."

These parallel attitudes—loving Mexico's people but being cynical
about their perceived historical tendency to play the angles—is not
uncommon among gringos here. Yet, Dick and Cheryl are among Sayulita's softest touches, lending and donating and volunteering. Dick tells
of the time he was at a meeting of Puerto Vallarta's International Friendship Committee. He "remained standing when everyone else sat down,"
and became one of the charity's leaders.

At the time, a few years ago, the committee began donating supplies to about eighty dirt-poor families who lived at the city dump. The
adults and children made a living selling scraps and slept under corrugated roofs without electricity or sanitation. Dick and the committee
decided to buy toilets for them. They paid for and installed the toilets.
A month later, they were invited to a ceremony at the dump organized
by a social worker. Dick and the other committee members were asked
to stand as a delegation of children from the families presented each
of the Americans with a Coke and a cookie. Then a leader of the families led them to one of the toilets, where two children held one end
of a ribbon across the door, which was then cut by the leader, to much
applause.

Dick mentions his gardener, Valentín, and the difficulty he feels
some Mexicans have in adopting newer ways. For their luxuriant garden, Dick bought the latest sprinklers and timers and urged Valentín to
use them to make his job easier. Valentín said thank you, and the sprinklers remained in the tool shed, unused. So Dick bought spray nozzles,
hoping that at least those would be welcome. Valentín smiled and
thanked him. Dick looked out the next day, and Valentín had unscrewed
the spray nozzles and was using his thumb on the hose to water the
plants.

Again, I disagree with the extrapolation. I have seen too many Mexican youngsters bent over computers at Internet cafés to think there's
any kind of national reluctance to adapt. Beto may do without modern
cement mixers, but he has researched a demolition hammer he wants—
looking over the shoulder of a friend at his computer screen.

Dick says also that Valentín and other part-time male employees
find it hard taking orders from Cheryl or any other woman; their sense
of dignity is affronted. That surprises us, because not only has Cheryl

supervised the building of a casita on her property, but she, and the women we are friends with, are respectful when they give direction. And, again, that has not been our experience. Perhaps it is just Beto's crew, but Thia has encountered no attitude whatsoever.

As I've observed, our workers seem to dote on Thia. They know that when she is looking around frantically, it is because as usual she cannot find her tape measure in her oversized bag, and one of the men comes over to offer her his. One afternoon we are walking away from the site, and find ourselves several hundred yards down the road. There is a shout, and Govany begins running in the heat toward us to catch up: Thia has forgotten her notebook. Often, we go to Conny's around the corner for lunch, but in the stifling heat, Thia just plops down next to the men cooking tortillas on the ground upon a round metal slat. She joins them with a beer and a banana, the only thing she was able to find at a small grocery store, and it becomes her lunch of choice.

She can get fixated on certain incorrect Spanish words. I have gently corrected her verbal confusion of the word *entrepaños*, shelves, with *empanadas*, the tortilla sandwich. Yet even when I come upon Thia telling Beto yet again that the house closets should have thin, rounded-off tortilla foldovers, I am impressed that Beto knows just what she means and does not comment on it.

In *Mr. Blandings Builds His Dream House*, the Cary Grant–Myrna Loy classic later remade as *The Money Pit*, there is a scene where the Myrna Loy character is explaining the color she wants on her walls. She says earnestly about one, "I want it to be a *soft* green, not as blue-green as a robin's egg, say, but not as yellow green as daffodil . . ." She takes Mr. Delford, the contractor, through the other rooms, describing subtle shadings of colors for each wall, as he nods vigorously at each description. She finishes with a request that a wallpaper be matched with "an apple red, somewhere between a healthy winesap and an unripened Jonathan." When she is called away, Mr. Delford turns to the painter and asks, "You got that, Charlie?" Charlie nods and says, "Red, green, blue, yellow, white." "Correct," says Mr. Delford.

Thia has definite ideas about the colors she wants in the house, and after one coloration discussion with her, my eyes glaze over. I expect that any day now, she is going to have her own Blandings moment with Chava, our chief tile and paint man. These are, after all, more basic and earthy guys than even Mr. Delford.

That moment arrives. One morning I see Thia describing to Chava the color she wants to match a tile with, in her mixture of English, Spanish, and Italian, saying something like, "If we can *buscar* an *azulejo que es* lighter than a *rioja,* but *más fuerte* than a *rosa* . . ." I wait for Chava to give her a tolerant expression, to nod patiently as he makes a mental note to find a plain red tile. But his answer confounds yet again any easy judgment: he pushes back his painter's hat and nods. "I think I know," Chava says in Spanish, "you want something that is not red like a cherry, but crimson like a *vino tinto* . . ." So much for Mr. Delford, and so much for Cary Grant.

Victor Islas, our door and window maker, comes from a family of carpenters in La Peñita; his four brothers and two sons work together. He belies the roguish reputation of carpenters in the region. Victor is wearing long pants and a T-shirt, has a neat mustache, and a somewhat melancholy smile. He has come over to the site to take measurements and nail down the details of his estimate. He explains that he personally has to choose the parota, after which they are cut down and then dried. For this reason, he will need half his money ahead of time.

The stories about carpenters are so rife that I decide I want a little assurance—a written contract. I have our local attorney, José Luis Barrios, draw up an agreement on the wood products we have ordered and the date on which they are to be delivered. Naturally, I haven't a prayer of trying to enforce it—how could I?—but I figure it will put a little incentive into the transaction. He is Beto's colleague, and that says a lot, but Beto himself has been skeptical of carpenters as a breed.

I accompany Victor on his measuring rounds, and as we walk down the now-cemented stairs, I ask him about something I've heard about parota wood—that it can be toxic, not healthy to work with. Thia and I have even asked ourselves if we should contribute to a worker's potential health hazard. The answer seems to be that there is no other wood that can be used in this climate, and that the solution is face masks.

"Yes," Victor says, "parota is toxic if the sawdust is breathed in volume and no face mask is used."

"So you must use a face mask," I say.

"No, it makes it too hot and clammy to work."

"Well, isn't that asking for trouble?"

Victor gives wry shrug. "I already have half a lung full of the stuff. Why should I care?"

I'm not taking this in the fateful Mexican way. "But Victor, if it ends up making you sick or you die . . . Look, we would be happy to pay for as many face masks as you would like if you would consider wearing them."

He gives me the same wry look. "By the time I'm fifty," he says, "if I'm dead, one of my boys can take over."

We spend much of the summer telling ourselves that we are staying on top of things at the site, because, as Dick says, "you have to watch your people." Between the language barrier and the culture gap, things will happen that you don't expect. And indeed, one row of tiles above the kitchen has had to be chipped away and replaced because Chava misunderstood what Thia asked for. But in a larger sense, it is Beto who is staying on top of things, and we are dancing to his tune. He is so well organized, and work flies by at such a pace, that we constantly have trouble keeping up with him. We gringos are invariably late; he is always early. He has advised us, for instance, that we must be ready to choose, and order, our floor tile. We have been taking our time, visiting tile places locally and in Puerto Vallarta. This is the fun part, and we are enjoying it.

But one morning in late July, Beto approaches us.

"We will need to have the floor tile. The men are ready."

"Ah," I say. "We're very close to a decision."

We have not, in fact, come close to deciding.

"I do not want to fall behind," Beto says. "When, exactly, can I expect the floor-tile decision?"

I look at Thia, who has a pained expression. She does not like being rushed on something as important as floor tile. I feel a stab of anxiety myself. I do not like to look indecisive to Beto. I know it will be several days, at least, before we can get to the stores we haven't yet visited. But I have to say something; I do not want to disappoint him. Before I know what I am going to say, it flies out of my mouth.

"*Mañana,*" I say.

CHAPTER 26

Benny and Hilda . . .
My Grandfather . . . Que Viva Villa!

At Choco Banana, the breakfast café by the plaza, we meet the third in the line of Mexican professionals who will decisively influence our lives. They are a husband and wife team named Benny and Hilda. We had begun to talk to people about landscaping. The wall around our lot offers a comfortable sense of privacy and makes it perfect for one of those lush enclosed gardens we see in so many Mexican picture books. Though our bank account is getting lower, we have saved a sum for landscaping, and Thia especially wants to find someone with an original design flair.

At the same time, as the structure has gone up, we have begun to wish that someone with a fresh eye could help us put the finishing architectural touches on the house. Though Aurelio gave us excellent floor plans, he never really offered us elevation plans, something that showed what a house should actually *look* like. There was a computer-generated elevation sketch that showed the correct proportions of the house, but never anything with the detail we had hoped for. Since Aurelio is also a builder, it's likely that he was designing as if he might build it, leaving out specificity in favor of the on-the-spot improvisation so many builders here prefer. But now that we are seeing it in brick and mortar, it is looking a little plain and boxy.

Benedicto Aristides Flores Flores and Hilda Servan run a landscape design firm and nursery on the outskirts of Puerto Vallarta. Our gurus,

Bruce and Maggie, hired them after weeks of dedicated ferreting They interviewed landscape people up and down the coast, and decided on Benny and Hilda. We have interviewed several ourselves, and there is no dearth of talented landscapers, but once again we will be the beneficiaries of our friends' dogged legwork. Most of all, we like what the couple did with Bruce and Maggie's garden.

I call and ask Benny and Hilda if they can come to Sayulita to meet us. They say they will be in the area this morning but are rushed, and can spare less than an hour. They ask for the address of our building site, so they can look at the property on their way in, and they suggest we meet for breakfast at Choco Banana. Thia and I walk over. Sitting at one of the small, round tables is a slim blond woman and a large, somewhat rounded man wearing a safari hat and holding an oversized plastic mug of coffee he has asked the waiter to fill for him. In the months to come, I will never see Benny without his mug—or a distinctive sun hat from his vast collection.

We introduce ourselves, and Thia tells them what we hope for in a garden. I hang back; this is more Thia's realm than mine. They nod and tell her that they have some ideas they will run past us. Hilda speaks fluent English—they have spent a lot of time in the States—and Benny is one of those people who says he cannot speak English but understands everything Hilda and we say in English.

"By the way," he says, taking a swig from his mug, "I designed a house for your lot that was never built." He waits for Hilda to translate, but I am already raising my eyebrows. I express astonishment at the coincidence, and Benny explains that he is a licensed architect and has designed and built many houses in the area. Several years ago, he was hired by one of the previous owners of our lot to design a modern Mediterranean-style house on the property. It was nothing like what we want, but it means Benny is very familiar with the lay of our land, as well as its general measurements. Kismet again.

They are a well-educated, well-traveled couple, with children who attend the American School in Puerto Vallarta, one of whom is at home studying for his SATs. Benny decided that by teaming up with his wife and offering a total house-and-garden package, they could do better in business, and their reputation is indeed excellent. As they talk about their ideas for the garden, I begin to sense they are vibrating on our wavelength. I like everything I hear.

I have brought the plans with me, including the computer-generated elevation sketch. Though we are straying from the garden topic, I begin telling Benny that we wish we had something more stylish going on with our house's facade; at this point, I say, Beto and we are improvising some of the design details that remain unspecified, and are not always sure of ourselves. There is a wistfulness in my voice that Benny responds to. He reaches into his carrying case, pulls out a sketch pad, and there, in Choco Banana, begins redrawing the front of our house.

In fifteen minutes, with swift strokes of his black pen, he creates a detailed sketch that turns our boxy exterior into a wonder of pediments and columns and wrought iron, all cascading with flowers and vines. And then, an inspired touch: two arches, done in old-aqueduct style, that frame the entrance from the driveway, and cross the corner of our garden, ending in a jagged half arch with water from the top spilling into the pool.

I stare at it. I look at Thia. She nods happily.

"You're hired," I say. "When can you start?"

We discuss terms, and agree that Benny will do scale plans of the exterior and the outside structures, and he and Hilda will help us plan our garden, providing us with architectural and landscaping advice, as well as the plants themselves—all for one price. As Hilda and Benny walk back to their truck, the plastic cup gripped firmly in Benny's fist, I realize that we will have a fresh, unusual new look for both our house exterior and our garden. All of twenty-five minutes have passed.

Whoever said things move slowly in Mexico hasn't been to Choco Banana, in Sayulita, in August.

It is a Saturday, and the workers should be knocking off work at one. I have brought the soda and beer, but three or four of the guys are engrossed in getting the columns raised and set for the second-floor terrace. Beto does not give overtime, so it is their decision to stay with it. I am touched, and cannot help it—my comparison reflex kicks in. Workers in the States work hard, too, with far better tools, but working beyond the quitting hour, for the pleasure of finishing a job, without overtime? Haven't seen it much.

I go upstairs to watch them set the columns. I see Roberto and Ramiro holding iron rebar in place at both corners of the terrace. Pablo brings over two thick cardboard tubes and inserts them over the metal rods. Manuel drags over a steel drum and stands on it. They pulley up a bucket of wet cement, and he pours it into the tube, which is held in place by Roberto. Then he does the same on the other end, giving the cardboard tube a whack on the side to make sure the cement is packed. Both columns are now swaying back and forth. I wonder what technique they will use to make certain the cement columns dry upright, and at the proper angle to the roof above. Pablo looks around for a couple of thin brick fragments and pieces of wood and jams them into the bottom, to wedge the tubes upright, very much like slipping a matchbox cover beneath a rickety restaurant table.

When it looks as if the wedged fragments might not hold, Pablo takes out a couple of long nails and hammers them through the brick fragments *into* the concrete terrace. He sits back to look at his handiwork. He looks around and sees a couple of cement building blocks. He has them brought over, and piles them onto the brick and wood, securing the columns more firmly. Finally, Chava is called over with his string and plumb. He hangs it from the top and says to the other guys, "A little forward . . . a bit more here." When he is satisfied, Pablo calls for several tall wooden beams and leans them at an angle against the cardboard columns so they will harden in the correct upright position. The procedure is repeated with the other, and the guys finally knock off.

Downstairs, in the shade of our new living room, beers have been opened, bottle cap against bottle cap. There is less alcohol drinking on his team, Beto says, than most. His men will have beer, but most prefer the soft drinks, and like to get home to their families. They spend a half hour drinking and joking—the Spanish they use for my sake has, on their own time, speeded up to an unintelligible tumult of which I pick up mainly *cabrón* and *chingadera,* the oaths that lace so much male conversation.

"Pay time," Beto announces, and they come over to sign Beto's notebook, the one with Daffy Duck on its cover, after which he hands each man his cash. They all take off, and I remain behind. I look about me and notice the ceiling under the shed roofs Beto has installed. On the flat exposed bricks he used, beneath the tiles, there are one or two paw prints—a small dog in one case, a cat in another. When I first saw them, I assumed they fell into the category of the charm of handmade imperfection. I mentioned it to Hilda, but she said no, that these are mass-produced. Once some years ago, while a factory was drying sheets of these bricks, a dog got loose and left his paw prints on the wet material. The bricks were sold and showed up on a gringo's house. The manufacturer heard about it and offered to replace the bricks. It turned out that the home owner, and other gringo friends, found the prints charming— and a good luck sign—so the manufacturer decided to make *all* its bricks that way, giving a few select dogs and cats final print privileges. Many new homes in Mexico have these prints somewhere on the flat bricks.

I close the outside gate and look back at the two columns now standing upright above the roofs, on the second-floor terrace, propped up by boards. It is windy, but they do not sway. They seem as sturdy as the Parthenon.

It is now early August, and time for our drive back to the States to pick up the house stuff we have shipped to California from Connecticut. We will also go shopping for what Thla says she prefers to get in the States—mostly sheets and towels, but some lamps and fixtures. The day is past when, as was the case two or three years ago, Americans would buy everything from hinges to faucets in the States and bring them down here. Now, since NAFTA, there is little for the household that cannot be bought here, though not always of the same quality and variety. The trip back will be our one-time household-goods importation, but it won't be a big haul: the boxes from Connecticut, what we buy—just what will fit into our SUV with the seats down.

Before we go, I have asked Beto if there is anything he would like from the States that he cannot get here. He gets animated and talks about a powerful Bosch electric demolition hammer—he and his men spend half their life drilling into concrete. I look up its price at Home Depot in the States, and it is expensive: over eight hundred dollars. I tell Beto that, and he shrugs and says, "I have to buy one; we need it badly." I decide to help subsidize the purchase, splitting the cost with him. When I tell him that, he blushes and thanks me.

Our two-day drive up to Arizona passes without incident, and on the afternoon of the third day, we arrive at Paul and Cindy Prewitt's house in Laguna Beach. There is no real time for an extended visit; they know we are on a cargo run and generously tolerate the boxes we have stacked in their garage. We are here to pick up our stuff, dip into Orange

County's cornucopia of malls, and then head back. I am also here to go to San Diego's Mexican consulate, where, as a Mexican resident, I will get authorization to import our household goods. I spend long, tedious hours listing the contents of each box, taking down the serial numbers of the electronic equipment we had delivered from Connecticut, making sure our newer purchases look used. (Like a tourist visa, the idea is that you can import your own used stuff, not what you've just bought.) To my chagrin, I find myself rubbing dirt on a new printer-scanner that I bought to replace the one that got fried in one of Sayulita's merry brownouts.

When we take off again for the Mexican border, we go through our now-normal paranoia about customs. The stories come back to me about people being red lighted and pulled over, one-time permit notwithstanding, and being charged high duties at the whim of an inspector. Tensing up as we approach the crossing in Nogales, I cross over, follow the sign that says Foreing Cars [sic] and await inspection. I am reading over my two sheets of closely-typed lists of articles, looking to see if I spelled everything correctly in Spanish. A customs officer approaches, looks us over, asks for the list, and without looking at it, waves us on.

I cannot help it. I feel cheated. I am a writer, and I wrote that list. He could at least have *skimmed* it.

On our way back, we realize that since taking off, we have been in more of a hurry than we need to be. And now we are in northern Mexico, with no obligations waiting for us—aside from being back for the house. For some time, we have been considering when we might make a certain road trip, and this seems like the opportunity. We decide that we can take a couple of days off, even with our fully packed vehicle. We detour east, past the Sierra Madre that divides Sonora from Chihuahua. Once in Chihuahua, we point ourselves in the direction of Parral de Hidalgo, an old mining town that means something to my family. This is Pancho Villa country. This is grandfather country.

My grandfather, Bernard Golson, was a Frenchman who left Paris in the early 1900s to seek adventure and fortune in the mining boomtowns of northern Mexico. Half a century later, settled in California, he was the man I was taught to call *Grandpère*; I could only manage "Gopere," and it stuck. Earlier, Gopere had brought his teenage bride with him to Mexico and took a job clerking for, and eventually managing, a gold, silver, and lead mine near Parral.

He met Francisco Villa, better known as Pancho, around 1910. Pancho was then committing mostly minor acts of pillage. But he was developing a keen interest in the rich mines that were mostly owned by Americans, Europeans, and cronies of Mexico's longtime dictator, Porfirio Díaz. From time to time, Villa would drop by the mine at which Gopere worked, and the two apparently hit it off. Villa, barely literate, was interested in all things French, since over the years the French had thoughtfully sent Mexico troops, culture, and a short-lived emperor. Gopere obliged with ripping good yarns about bloody revolutionaries like Robespierre and Danton; Villa loved hearing the stories, the bloodier the better.

The Mexican Revolution of 1910 dragged on for five years, and when Villa and his compatriot in southern Mexico, Emiliano Zapata, led their peasant revolts, the countryside was plundered, and wealthy landowners and some mine operators were picked off and killed; many foreigners fled north to Texas to sit out the unpleasantness. Gopere stayed. One afternoon at the mine, a ragtag platoon of Villa's soldiers galloped up. At its head was not Villa, but a newly self-minted colonel my grandfather knew well—he was a paymaster Gopere had fired a few weeks previously for stealing more than nuggets.

Military justice, as meted out by Villa's men, was not long on due process. The paymaster colonel immediately had my grandfather put up against a wall to face a firing squad. Gopere, his back against the wall, reminded the colonel of the old Mexican custom that a condemned man has the right to say a few words before being executed. He chose as his topic the French Revolution, which he compared at great length to the present glorious Mexican Revolution. As he later told it, the soldiers were sufficiently interested to put down their rifles for a bit to listen. He managed to keep his lecture going long enough that Villa himself arrived, galloping onto the scene, where he cussed out his colonel, and set his friend the Frenchman free.

But with the revolution intensifying, Gopere realized he had to leave, and got a safe-conduct pass from Villa to go through the lines to the U.S. border. Not finding a car or a horse, he hitched six donkeys to a stagecoach, put my grandmother and her infant son—my Uncle Charles—on board and wound their way for three days through the fighting and the mountain trails north to the U.S. My grandmother was pregnant at the time with my father, who was born in Long Beach, California.

Gopere's relationship with Villa endured through the years, and he was called on by the U.S. government to take messages to Villa and to translate for him. Twice he was asked to intercede after arrogant gringo negotiators had affronted Villa. As I understand it, my grandfather's intercession, always respectful of Mexican sensibilities, repaired the damage. It always pleased me to think that Gopere made his mark in Mexico not just as one of the foreigners profiting from Mexico's mineral wealth—which he did—but as one who also prospered because he learned about, and respected, Mexico's people. He loved the country, and in later years had his two sons—Charles, and my father, George—come down from the States on college vacations to get their hands dirty working down in the mines with his Mexican crew.

As Thia and I arrive at Parral, we see a thriving, robust, somewhat shabby city spread out among hills that once contained some of the richest, longest-exploited ore deposits in North America. But its true claim to fame is its association with Villa. At various times, he lived there, occupied it, ransacked it, and gave it schools and orphanages. He once said he'd like to die in Parral, and he got his wish. In July 1923, as he was driving his Dodge roadster into town with several men, armed assailants burst out of a building and shot up the Dodge and its occupants, pumping Villa with more than fifty bullets. Who did it and why were never made absolutely clear, but it made an impression on Parral. On its official brochure, adorned with Villa photographs, is its city motto, whose ambition has to be admired: "The Capital of the World."

The mine that Gopere managed is still operating in Santa Barbara, a small town some twenty miles from Parral. We drive there. It is a real company town, with a miner's memorial in the central square. We ask a few questions and locate the mine we are looking for, now renamed, which is still yielding silver and lead. High on a scrubby hill, I peer through a fence at the mine shaft where, two lifetimes ago, my grandfather and his two sons, their faces begrimed, mining helmets fastened, worked the vein together.

Driving back through Parral, we stop at the large statue of Villa on a raised pedestal at the entrance of the city. It is a wonderful likeness of the old brigand, pulling at the reins of his horse, bronze bandoliers and sombrero shining in the sun. I climb up on the pedestal and pose by this one-time friend of the family, this larger-than-life bandit and national hero who, with the swivel of his revolver in the direction of my grandfather, and a snarl-like "*Basta* with your French nattering!" followed by a pull on the trigger, could have prevented my existence. As Mexican drivers wheel past the roundabout, they see this silver-haired, mustached gringo perched up on the pedestal, waving to his camera-pointing wife, and several shout out their car windows, *"Que viva Villa!"*

CHAPTER 27

A Thing of Beauty . . .
Staying Cool . . . Aztec Chairs

Arriving back in Sayulita, we find it even hotter, if possible, than when we left. The dirt roads on the north side are deeply rutted, in places impassable, from the rains. The public-works department figures there's no point in doing something more than once, so it leaves the roads as they are until the rains stop, a period of about four months. We are weary from the drive, but I am so pleased at having found the demolition hammer Beto wanted—I visited four Home Depots in Orange County before finding the right one—that I want to go straight to the site and present it to him.

We drive, or, rather, trampoline, our way over the ruts to the site and park in front. I go in, Thia says, "Hola, casa," gets her replies, and I go in to find Beto. The ceilings are finished on the top floor, the walls are being painted, and it looks like everything is in its normal forward rush. On the roof, where once the third floor was to be built, Beto has erected pediments. He tells me that he has buried rebar inside them, in case we ever want—or can afford—to build a third floor. Hope.

But some things happen for a reason. As I looked at the structure when we drove up, it struck me that the building had a certain harmony, and was the right proportion. Another floor would have looked gawky, ungainly.

I ask Beto to follow me outside. With Thia standing by, I go to the car, open the back hatch, and take out a heavy blue case that has mud streaks on it. "For the customs," I explain to Beto. I wipe off the case and open it, and there it is: Beto's shiny, new demolition hammer.

"This is for you, Beto. We decided we did not want to share the cost with you, but to give it to you. Our present."

Beto is both beaming and blushing as he picks up the gleaming apparatus and hefts it in his hand.

"*Qué preciosidad,*" he says. What a precious thing, what a thing of beauty.

Beauty isn't what comes to my mind, but I am delighted that he likes it and that Beto can be so . . . delicate in his appraisal. Knowing him, it won't be long before it is in use. We look around at the progress. As we drive away a while later, sure enough, I hear the heavy rat-a-tat of a beautiful thing demolishing concrete.

Keeping cool in this torrid jungle weather requires a big, big effort. You go for an ocean swim in what feels like warm bathwater, and have to dive down to get the cooler currents. As you walk back to where you dropped your stuff, you dry off, and then, improbably, begin to get wet again—from perspiration. (Jeanne, who spent a summer here when she and Rollie first moved down, swears she sweats while *in* the ocean.) When you get home, you take a cold shower, then step out and towel off while still cool. By the time you get back to your bedroom, you are starting to glisten again—from perspiration. By noon, it so hot that you are enervated, limp. We begin taking siestas regularly, and need to. No gringo will ever make a siesta joke again in my presence.

We have air-conditioning in the bedroom, and it's a help at night when we're asleep, but not elsewhere in the apartment during the day. We find more than the usual reasons to do errands by car, to get blasted by the cold air of the air conditioner. But as I look around town at my neighbors, I feel the indulgence of having *any* air-conditioning at all. It is a feeling I have not had in the United States, where we avoid summer heat altogether by moving seamlessly from one machine-cooled environment to another. I do not rationalize by thinking my neighbors are acclimatized. I can see Mexicans around us wiping their necks with bandannas, seeking shade anywhere they can. It is just as hot for them; I know this because those who can afford it have begun to install air-conditioning units they can now buy affordably at Sam's Club. Happily, this has been happening here more and more.

The days go by in a steamy blur. Across the street from our summer apartment is the side door to the church, where we hear the hum of prayers and the chant of hymns most mornings. The majority of the worshippers are women. Next door, directly across from us, our neighbor takes delivery of a large catch of mahimahi before seven each morning and spends an hour gutting them for dispersal to the markets and restaurants of Sayulita. In another six weeks, the gringo residents and the tourists will return, but for now this is a quiet main street. The dogs are bolder in their indolence, stretching out in the middle of the street with their paws in the air, giving themselves a cobblestone back massage. There are no customers for the horseback-riding center, but the horses must be walked, so, a little old, a little new: the center's owner rides a minimotorbike down the street, holding a handlebar with one hand, and in the other, the reins of a horse that trots along behind.

One afternoon I have a flat. Changing a tire in this kind of heat and humidity is unappealing. There is a *llantero,* a tire repairman, in neighboring San Ignacio, a village of a few dozen shanties five minutes down the highway. There I meet Agustín Pereida, a strong, swarthy man with grease and tire-muck on his worn work pants. I watch him jack up the car with a handle and unscrew the tire bolts with a manual lug wrench, sweat pouring down his arms onto the tire. I ask him if he's ever considered investing in a hydraulic pump or an automatic lug wrench; they are now available here for a reasonable cost.

"No," he says. "Then I'd have to invest in a new compressor. It could end up costing me."

"But not that much," I say, "and think of all the wear and tear on your arms."

"Ah, American," he says. "You like to improve things, eh? But you know—*it's all right the way it is.* I get good exercise, and nothing breaks down."

I tell him he sounds as if he has known lots of Americans. He says yes, that although he was born in this very village, he's lived in the States for several years—in Texas, in North Carolina, in Arizona. I ask him for his impressions.

"Well," he says, spinning my tire in a tub of dirty water to find the leak, "the people in Texas and North Carolina treated me like a dog, like a mangy cur. And do you know who were the worst to me? The absolute worst? The *Chicanos* of Texas. They knew how to make a Mexican feel worthless."

And the best?

"Arizonans. They talked to me as if I existed."

Thia and I continue to visit the site almost every day and are impressed with the solid workmanship that emerges from such basic tools and such purely physical, almost entirely manual, labor. Thia has bought tile in a variety of places locally and in Puerto Vallarta, and is happy and in her element, even though she sweats through three or four kerchiefs a morning. At night we go out to dinner with the few friends that are here, at the few restaurants that are open. A couple of times we wander over to Don Pedro's, on the beach, to watch the young Mexican couples dancing salsa. Thia looks wistfully at me, but her longtime lament is that American men in her generation don't dance. (At Mrs. Plum's, in Mexico City, they taught us the foxtrot and waltz, not merengue and salsa. Rock and roll, of course, we picked up on our own.) But mostly, throughout the late summer, we entertain ourselves in a solitary way. We consume books by the shelfful.

I have found journalistic work that I can do online. Thia is preparing for the day we will become vacation landlords by boning up on house rentals. She reports that if we are going to offer competitive amenities, it is going to be—surprise, surprise—more expensive than we thought. I find even *more* journalistic work I can do online. It does not escape my notice that I am now accepting work for fees at a fraction of what I used to earn for similar work in corporate America. Adjusting to one's new market value does not happen just once in "retirement," it is a slow process, with many small moments of rueful recognition.

We see a lot of Benny and Hilda, and visit their home and adjoining nursery just outside Puerto Vallarta. Benny has, of course, designed the home, which feels like a floating pavilion, with stretches of cool marble in columns and tiles, and Colonial armoires of old wormwood. We share drinks and stories around their large glass dining room table, seated in chairs decorated with brightly colored parrots. With children a bit younger than ours, their concerns and interests are similar to ours: popular culture, music, movies, keeping up with their careers, making sure the kids are in good schools and aimed at private college. Hilda loves her horticultural work. She shows us around her meticulous garden, and when she picks a leaf off a tree, she says, *"Con permiso,"* begging its pardon. Benny, broad and ebullient, is a cheerful host, pulling out a sketch pad from time to time to draw some idea that has just come into his head.

It seems to me that the image of Mexico as a country where the privileged get an education and the rest live in ignorance is another shaky generalization. There is no question that the primary-school system is flawed. In villages in our region, primary-school students have a half day of school. Modestly paid teachers sometimes do not show up; when they do not, there are no substitutes, and the kids are sent home. High schools are often several towns away. Too many parents, thinking their kids' best career prospect is to join the family trade, encourage their children to drop out early.

At the same time, there are some fine secondary schools, rigorous public universities, and an admirable tradition of universal public service not found in the United States: High-school students are offered subsidies and time to go on service missions to teach children in remote hamlets. Graduating medical students, as we heard from Dr. Mauro, must perform public service as a condition of practicing in Mexico—which is the reason that nearly every village has some kind of basic medical facility.

The difference from what I've known in the United States and Europe, with their prosperous middle classes, is that here I have run across many people who have a basic education or less but who are sophisticated and cultured in unexpected ways. There is Aurelio, torn from his architectural studies, with his baroque sweet talk and shrewd understanding of gringo character. Ramiro, the literary mechanic, who can fix a metaphor but not an alternator. Doña Lety, who may not have finished primary school but can discuss the "physiognomy" of her customers and the politics of graft. Armando, the plain carpenter, who names his sons after Greek mythological characters and takes time off for petroglyphs. Beto, the fifth-grade dropout, who taught himself craft and integrity, and wants more than anything to visit Machu Picchu.

I suppose the notion of Mexico as a Third World country, split between a rich elite and the masses of poor, is a stereotype that is still statistically true in places—certainly in the slums surrounding its major cities and in the remote rural areas we visited. But it's been instructive to meet striving middle-class professionals like Benny and Hilda, with their advanced degrees and their kids cramming for SATs. What we haven't encountered much, probably because of our circumstances, is another type: the upper-class Mexican, a breed more or less universally derided, both by other Mexicans and gringos. These patricians, mostly *Chilangos* from Mexico City, are said to be arrogant and demanding toward Mexicans beneath their social class. Mexicans we know—from laborers to professionals—say they would rather work for gringos than for rich Mexicans, who do not tip, or pay well, or treat their help respectfully. It is probably just one more class stereotype, easily disproved by individuals who contradict the image, but around here it is pretty much a universal appraisal.

Shopping to furnish and decorate a new house in Mexico is supposed to be the dessert you get for enduring the first courses of jackhammer and concrete, and we have been looking forward to it. The right opportunity arises when Bill and Barb decide to spend their three-week vacation (yes, they call getting away from their tropical inn a vacation) in Pátzcuaro, in the state of Michoacán. They have San Pancho friends who live not just the good, but the excellent, retired life: this couple spends a third of the year in their house in San Pancho, a third in their house in Pátzcuaro, and another third on their farm in Colorado. They have offered Bill and Barb the use of their Pátzcuaro in-town home, and we will get to join them for a week.

What makes shopping in Pátzcuaro and its surrounding villages so appealing, we are told, is the opportunity to furnish and decorate a house by seeking out the work of local artisans: wood and stone carvers, weavers, ironmongers, pottery makers. Our plan is to explore these villages for a week, then drive north to spend a day or two in Tonalá, on the fringe of Guadalajara, where we will buy what we can't find in Pátzcuaro—more practical stuff, like lawn chairs and fabrics. We have met gringo home builders who have furnished and decorated slowly, one piece at a time, over years. But we want to be able to rent out our place this winter, so we're going to do it all, or most of it, in the week that we're there. Again, we will benefit from our friends' experience; Bill and Barb have been to Pátzcuaro several times and know the local ropes.

We ask Benny, our creative counselor, if he has any advice on our shopping expedition. He knows we are interested in buying equipale, the handcrafted leather-and-cross-hatched wood furniture first designed by the Aztecs. (*Equipale* comes from *icapali,* a Nahuatl word.) Thia wants most of our living and dining room furniture to be of this kind, since it is handsome, relatively inexpensive, and lasts.

"Go to Zacoalco de Torres," he says. "It's a small village between Guadalajara and Pátzcuaro, and that's where a lot of equipale originates. Practically the whole village makes this one kind of furniture, and you can get the best prices."

We hope that finding Zacoalco is easier than saying it.

We leave late, as is our wont, and drive to Guadalajara, about three and a half hours away. On the map, we have found the tiny equipale village to the south, and we take the toll highway. I happen to ask a toll attendant how far we are from Zacoalco, pronouncing it a couple of ways. He says that it is ahead, but there is no proper exit for it; we should have taken the free road. We have to watch for kilometer marker 24, slow down, and take a dirt path off to the right. We find a rutted road that takes us into a drab little village bisected by train tracks.

I drive slowly through the village ruts, looking in at modest block houses and shanties, many with open workshops where piles of half-built equipale can be seen. We know it is going to be a matter of luck as to whether we find a good or a mediocre craftsman. Thia only knows that she wants to buy equipale that has more fabric than the pigskin leather, since fabric is a cheaper replacement when the Nayarit sun has its charming way with furniture. But they are not as common as the all-leather chairs. As we pass by one place, she tells me to stop. We go up to a small stone house with clothes hanging from a line on one side and a cluttered workshop on the other.

We introduce ourselves to Antonio Margarito Bermejo, a copper-skinned man in his early thirties wearing work pants and a colored shirt. His pretty wife and infant son are moving around in the back of the shop, and a dog sleeps on a half-made chair. Thia has spotted just the kind of fabric-tufted equipale she is looking for, and we ask him to tell us about the kind of work he does. He shows us two chairs, challenges us to pick the better one, and points to the slats in the one he says is best. He says that most middle-priced equipale found in big cities are made with cheaper wood and sold at a markup of several times his prices. His are made to order, at any length, and with any fabric we choose. Thia asks if he uses staples or sews it with leather thongs, in the traditional Aztec style. He acknowledges that almost everyone uses staple guns today.

We tell Antonio that we are looking for twenty pieces for our two floors, which we describe, and we ask for an estimate. He goes to the back of the shop and confers with his wife. When he comes back, he offers us a price that is about a third of what we'd seen in Puerto Vallarta. He says that if we bring our own fabric, we can tell him what we paid for it, and he will subtract it from his estimate. We tell him we will get back to him with our decision within the week. We drive around Zacoalco a while longer, make two more stops to comparison shop, and ask for estimates, but we don't find anything better than Antonio's. We drive back to tell him he has a deal and that we will return with our fabric in a week.

Back on the highway, several hours later, we drive a couple of thousand feet up into the mountains, and as we approach Pátzcuaro, the weather changes abruptly. We notice it has gotten downright nippy. The countryside has also changed, from agave plains to pine-tree forests. There are kilometers of tricky curves, but finally we come up over a rise and see a large lake before us, turning mauve in the descending twilight. Several small towns are beginning to turn on their lights in the valley. We are still a way from Pátzcuaro, but it is a breathtaking change in scenery—and temperature—from the steaming jungle of our home, or the gnarled plains surrounding Guadalajara.

One guidebook calls Pátzcuaro the most picturesque city in Mexico. Its setting reminds us of the lake district of Italy and Switzerland. But it's more than the landscape. As we drive into the city's main square, we pull over to gape, even though we are late for dinner with Bill and Barb (as usual). The plaza is very large and broad, tree-lined, and surrounded by ancient Colonial-era buildings gleaming from the square's many black wrought-iron lanterns. Like Querétaro, it is spotless. The signs and colors of buildings in the city are stylized in the traditional Michoacán manner; the bottom portion of buildings is painted an earthy red, the

top portions are white. All the signs have an initial capital letter in
Pátzcuaro red, and the following letters are black. This traditional let-
tering is pleasing and harmonizing, and includes not just the artisan
and handicraft shops, the municipal offices and grocery stores, but the
Internet café offering broadband.

We find the address of Barb and Bill's friends, just a couple of blocks
off the plaza, but we are not sure we have got it right. The street number is on an old wormwood door that has a knocker on it, as common-
place as the other neighboring doors. It looks like it could be a small,
shuttered scrivener's shop in a Dickens novel. We knock, there is a
shout from a familiar voice ("Well, it's about goddamn *time!*"), and Barb
throws open the door, wearing the first city skirt and blouse we have
seen her in. Bill is close behind, a wine bottle and several glasses in
hand.

The little scrivener's office (in fact, we find out later it used to be a
print shop) opens up to a vast, long corridor of a house. It is an old Mexican truism that one never knows just what may lie behind a modest
door; rich grandees never wanted to be targets for torch-bearing peasants in the next uprising, so they learned to be discreet about their
wealth. The house has bedrooms done in museum-quality artisan
decor, a lit courtyard with fountain, a huge kitchen, all lined with enormous clay urns, huge copper pots, exquisite pottery, and porcelain stat-
uettes. Everything is authentic wood, brass, and old iron, done in
terrific taste—here, at last, is what you can collect in Mexico if you take
your time, as these owners have after living in Mexico for eighteen
years.

After supper, a couple of bottles of wine, and some conversation
about how we are going to start our shopping week, we go to bed in a
wood-timbered room. It is early September, but there is a huge com-
forter on the bed and a space heater in the corner. The air is cool, and
for the first time that I can remember, I wear socks to bed.

CHAPTER 28

Commando Shopping . . .
Monogram Mania . . . Comely Catrina

Expats in Pátzcuaro call one of the attractive plaza colonnade cafés by the uninspiring name of the Office, as in "I'll meet you at the Office after our siesta." Perhaps it is a way of telling themselves they are keeping busy, if busy means long, languorous meals over chitchat and shopping lore. We four sit down for an early morning breakfast of *"huevos divorciados"* (two separated fried eggs, one with green salsa, the other with red) along with Kahlua, the boisterous puppy Bill and Barbara recently adopted. It is a rare restaurant in this part of Mexico that does not welcome dogs. Kahlua is strong and frisky, yanking at the leash tied to a table leg, jostling the silverware and plates, briefly reconciling my divorced eggs.

The plaza is as lovely in the morning as it was at twilight, and, despite the handful of gringos sitting at the Office, I notice that most of the people I see crossing the square are locals, on their way to work in the multitude of shops and boutiques ringing the plaza. This is still the off-season in early autumn, and although we see preparations being made for the upcoming Independence Day celebrations on September 16, there is a drowsy, tranquil aspect to the scene.

Independence Day is a less glamorous holiday in Pátzcuaro than the one that will be held six weeks later, on November 2, the Day of the Dead. On that day, somnolent Pátzcuaro comes alive with one of Mexico's most funereally festive celebrations, its inns and hotels packed with visitors from all over the world. Michoacán artisans bring all their best wares to Pátzcuaro for the giant street fair. At night, as tourist onlookers flash away, the local cemetery is filled with candle-bearing townspeople who bedeck the tombs with marigolds to celebrate the memory of those who have passed.

But for now, the square is quiet. A stooped and shriveled old man, dressed in Indian white, is tottering across the street at an excruciatingly slow pace. When he reaches the opposite curb, he tries, but cannot step up onto it. Before Bill or I can get up to go assist him, a woman street cleaner walks over, lays down her broom, and, offering him her arm, helps him tenderly onto the curb.

Since the theme of the week will be shopping, we talk a bit about the uncommon experience of buying merchandise in Mexico. To a gringo, there are differences not usually noted in the guidebooks. For instance, how well an item sells is often unrelated to how quickly it will be restocked or be available in the future. We have all noticed that if a shirt, or a vase, or a delicacy sells out, there is no predicting when, or if, it will be available again in a particular store. Ask, and a shrug is the usual response. Bill says it is almost as if a merchant may not *want* to restock it because it sells too easily and may discourage the purchase of slower-selling items. In a similar vein, an item that sells well during a busy season may be put on sale for the slow season, but at a *higher* price. The thinking, I imagine, is that if fewer items are being sold, selling each at a higher price is a strategy to make up the lost income. Nobel Prize economists have fought each other bitterly over just such issues.

Barbara tells the story of a street vendor who was selling pistachios in San Pancho. Barbara was having guests that night and stopped the vendor to ask him if he would sell her his entire inventory, about thirty bags of nuts. "'Oh, no, Señora, if I sold you all my bags, what would I do for the rest of the day?" Barbara laughs, but says, "In a way, it's a perfectly logical way to think about it. It's not just about income but about nurturing a business."

We turn to our goal of commando shopping—furnishing our house in five days—and plan our line of attack. We agree to reconnoiter the terrain first, and we spend a couple of hours ducking in and out of Pátzcuaro's shops, not only those ringing the plaza, but up narrow streets and alleys, in and out of the city's famous House of Eleven Patios, a former convent turned into a series of upscale shops. We look

at embroideries, urns, ponchos, plates, serapes, all done in traditional
Michoacán patterns, as we pad along corridors where nuns once recited
their vespers. The city is our staging area; in the afternoon, we fan out
to visit the villages in the area, each of which specializes in a different
craft.

Pátzcuaro and the towns surrounding the lake owe much to the
sixteenth-century churchman Manuel Quiroga. He was a scholar sent
by the Franciscan order to undo the damage done by an earlier Spanish
governor, a tyrant who tortured and dispatched the Indians under his
rule. Quiroga was a humanist influenced by the writings of Sir Thomas
More, and it was in More's *Utopia*, Quiroga believed, that the answer to
the survival of New Spain's Indians could be found. Drawing on More's
ideas, Quiroga organized the Indians into communal units. To avoid
debilitating competition among localities, he decreed that each village
should specialize in one craft—one would do weaving, another stone
carving, a third tapestries, and so on. The system gave the Indians
dependable work, and it persists to this day. For gringo shoppers, it
means researching the villages and markets for their particular crafts—
which anyone in Pátzcuaro can tell you about—and planning an itinerary around the region's back roads, like visiting some vast, hilly mall
made up of shanties and shops and chicken-coop showrooms.

We head for the bedroom-furniture village. There are few marked
roads, so you need good maps, a good guide, or good friends like Barb
and Bill, who remember their way from their own earlier expeditions.
We enter a modest, nondescript village, and tumbling out of every
workshop are wood-carved beds and chests of drawers and nightstands.
An armoire of good solid pine with intricate carvings, some with Diego
Rivera's girl-with-lilies motif, will go for $175 to $250, a fraction of
what even this rustic furniture would go for in the States.

This is a get-acquainted tour, so we visit four or five other villages,
some specializing in large clay vases, another in shiny burnished copper ware, another in stone garden statuary, much of it well made, all of
it cheap. It is definitely low season; we are the only shoppers on patrol.
At one stop, along a row of workshop shacks, we see some nice bed-
steads, and we troop over to knock on a tar-paper door. A woman comes
out, looks us up and down, then ducks back in. She reappears with a
dusty bullhorn in her hand and pushes politely past us. When she is
within visual range of her neighbors, she shouts into her bullhorn,

"Hay gringos!" Gringos here! Doors open in the shacks around us at this neighborly announcement, and the residents poke their heads out to wave at us, asking us to stop by. It takes us an hour to make our polite way through a number of workshops, most of them showing similarly styled wood furniture.

We discover the village of Tzintzuntzan (pronounced, more or less, Zeen-Zoon-Zan), named after a Tarascan word that mimics the sound of hummingbirds that used to abound here. The village is laid out so that you can flit from this artisan shop to that market stall, all brimming with craftwork of all kinds. On many of the tapestries are embroideries of the rich folklore of the region: village women with brooms, fishermen with their catch, and one, a big favorite around here, the Dance of the Little Old Men.

We end our day making just one whimsical purchase, a tiny sewn cap and apron meant to adorn the top of an olive-oil bottle. "Let's review our progress for the day," says Barbara on our way back. "You came to Pátzcuaro to furnish a house, and so far you've bought a bib for a bottle. Am I right?" That night we go out to a restaurant specializing in regional dishes and stroll afterward to a café for ice cream. A trio of the oldest, most wrinkled and withered singers I have seen on any continent come by and serenade us. One has a guitar on whose strings his bony fingers make hardly an impact, another bows his violin in a feeble screech, and the other closes his crinkled eyelids to sing in raspy croak. We are not sure that all three of the old gentlemen will outlive the performance, but it adds a certain patina to the evening.

The next day, we head back to Tzintzuntzan, and hover at a couple of workshops we noticed the day before, where the bedroom furniture, though similar or identical in style to many others, seemed to have more detail and better workmanship. At one, we meet Gorgonio Reyes, a diminutive, energetic man who directs the family enterprise of headboards and bed stands. We find several headboards we like, and ask him if he can match bed stands and bureaus to the headboard style. *¡Cómo no!* Of course! We order three bedrooms' worth, including bed platforms, as his wife, Mayela, carefully takes notes and jots down the estimates. To measure a bed platform for us, Gorgonio takes us into his own bedroom in back. It is an unadorned room with bare walls, a large television set, and, on the cement floor of this maker of fine bed furniture, the couple's bare mattress.

A few hundred meters down the road, we stop at a place whose tables and bureaus we had seen the day before; they too seemed to have a special flourish. Here, Pablo, expansive, round, and varnish stained, shows us his wares as again, the wife keeps a watchful eye on the proceedings. While I talk to Pablo, Thia wanders to the back of the workshop, where, she reports later, she finds a shrine bedecked with votive candles and flowers. Tacked on the wall is a framed picture of a haloed man on a horse, with this inscription underneath: "Oh, Saint Martin on Horseback . . . may I never lack for health, work, or support. God bless my job, my business, and my customers." Other times, at marketplaces, we have seen older women make the sign of the cross after making a sale.

We like an Aztec-style carved wooden table, and ask Pablo if he could adapt some of the same designs to a specially made armoire. ¡Cómo no! These craftsmen have been creating similar, if not identical, patterns for years, if not generations. The challenge of mixing the patterns together into something new, or even of fashioning something altogether novel, appears to intrigue Pablo. He cocks his head, rubs his chin, and nods. ¡Cómo no! It is hard for a prosperous foreigner to reconcile the simplicity of these lives—their meager education, their poor living conditions—with the richness of their artistic sensibilities. I recall what novelist Waldo Frank wrote: "Perhaps Mexico is unlike any other place in the world, the cradle of genius. From the first Mayans to the modern peasant artisan, Mexico has done no more than lavish incessant beauty. The songs, the dances, the sculpture, the pictures, the ceramics, the tapestries, toys, jewelry—all testify that these people, from immemorial time, have somehow known truth."

Pablo names a price of $1,100 for two armoires, a hutch, and the Aztec-calendar dining room table. The preferred method of payment is half down, the other half on delivery. The problem is, we're ordering work we haven't seen and don't know if it will be finished on time. To give Pablo an incentive, I suggest to him that if the furniture is finished on schedule, and the work is as good as we hope it will be, we will give him a $100 bonus on delivery. He seems surprised, then pleased. As Thia leans over with Pablo to confer on which Aztec chieftain heads might make the traverse from table to armoire, I reflect what an exceptional moment we are having. In the United States, to buy in such a personalized, made-to-order way is an experience that, for the most part, is reserved for the wealthy. For most Americans, buying off the shelf or out of a catalogue is all there is.

I get carried away by the idea.

"Remember when I got those monogrammed shirts?" I say to Thia.

"Yes," she says carefully.

"Well, how about we carve the house's initials on this stuff?"

We have decided to call the house Casa Gala, after the family nickname of my late mother, who spent some of her happiest years in Mexico in the 1950s. It also means "celebration" in English and "finery" in Spanish. So: CG! Thia is hesitant and wonders if we are taking this too far. She sees the hurt, adolescent expression on my face and gives in. We place our orders for living room furniture with Pablo and head back to Gorgonio's to ask him if he can carve the initials *CG* on the headboards. *¡Cómo no!*

The next day we stop at an ironwork furniture maker by the main road that specializes in outdoor wrought-iron chairs, tables, and benches. A young man named Miguel comes forward to show us around. Inside the big shed, a dozen workers are forging steel, vats of molten iron gleaming, and yellow sparks are flying from the welders under the hot roof. For a second, it looks to me like a scene from Dante's *Inferno,* or at least one of those sweatshop factories along the border. But peering into the dark, I see that the workers, most in Adidas sneakers, are sipping beers, listening to their radios, and swapping cheerful insults back and forth while looking down at wrinkled client sketches. Tough work, but here it seems to me they are taking an infernal pleasure in their labor.

We ask Miguel if we can substitute our own design for the daisy pattern in one style of chair-and-table set. *Cómo no.* I sketch a four-sided *rosetón,* a kind of cloverlike shape we like that we plan on using for our wrought-iron railings. Miguel looks at it, and nods. Anything else? I write the letters *CG* on the scrap of paper. Thia rolls her eyes. Can you integrate that into the design, I ask? *Cómo no.* We order three sets of two wrought-iron chairs and a table each, and a long, handsome bench, all in heavy metal and black-matte finish. Miguel asks for half the five-hundred-dollar total in advance. I tell him that we will pay him six hundred dollars and that we expect he will take special care with the order, and deliver it on time, six weeks from now. Miguel blinks at me slowly, surprised, then writes up the order with what seems a special relish.

When we add it all up later, it appears that we are furnishing our house—both units, with two separate living rooms and kitchens, and all four bedrooms—for under seven thousand dollars. Of course, the stuff will be rustic, and would be out of place in an American suburb or city apartment, but we recall that a New York City friend recently spent that much on a couch. This, I think, is what makes the real difference in the cost of living between the two countries. (This, and woefully low taxation.) Real-estate values for land and finished houses in desirable Mexican locations will continue to rise to a point where they are no longer whopping bargains. But to be able, still, to choose the affordable artifacts that you will surround yourself with, and to do so with great individuality and a sense of personal style, is a singular experience.

We do not bargain much. Neither Thia nor I is much impressed with the tendency of American visitors and expatriates to haggle with every beach and street vendor who proposes a price for a pair of sandals or a necklace. While it is true that there is a gringo pricing system, and that the first price offered is often inflated, the question is, inflated from *what*? To talk an old woman selling a rebozo down from eighty to sixty pesos to gain bragging rights among one's American friends strikes us as uncharitable. The profits most vendors get from their work are already so meager; if they get a bit more from an American than they would from a Mexican, so what? We have tried to keep in mind what the value of a purchase is to *us*; if it seems right, we pay the price suggested. And on those occasions when we offer more than the going price, as we have with several of our "big" purchases in Pátzcuaro, we are betting that Mexicans, no less than their American counterparts, will be motivated by incentive. In fact, our experience thus far is that many Mexicans, surprised *not* to be busted down for a few less pesos, react to unexpected gestures with extraordinary generosity and hard work.

Thia says she will need a day of shopping with just her girlfriend Barbara for kitchen pots and garden vases and wall hangings. I suspect it is because she fears that if I come along, I will insist that the kitchenware be monogrammed. I agree that I will take a break, and Bill and I spend a day sightseeing. We visit a sixteenth-century convent nearby, and the mossy ruins of a Tarascan pyramid. When the women return, the SUV is filled with housewares for Casa Gala. They tell us that they packed so much into the vehicle that they had to shove Kahlua out of her backseat perch. When they crammed their last basket in, they looked up to see an old woman standing in front of the car, staring through the windshield. The dog had looked for the only vacant space left—the driver's seat—and had her paws up on the steering wheel as the car idled.

The next day we discover Catrina. She is the skeleton doll, a local favorite, made and sold in shops and roadside workshops. The doll comes in many styles and textures—clay, ceramic, porcelain—and is one of the more flamboyant symbols of Mexico's flirtatious relationship with death. Based on the nineteenth-century newspaper illustrations of José Guadalupe Posada, who used to satirize the pretensions of high-born Mexican ladies and their infatuation with French style, these dolls have become a witty, macabre cottage industry in Michoacán today— and sell elsewhere for an impressive markup. With their rictus grins and movable skulls, Catrinas are usually decked out in outrageous ruffled gowns and rococo bonnets, jewelry jangling from their arm bones, their long, tapering skeleton fingers sometimes holding a cigarette or a cigar. Bill and Barbara are already crazy about the dolls, and Thia and I decide on the spot to start collecting them.

At several shops near the plaza and in roadside shack sheds, we buy six or eight of the figurines for an average of about fifteen dollars apiece. One skeleton lady is a revolutionary señorita, with crossed bandoleers, another a vamp with low-cut dress exposing a daring breastbone and ribs. At one little shed we buy three dolls of dark terra-cotta from a for-mer fisherman who says he turned to designing his own Catrinas when his catch dwindled. His wife wraps the dolls carefully for us in a long roll of toilet paper. As we leave, I hear the wife say to her young daugh-ter in Spanish, improbably enough, "There, now we can buy those shoes you wanted."

Every craft has its supreme artist, and we are lucky to be in the vicin-ity of the hacienda of Juan Torres, a world-class painter and sculptor whose labor of love is the Catrina doll. We drive up to his stone-cut gallery and walk into a room filled with spotlighted über-Catrinas, twenty-inch-tall skeleton divas that astonish us with their style and humor. Here, the bonnets are wild and extravagant flowery concoc-tions, with saucy skeleton legs protruding from slit dresses. We buy one gorgeous grand dame for two hundred dollars (they cost three times as much in upscale crafts shops in Puerto Vallarta), whom we immediately call Señorita Gala, and Barb and Bill buy another. No toilet-paper wrapping here: the dolls are lovingly entombed in Styrofoam and cardboard, and we go proudly back to the Office in Pátzcuaro for afternoon coffee.

While the women head off for one last burst of shopping in the plaza stores, Bill and I order coffee and talk about the Catrinas we have just splurged on, marveling over the detail in the bony fingers that Juan Torres sculpted, and the pointed stiletto heels on which he lavished such care. As we sit there sipping our coffee, we grow quiet. We are staring out at the plaza. I turn to Bill, who is scratching at the stubble of his two-day beard. I raise a topic I know is on both our minds.

"Did we just spend a whole bunch of time talking about . . . *dolls*?"

Bill continues to stare out at the plaza. "I think we did, yes."

We avoid each other's gaze. We take a couple of more sips of coffee. Bill finally speaks up.

"How about them White Sox?" he says.

CHAPTER 29

Oscar Willy . . . Advice from Benny . . . Pancho's Detail

We have left one full day more to shop in Tonalá, and so now we shift from commando to blitzkrieg. We have heard that to get around Tonalá's crowded, shabby warren of everything-must-go shops, a personal guide is best. Several gringos have mentioned Oscar Willy Klauditz to us, and a day before we leave Pátzcuaro, I call his Guadalajara-area telephone number and introduce myself. I am told it's a good idea to prepare Willy for what we want, so the day can unfold efficiently. We won't be taking the scenic route; there is no "scenic" in Tonalá.

Thia has prepared a list of what we will need: Talavera dishes, glassware, sun-resistant fabric (for the equipale furniture), a large lantern, pool furniture. Oscar Willy, who speaks accented English well, says merely "Yes, yes" to each item. He seems oversure of himself, so I throw him a ringer: terra-cotta angels playing instruments. They are the inspiration of Benny, who thinks that arranging a little celestial orchestra in a nook of our garden would be just the thing. I mention this to Oscar Willy, and there is just the merest pause, and he says, "Yes, yes."

Early Saturday morning, we begin to pack the Pátzcuaro purchases that we are transporting ourselves by piling them outside on the sidewalk by our car. We stand there, contemplating how to fit the boxes, packages, and toilet-paper-wrapped figurines into our SUV. Thia ducks back inside to collect her purse, and I spread the stuff out on the sidewalk to sort it out by size. I am dressed in my work clothes. My beard growth and drooping mustache must make me look like a local, because an American tourist happens by, stops, and points to a couple of clay pots I have leaning against the wall.

"¿*Cuanto cuesta?*" he asks.

"*Trescientos* pesos," I say, not missing a beat. The tourist shakes his head—too expensive—and walks on. A moment later, he looks over his shoulder and gives me a look as he sees his sidewalk vendor lifting the pots into the back of a Connecticut-plated SUV. I don't know why, but this gone-native encounter gives me as much pleasure as anything else that happens that morning.

Oscar Willy is a short, bespectacled, ruddy-faced fellow who works out of a cluttered office just off Tonalá's main street. As we set off for our purchases in his oversized, battered SUV, he tells us that he has been a personal shopper for the past fifteen years. The son of a naturalized German immigrant who fled the Nazis and settled in Guadalajara, Oscar Willy is organized and efficient. Beto and Aurelio keep everything in their head; Oscar Willy has a written list, and he checks off each item we purchased as we make our stops. We tell him we are on a tight budget and are looking for value. He says, "That is my job—to keep you on your boodg-et."

Our first stop is a Talavera dish factory, and Thia, who has been looking forward to this purchase, goes merrily mad. She zips around the store, lifting dishes and holding them up to the light, chattering to herself. She settles on two patterns, one for upstairs and the other for the main kitchen, and asks for a lighter color than the sample she is shown (*cómo no*). She orders twenty teal-green place settings of plate, soup bowl, saucer, salad plate, and dessert plate for a total of $276, delivered to Sayulita. She is bouncing on her feet as she gets back into the car, crowing about single settings in the States that cost as much our total. As I take out my tape recorder to remind myself of the prices we're paying, I recite, "Two hundred and seventy-six dollars for twenty settings," and she grabs the recorder from me and shouts into it, "That's *fourteen dollars* a setting for *Talavera,* ladies!"

We get equally good buys in glasses, pool chairs, and, yes, five terracotta angels playing a harp, a mandolin, a saxophone, a flute, and a harmonium. To illuminate the huge stairway at Casa Gala—the one we just barely got Aurelio to reduce—we stop at a Tonalá forge and order a candelabra-type iron lantern of our design. I feel sure it would have pleased the Phantom of the Opera; its price is pure operetta: $135. Oscar Willy then announces that the only place to get good fabric is in neighboring Tlaquepaque, the pricier boutique district more frequently patronized by tourists. There Thia finds the equipale fabric she is looking for, though for more than what we had hoped.

We drive back to Oscar Willy's office in Tonalá, where we settle up. He has charged us $15 an hour, plus a fee for coordinating the deliveries (all the purchases will be taken to his office for shipment to us), and we take off for Zacoalco again.

This time we take the free, bumpy highway, and look for the turnoff. From this direction, the equipale village is well marked: instead of a sign, there is a giant Aztec chair lodged crookedly in a tree. Antonio is waiting for us with his wife and child. Thia takes out the fabric she has bought in Tonalá, unfolds it for him, and asks him if he can work with it. He says yes, but . . . His pretty wife is standing behind him, burping their baby, and she looks worried. I ask him what is bothering them. He says that he can see it is expensive fabric, and he knows that he promised us we could subtract the price of any fabric we brought from his original estimate. Now he must honor his word.

"Antonio," I say, after glancing at Thia. "We think your estimate was fair. Why don't we just say that the cost of the fabric is ours?" Unexpectedly, Beto comes into my mind as I say this. Again, I catch the glint of surprise. The fabric has cost us a couple of hundred dollars. It would probably have meant his margin of profit. He nods, relieved.

As we make arrangements for a delivery date four weeks later, Thia asks him, as she did the first time we visited, if he will use a staple gun to secure the fabric. It is her only reservation; in far more expensive equipale that we had seen, the seams were braided in leather. Antonio pauses, then shyly reaches across to pick up a long, narrow strip of uncured pigskin. Silently, he takes out his leather knife and slits it into three narrower strips and begins to braid them together. He holds out the braided strip to Thia.

"What if I were to cover all the seams with this?" he asks.

"*All* the furniture?" Thia asks.

"Yes."

"But, Antonio, it would be a lot of extra work."

"Well," he says, estimating, "it would mean I would need three more days than I promised."

"And the cost?" I say. I am doing my own estimating and do not know what three more days of work braiding our furniture would mean.

"It will be my pleasure."

We are touched. We leave a deposit and drive away as Antonio and his wife, still holding her baby over her shoulder, wave good-bye. I do not know if his offer to take the time to braid all the seams, three more days of work without extra pay, was directly related to our decision not to hold him to his fabric estimate. But I know this: in this little village, as elsewhere in Mexico, we have found our way into a new world of personal commerce. It is one of gesture and nuance, of favor and rejoinder, where the pursuit of monetary profit is not, remarkably enough, the sole standard of human exchange.

Back in Sayulita, we resume our routine of visiting the site every morning. The Beto juggernaut has continued, and there is great progress, even if we are a bit behind schedule. The construction of the house is basically finished. The corridor tile has been laid beneath the eaves, the stairway steps have been finished off in a pebbly granite, and, most conspicuously, the bulldozer is ready to break ground for the pool. Benny, whose lateness has begun to irritate Beto, finally arrives at midmorning. After consulting with us, he paces off the contour of the pool with Roberto, from Beto's team, pouring chalk behind him. He takes out his pad, makes a few sketches of the surrounding terrace and outdoor bar area, and hands them to Beto. Glancing at the sketches, Beto tells Benny he needs more detail and more precise measurements. So Benny walks over to the wall where the bar, sink, and outdoor bathroom will go, and draws lines with a red pencil on the wall, marking the measurements Beto has asked for. Both men feel satisfied with this improvised architectural rendering.

Benny is also here to help us decide whether we want a palapa or a tile roof as a pool cabana. By now, I am beginning to see where the final expenses of the house will lead us and am nervously looking to conserve what capital we have left. Although our expedition for furnishings was a big success economically, we are now facing major costs. The construction of a pool palapa, the terraces, and driveway were not part of

Beto's original estimate, as he has politely warned us. Nor is the viewing pavilion we have planned for our roof. As I began to pick up hints of what these are going to cost, I began to feel dread. It is one thing to begin with a bank account in the low six figures, as we did in early May; anything seemed possible. It is another when, after nearly five months of weekly cash disbursements and daily house purchases, that bank account dwindles into the low five figures. Very low.

Thia is oblivious. "What about putting up a wooden gazebo on the roof?" she says gaily. "Do you think we could afford something big enough so we could have mariachis come and sing beneath it when we have a party?"

I give her an exasperated glance and reluctantly translate. "Maybe a guitarist," Beto says dryly. The tension level between Thia and me has risen since our return; she is coming into her own, since these final weeks promise to be about aesthetic decisions, her domain, while I am convinced I am the only one aware of the coming crunch in our bank account.

Beto and Benny and I huddle over costs. I ask them how much they think the terrace, which Benny wants us to do in expensive broken cantera stone, will set us back.

"Well," Benny says with a broad smile, "it will stretch to the wall where we plan to put up our musical angels. Why don't we pray to them for celestial assistance?"

I tell him I am happy that our financial straits amuse him and Beto. And I am happy that my wife can entertain herself with whimsies of gazebos and mariachis. But we are going to have to finish this house without going broke, and it is a serious matter.

"Barry," says Benny in his best avuncular tone, "let me tell you what I've seen in my years of building and landscaping. As a couple approaches the final stages of a house, they have three sources of tension: they are running short of money; short of time; and they are getting short with each other because now the decisions are about how to dress the house, how to apply its makeup. The wife has her ideas, the husband has his. It's—how do you say it?—a perfect storm. And it's normal."

"And your advice, sage one?"

"My advice is Mexican. Why worry? If something is going to happen, then it will happen. If it's not going to happen, your worry was for nothing. Life goes on."

I nod, but tell him I am going to have to save the philosophy and deal with practicalities. Together, we decide that a palapa will be the most economical way to have a pool cabana, and that a pergola—concrete columns with wooden beams on top for partial shade—will be the cheapest, most attractive route to a viewing pavilion. Then we stand back as the bulldozer man begins to excavate the pool, and lifts dark, fresh earth into piles that will later be used to raise the level of the courtyard and lawn area. It is a big hole, and I think it is an altogether appropriate metaphor.

By now, our subcontractors are converging on us as well. Pancho Duarte, the wrought-iron maestro, is, like Victor the carpenter, a Beto recommendation. His bid for our terrace handrails, a spiral staircase to the roof, and for transforming our large iron gates from swinging to sliding doors was considerably lower than Aurelio's suggested candidate. In another Kismet moment, he tells us it was he who originally made the tall iron gates at our entrance. It looks as if we made a good choice. The ironwork samples he has brought us look sturdy and refined. ("Beto knows other Betos," was Thia's pithy observation.) Our Pancho is a large, bluff hombre whose loud, booming voice has become familiar to me over the phone.

We have planned iron handrails across the second-floor terrace and along all four edges of the roof. When Pancho asked us what design we wanted, we expected to leaf through a catalog. Instead, he handed me a begrimed piece of paper and a pen, and indicated that I should sketch what we wanted. It hits me again: though you *can* pay to have ready-made construction in Mexico, the default, from years of work-arounds, is to do it yourself. Thia and I conferred, and I drew our four-sided rosetón clover along the top frame of the railing; below, I sketched bow-shaped thin vertical bars I remembered seeing on elegant Spanish colonial mansions.

"Can you do this, Señor Pancho?" I asked.

"*Cómo no*, Señor Barry!" he shouted.

The day he arrives in his truck with the first sets of handrails, Thia and I are on site. We are excited because this is the first time we are seeing what comes after bricks and cement—what Benny calls the house's dress and makeup. Victor's parota doors and windows are behind schedule, so the railings are the first real evidence of what the finished house might actually look like. Pancho has a crew with him, and in a short time they have bolted the handrails across the terrace and begun attaching the ten-foot spiral staircase into position between the second floor and the roof deck.

I am out in the yard when Pancho approaches me.

"There is a *detalle,* Señor Barry," he says. A "detail" in Spanish, I have come to learn, has the same linguistic flexibility that mañana has: it can indeed be small and trivial, like a missing hinge, or it can be somewhat more serious, like a missing wall. Pancho leads me up to the second floor and points at the spiral staircase, now temporarily fastened to the roof by a thick rope. The steps lead nicely from the landing, twist upward grace-fully, and then end—in midair. The final step of the staircase fails to meet the roof deck and instead points away from it at a sharp angle, leaving several feet of open space and a cliffhanger. Pancho has miscalculated.

"That is the detalle," Pancho booms out, helpfully.

I am having a Mr. Gomez moment after all. It may not be a toilet located in the middle of a living room, but it is close. The casual way our Mexican workers do their measurements—in their heads, scribbled on walls—is charming, but sometimes it runs up against reality. I keep my cool and ask Pancho what can be done. Can the staircase be spun to meet the roof? Can a step be added at the bottom, lifting the stair-case above the level of the roof floor, with a step down?

Beto has joined us, and he, Pancho, and I study the detalle from every angle. They are both in good humor; this is an interesting prob-lem. I, on the other hand, am feeling a stab of panic—I can't see an easy way out. In the States, I think I'd insist that the staircase be removed and redone. But I know enough about the way money is spent here that that kind of solution will simply not happen—too much expense has gone into the off-kilter staircase so far. A solution will have to be impro-vised. Sure enough, Pancho says, "This is what we will do."

He says that by bringing in his soldering crew, he can cut away the cliffhanger, and substitute a short curved walkway with handrails that will meet the roof floor—farther away than was planned, but perfectly safe. So much for symmetry, but I agree—it is the best that can be done. It is in fact the most ingenious way out of the dilemma.

The decision made, a short time later I scamper up the staircase, take a flying jump over Pancho's abyss, and land on our roof. There, I stride over to our just-bolted railing and gaze down at our realm. Beto is below, directing the cement workers at the bottom of our excavated pool. Pancho's boisterous voice can be heard as he and his muchachos haul the last railings up what was once Aurelio's own staircase folly, now a handsome set of stone steps. Thia has her little umbrella hat on and is doing something with the tiles in the courtyard below. Another crisis past, all is as it should be. It is good to be king, even when everything doesn't quite measure up to one's regal expectations.

CHAPTER 30

The Gringos Return . . . Vallarta Time . . . An Electric Moment

On October 1, the swallows—the earliest winter gringos—return to Sayulita. The lead swallows, as far as we are concerned, are Jeanne and Rollie, who arrive to give themselves a month before getting the restaurant up and running. When Jeanne shows up at our apartment door with a wide smile, her green eyes flashing, Thia and I nearly smother her in an embrace. We have joined the battalion of hardy summer survivors like Dick and Cheryl and Bill and Barbara, and we are now hardened veterans. And we're glad for the fresh reinforcements.

Rollie, who is behind the wheel of a new, idling giant SUV he bought in California—"Meet the Beast!" he calls out, pointing a thumb at the cavernous cargo hold—waits while Jeanne and Thia exchange only the mission-critical intelligence that cannot wait. There will be more time to drill down when they are settled and we take up our bridge games once again.

Toward the second week of October, our three sets of close friends begin to comment on a certain level of tenseness and irascibility we two are beginning to exude. I have less patience for watching the videos all the way through that Dick and Cheryl show at their house by the beach. Bill and Barbara email us from San Pancho that they've hardly seen us since Pátzcuaro. And Jeanne and Rollie murder us at bridge, leading Jeanne to ask if we're really having any fun finishing our house.

The reason is this: confident that we would be through with construction and the garden by November 1, we have invited six members of our family to fly down and join us for Thanksgiving. They will be the inaugural visitors to our new house in paradise: my sister, Michele, and her husband, Tom; my brother Chris and his wife, wary Kit; and, most meaningful to me, my eighty-nine-year-old father, the one who'd first brought me to Mexico—as his father had brought him—and his wife, Bernadette. To top it off, Kit's daughter by an earlier marriage, Lisa, and three of her friends, are vacationing in Puerto Vallarta at that time, and they will be partaking of turkey with us as well. We calculated that with three weeks to move in the furniture, and for Thia to decorate with her usual flair, we would be in good shape when they arrived.

But Benny was right: finishing a house is a perfect storm, and it has been reaching new levels of tempestuous perfection every passing day. Because our doors and windows are late, the usual state of affairs with carpenters, Beto has postponed the painting of the house. Because the house interior is incomplete, Beto has not been able to move his workers out as he wished, to concentrate on terrace and driveway construction. The pool tiles Thia wanted are not available, so that will be another postponement. And we are getting increasingly nervous about where we will stash the two truckloads of Pátzcuaro furniture due to be delivered in about a week.

Beto himself is getting snappish, because none of these delays are his doing; they are the subcontractors' fault, but he feels responsible. He is a man of deadlines, and the deadlines are being pushed by forces outside his control. There are also literally hundreds of purchases to be made—we are responsible for everything that is "visible," after all—which means almost daily trips into Vallarta by Thia, who does not trust my instincts when it comes to what is visible. I volunteer to do some of it, and have promised her I will squelch any lingering monogram impulses I may have; we are down to faucets and shower heads, and I don't see what harm I could do. But she wants to do the final marauding on her own.

And then there is the matter of plumbing and electricity.

Francisco, our electrical and plumbing specialist, is a handsome devil, a smoothie in his thirties with decent English and dark liquid eyes that made Thia call him the Johnny Depp of Nayarit. He is another Beto subcontractor, to be paid by him under the terms of the overall budget. But Francisco has had trouble showing up when he says he will. He and his crew of two have installed the main plumbing and electrical lines, but they have not been seen for weeks. The countless decisions that need to be made—all the light switches and outlets, the fan controls, the faucets, the boiler, the water pump and pressure tank—have been left hanging as Francisco breaks appointment after appointment. A couple of weeks earlier, around the second week of October, I expressed my concern to Beto, who was himself becoming frustrated.

"What is going on with Francisco?" I ask.

"I've worked with him before, and he is the best," he says, "but I think he has taken on too much work. That is always the problem I find with people who are not part of my team; they will not tell you when they cannot do something."

"Can you light a fire under him? Call him? You're close to him."

Beto has told me that Francisco is not only a colleague and a friend but a compadre. They play soccer together.

"Well . . ." Beto shifts from one foot to another uncomfortably. "I do not like to beg anyone."

Ah, pride. Even if a problem is becoming acute, dignity must be upheld.

"Then *I'll* call him," I say.

Francisco returns my call a couple of days later and could not be more gracious. Other commitments, a stalled truck (one of Benny's favored excuses), a sick sister, have all conspired to keep him from his work with us, which he remains enthusiastic about. He will be at our site mañana, at eight sharp.

Two days later he shows up in the afternoon, all smiles. I tell Thia that I intend to confront him. She restrains me, saying it will do no good. Francisco walks us through every room, asking Thia where she wants the outlets and the switches, what kinds of dimmers are required, where the fans should be located, and where the controls should go. He is taking notes, and I take that as a good sign at last. I take him up on the roof, the two of us leaping across the spiral void, and there we decide what kinds of lights to put on our posts, and where the air-conditioning units will be wired.

We finish by taking a break and leaning over the railing to look out at our palm and village view.

"You know, Francisco," I say, "we have come this far this fast with Beto because I have implicit trust in him. He is one of the most honest men I have met, and this would not have happened without both of us relying on each other's promises."

Francisco gets what I am saying. "Of course," he says. "I have had some distractions up until now, but you can rely on me as well. You can have the same trust—*confianza*—in me as you have in Beto. Count on it."

It is the last time I ever see Francisco.

He breaks several more dates to show up at the site. We then make a firm appointment to meet in front of Blockbuster in Puerto Vallarta. Francisco is going to spend the day taking me to electrical appliance stores, getting me "Mexican prices," and advising me on brands and quality. I drive the forty-five minutes and show up at nine sharp. No Francisco. I wait. I use my telephone card to call from a battered pay phone and leave messages on his voice mail. Three hours later, I give up and drive back. Fuming, I leave more messages on his phone. A couple of days later, he calls back and, in a charming manner, asks why I didn't meet him. I tell him through gritted teeth that I was there at nine, as agreed.

"Was that Vallarta time or Sayulita time?" The difference in time zones is one of the most honored excuse stratagems in the Pacific Coast region. It has served its residents well through the years, as students show up for tests, patients show up at doctors' offices, and pizza delivery boys show up at beach houses, all with the same refrain: "Oh, you meant _____ time?"

But I am onto that ploy.

"What time zone did *you* show up at?" I ask.

I've got him cornered. "Vallarta time," he mumbles.

"Me too," I say.

"Well, I was there—how strange."

Strange indeed. Rather than call to break the appointment, or even to tell me that he really could not finish the job for us, Francisco chooses to lie in a way that is so blatant, so disprovable, that for a while I wonder if I could have been wrong. But I know there is just one Blockbuster in the section of Puerto Vallarta where we are going to shop. Francisco has decided to tough it out. He will not directly disappoint,

neither will he admit error, nor will he confront. Some Mexican tradi-
tions die hard, even among the young and moderns. I fire him.

But now we have a major *detalle* on our hands. Beto is embarrassed
about his compadre, but is vague about finding a replacement. He calls
another friend, Pablo Santander, who he says does fine work, but he is
too busy. I scramble, get a couple of recommendations, but the village
is shaking off its summer and fall torpor as more gringos drift back for
their winter stays; work has picked up. Everybody is busy. Several days
later, as time is beginning to really press, I track down Efrén Robles, a
vigorous, confident type who comes by to look over the work that has
been done so far. He spends an hour at the site with a clipboard, picking up wires, taking notes, and asking brisk, impatient questions of
Beto. I can see instantly that my construction chief has taken a dislike
to my electrical and plumbing candidate. One does not *do* brisk and
impatient with Beto Ramos Balcazar. One does not show disrespect. I
have never even switched from the formal *usted* to the familiar *tú* with
Beto, as I have with Benny and others. Efrén, finished with his inspection and alienation tour, says he is ready for a sit-down with me.

Beto has told me that, of the disbursements I have been giving him,
he has sequestered thirty thousand pesos (about three thousand dollars)
for his electrical and plumbing work beyond what has already been
paid for, and hoped to do it for less. Since Beto and I are in this
together—his budget is ours—I know the neighborhood we are prepared to pay. Efrén begins by criticizing Francisco's work, telling me
stronger cables will have to be put in, warning me that he will have to
open up walls and jackhammer cement. But he can do it, working late
and on weekends. The cost will be fifty-two thousand pesos.

I swallow hard, and walk over to Beto to see if has any new candidates, or new ideas. When he does not, I take Efrén back to our apartment and try to get him down on his price (this is not one of those
times I disdain to dicker), but when he will not budge, I sigh and say
that we will hire him. I am not looking forward to telling Beto what
Efrén has proposed. He will not find it a fair price, and fairness is essential to him. In any case, Efrén accepts and says he will call in his team
this very weekend and work until dark every day until the week is done.
I am impressed by this.

The next morning, a Saturday, I call Beto at his home and ask him
to come by the apartment before he goes to the site for a half day of

work. He shows up, and when Thia offers him coffee or orange juice, he thanks her and asks for a plain glass of water. I sit down with Beto on the back porch, and I proceed to tell him about Efrén's fee and my decision to hire him. He asks me how much the fee will be, and I tell him. He flushes red and becomes agitated.

"Señor Barry," he says, "you *cannot* let this man rob you this way!" He hits an open palm on the table. "I *hate* this about some of the people around here. They take advantage of a situation, or of a foreigner, and then *all* the *gringada* hear about it—and then all our reputations suffer!" *Gringada* is a term I have not heard used before. Although *gringo* has long since passed into casual use among expatriates, it's relatively rare that you hear a Mexican use it in a conversation with an American. It's not exactly insulting, just mildly impolite. But *gringada*—which seems to mean "every damn gringo out there"—is even rarer, and it is an indication of how worked up about this Beto is.

"But Señor Beto," I say—the conversational etiquette is getting complex, and we use the polite *señor* with each other because tempers are rising—"we don't have a choice. You know my family is coming to visit. You know my ninety-year-old father will be staying with us." This is a bit of a face-off, so it's fair for me to use my father, knowing the emotional pull that will have on Beto. "I cannot have my respected father without plumbing or electricity."

I tell him that I think we should split the extra charges Efrén will cost us—half from Beto's budgeted funds, half beyond the budget, which I will pay for. Beto digs in his heels. He says, uncharacteristically, that *he* will not pay that man a centavo beyond what he had budgeted; if I want to, that would make it my business. I stare him down. I don't believe he means it.

He doesn't. He gets up, begins pacing around, and says, "It is extortion, what that man is doing! Why, I offered Pablo twenty thousand pesos, and the only reason he did not accept is because he has other commitments." He draws himself up short. He has an idea. "I know what! I think that if we offer Pablo ten thousand pesos more to excuse himself from his other commitments, to make that great effort, I know he would come to work for us!"

I am dubious. The work-around, the improvisation this time is to leave some other home builder hanging. But I am desperate. I've thrown my aged father into the ring, why should I have scruples about other home builders? They, unlike me, probably have no Thanksgiving deadlines. They are probably used to having Mexican workers plead excuses for postponement. If not, it would be a learning experience for them, as it has been for me. It begins to sound better.

In addition, there is the personal element. If I insist on a sure thing—Efrén—we may be facing a week or more of cold war between the two men. There needs to be cooperation, and, since Francisco's departure, without leaving written plans, Beto and his crew are the only ones who know where all the bodies—the plumbing and electric lines— are buried. I am pretty certain an American management consultant would charge a hefty fee to guide me through this.

"How soon could you contact Pablo?"

"He is probably off on a job. Probably by this afternoon."

"What about Efrén?" The night before, Efrén called to say he was "importing" several workers from Tepic and was paying to put them up for the duration. He is probably preparing to go to work on the site right now.

Beto turns his palms up. My problem. His role is to throw himself on the tracks to prevent my being overcharged. If he can get Pablo to come over, his job is done. The rest is up to me.

I wait until about three o'clock, when I get a call from Beto. Pablo is willing to do it! He will come to the site tomorrow, Sunday, and assess the situation. I am relieved, and go over to the site to give Efrén the news. He takes it well. Though he has paid for some materials, and for his out-of-town workers' accommodations, when I offer him five thou- sand pesos for his time and efforts, he accepts, and we part as amigos. My little escapade has cost me a quarter of the sum this entire imbroglio is about.

When I meet with Pablo the next day, I find a blue-eyed, sandy- haired man with a soft voice and manner. Between inspection rounds, he tells me that one of his ancestors was an American, and that he is known as the Güero, the Fair One, like the fisherman who served us oysters during our outing with Armando. He seems entirely profes- sional, and modest, lacking the bravado of Efrén. Like Beto and Victor, his family is in the same trade—both his sons will be helping him. He says he can work with what's been done so far. I'm going to like him. As we come to the end of his inspection, having ticked off the dozens of fixtures, inside and out, that our Colonial circus of lights is going to require, Pablo says, "This is quite a job, bigger than I understood from Beto. Much bigger. I will have to take more time and work past dark every night to make your deadline."

He says it in such a way that I believe he is telling me the sacrifice—the time away from home, the excuses he will have to give his prior clients—is going to be considerable. His sons are going to have to miss soccer practice. I tell him I understand and that there will be a bonus for him when we finish. He nods in appreciation.

"Then let me get busy," he says. "Let's get your toilets flushing and your house lighted. You have a *lot* of lights, Señor Barry."

I tell him it will be a great day when the lights go on.

I walk back to the apartment and stop in a grocery store along the way. Thia is out with Jeanne, and I sit out on the dark porch by myself, taking a surreptitious puff of a cigarette from the pack I picked up. Damn it, they cost less than two dollars down here, and I stopped smoking years ago. I only backslide during, or after, very occasional moments of stress. I feel ashamed of myself. What was I stressing out about? It's all working out, isn't it?

CHAPTER 31

¿Mi Casa, Qué Pasa? . . .
Got Water? . . . Got Sterno?

It is now the fourth of November, and our family begins arriving in just sixteen days. Friends and neighbors have been dropping by the site, looking things over, murmuring little compliments—until we tell them we are expecting our first guests in two weeks. Their eyebrows go up, and they say, "Is that right? Two weeks?"

The front yard is a dirt lot. The pool is a cement hole; workers are just starting to lay the tile, which arrived belatedly. The palapa man hasn't shown up, so we have a pool terrace without a roof. We also have a pool equipment room lacking, as of now, any pool equipment. In the house, there are lights and fans downstairs, but nowhere else. (Pablo has found that most of the fans we bought lack expandable rods, so he and his sons are improvising from hardware store tubes.) The arches, those ancient aqueducts that will adorn our garden, have been erected, but stand there in raw, modern brick. We still have no boiler, no pressure tank, no front terrace, no driveway, and nothing on the roof except six cement pillars; the roof beams we ordered are not available. Water is not yet running, no toilet has as yet been flushed. The outside walls of the house have not been painted, nor have the walls of the hacienda fence.

The thought of turkey for Thanksgiving is beginning to have a dire, dreadful significance to me.

Beto is glowering more than usual. His five-and-a-half-month deadline is just past, and this is a man who does not like to come up short—

or long. He mutters to himself as he strides around the lot, urging his men on. Benny does not endear himself to Beto by arriving on the scene and inquiring pointedly when "Don Beto" will find it convenient to have his men finished with their outdoor work so that he and Hilda can begin planting. The *Don* is a patronymic the two maestros use with each other when they are being exquisitely, emphatically polite. Beto's curt response: when everyone else fulfills his commitments. By that, he says, more curtly, he means the carpenter, the electrician, the plumber, the air-conditioning people, the pool-tile people, the pool-equipment people, the palapa man, the wooden-beam people, and the wrought-iron man. There are a couple of things Thia and I were supposed to get on a run to Vallarta for him, and before Beto gets around to adding us to his list, I slink away.

There is another crisis looming. Two twelve-ton truckloads of furniture are arriving, one from Pátzcuaro, the other from Tonalá, and we are beginning to realize they cannot be unloaded downstairs—or, indeed, anywhere on our lot. We begin to inquire about extra space around town. At the same time, our generous apartment-for-free landlord, Flip Baldwin, has come back to town, and he will need his place back. So we will have to move . . . *now*. We spend the better part of a day transporting our summer belongings to a small inn a couple of blocks away and move in for the duration. By now we have hired Andy Mehl, a young Californian apprentice sculptor-turned-handyman, living down here with his young Mexican wife. Thia wants an English-speaking assistant for the hundreds of things she will have to do and does not want to have to struggle in Spanish-Italian. Andy begins his two-week apprenticeship with us by managing the move. But as to the furniture bearing down on us like a chugging locomotive from the interior of Mexico, it is beginning to look hopeless. There is just no place to put it.

And then a bit of good news: Eagle George has landed. He and Shirley have flown back from their Canada summer nesting ground; I recognize the tall, skinny, slightly stooped figure from afar as he approaches our front gate. In truth, he doesn't take much recognizing. George has made himself comfortable upon arrival; he is wearing cutoff shorts and no shirt. His huge blue tattooed eagle, a bit shrunken from age, flies proudly across his eighty-four-year-old pectorals.

"George!" I shout, running across to pump his hand. "We've been waiting for you to come back!" Thia has heard, and rushes up as well.

George shakes our hands, and then continues in, walking around to our dirt courtyard. He begins a slow inspection of the place, slapping the walls, kicking the columns, peering into his beloved aljibe. We arrive on the second-floor terrace and stand there with him as his thin hands grip our thin handrails.

"Well," he begins in a slow drawl, "I'd say this is A-number-one construction, youngsters. And shoot, it's gone up as fast as anything I've seen 'round here."

At last! A flat-out compliment, just what we needed to hear. No defeatist talk.

"Course," he says, "I already heard you got family coming to town for Thanksgiving. That's cuttin' things pretty durn close, isn't it?"

We go back to George's palapa, greet shy Shirley, ask about their summer, and then Thia begins pouring her heart out. They listen sympathetically.

"I know what," says George. "We have a three-car garage out back—you probably didn't even know we had it. How 'bout I move our two vee-hicles into our driveway, and you youngsters use the garage for as long as you need to?"

We fall all over ourselves in gratitude. The trucks will be arriving in a few days. Now the furniture has a safe roost at Eagle George's. We chat for a while. I ask if George has been to Rollie's for breakfast yet, a tradition for newly returned gringos.

"Nope," George says.

"Why not?"

"He might sing."

George rises to see us out. He stops to gather up his road pick from a corner, which he carries in his wiry hand. I ask him what he intends to do with it.

"Someone let the road out front get purty smooth this summer," he says. "Needs some serious unfixin'."

A week passes, and the stress level mounts. The pool tiling is just about finished, and Pablo has given us a tour of the lighting fixtures and fans, most of which work, with little quirks and peculiarities. One fan begins to whirl so fast that its neck begins to wobble, and it looks as if the whole apparatus may fly off like a downed chopper. A *detalle*, Pablo explains. But the palapa guy has not shown up, nor have the roof-beam installers, nor the air-conditioning installer, and Victor the carpenter has taken a day off.

One big success: Pablo has connected the telephone wires. I signed up for a line earlier this summer. Although it is no longer so difficult to acquire a telephone line, I took no chances and began paying for service—Internet broadband included—as of June. It is a little perverse, but late that night, amid the dust and disarray, with one of Pablo's son's twisting wires together outside the window of the den, I connect the DSL modem and find that I can reach the Internet. What I *cannot* reach is the light switch, which is not yet working, and I sit there in the dark surfing the net in my shell of a house.

The electrician and plumber down here are often the same person; as Francisco, now departed, would have been. But because Pancho is so busy with the lights, Beto's brother Luis—better known as Pulido, after a popular singer—is tying together our tubes. He seems knowledgeable and is hard working, but the labor is slow. Elsewhere, Israel the painter has finished with the interior and is now putting on the outside coat, but there is an entire house to go. No garden, no terrace, no driveway, no propane tank, no pool equipment, no running water. Well, one seatless toilet flushes. I get an image of twelve family members, including Lisa's friends, fresh from slogging about our dirt lot, lining up at the one working toilet, waiting to heat slices of turkey over a can of burning Sterno, then dashing off to use the high-speed modem to send I-told-you-so emails to the rest of the family. Do they *have* Sterno in Mexico? Am I finally losing it?

The palapa guy, another smoothie named Eduardo, arrives to say that he showed up a week earlier, but, not finding anyone here, decided he must have had the date wrong. The site has been crawling with people from dawn to dusk every day, and I am facing another example of an excuse so blatantly disprovable that this time I do not bother to refute it. I just wave him in the gate, point tiredly at the corner of the pool where it is supposed to be constructed, and tell him to have at it.

The furniture arrives on November 11. Govany and a couple of the workers pitch in and spend the morning lifting boxes and bureaus and bed platforms and tables and twenty pieces of equipale from the trucks into Eagle George's garage. We, who had so simplified our material lives in the States, have now filled an enormous space with new *stuff,* a good portion of which will not be expected to survive five years in this climate. Still, it is a momentary thrill to see the carved headboards and the Aztec table poking out of their wrapping paper. Eagle George pays his garage a visit and pokes around, looking around at the visible furniture. "You've got some A-number-one carvings here," he says. George knows how to ease pain and suffering.

For a couple of more days, progress seems to inch ahead. At this point, we are no longer welcoming any onlookers, not since the last woman showed up ("Guests in *four* days? Are you sure?"). Electricity is now mostly flowing, as is the water; Pulido appears to know what he is doing. Thia is still making her daily trips to Puerto Vallarta, returning to the inn exhausted but summoning up the energy at night to plan her furnish-and-decorate campaign. The boiler has finally arrived but is not connecting properly. The propane tank has arrived but is not connecting properly. Victor has removed the main doors, and he and his brothers are sanding and oiling them, while Beto fumes because the interior was supposed to be clear of workers by now.

It is time to move the *stuff.* Govany and his fellows spend an afternoon finally clearing George's garage, lugging our furniture and cartons into rooms designated by Thia, who is now sputtering directions entirely in Italian. *"Govany, non cada quella scatola!"* Govany, living up to the name his parents gave him—they liked the Italian sound of it— deduces that Thia is begging him not to drop the box, which happens to contain our prize Catrina.

A decision has finally been made about the arches. Benny, as the house's exterior architect, began to show Chava how to chip away at the stucco on the arches to make them look ancient. He explained to him that they should look as if "horse-drawn carriages had scraped against the edges," and time and age had done the rest. Chava dutifully chipped away in the even, perfect patterns he has been trained in, and the arches now look like aqueducts imprinted with Frisbee indentations. Benny says not to worry, he will come up with something.

I have been, humiliatingly enough, sneaking more cigarettes, going behind my new house to smoke surreptitiously, as I used to when I was a teenager. The evening before we are scheduled to move into the house to sleep, I duck behind the house again for a quick one and am shocked to discover Thia there. She is leaning against the unconnected boiler, puffing guiltily on a cigarette—her old brand. She admits that she bought a pack as well, stubs out the butt against the unpainted wall, and says she does not want to discuss it.

On November 15 we check out of the inn and bring our clothes and toilet articles over to the house. As I trudge, trash-bag laden, through the dirt that Benny has promised us will be glistening grass in just two more days, I think to myself that this should be a special moment—we are actually *moving into our new house!* But the thought winks out as I hear Thia give a shriek upstairs; I lope up the staircase to see what, now. She has unwrapped one set of new sheets to lay them on our new bed, which is framed by our fancy headboard (with a really terrific set of initials carved upon it). She is pointing at the sheets in horror. The wood headboard and bed platform were treated with diesel oil and chapopote, the traditional termite resistant for pine. Which is fine, except that now Thia's new sheets are streaked dark brown with diesel oil and chapopote. They were supposed to have dried weeks ago.

We stay up most of our first night, wiping down the beds and headboards with rags, and at last fall asleep on the diesel-stained sheets, too tired to find fresh ones, pulling our new, multi-hued Pátzcuaro bedspreads over us, alone at last in our dream house by the sea.

I get up before the workers arrive, and I make my way into our bathroom which Thia has fringed in bright Mexican tiles. I turn on the tap and find that there is no water in the sink—or the shower, or the toilet tank. Maybe it is because Pulido has arrived early and is running a test of the pipes. I go downstairs in yesterday's shorts and find that no tests are being made. I look into the aljibe, the cistern that is supposed to keep us independent of town water, and find it empty. I run up to the roof and point a flashlight into the reserve tinaco. Also empty. I run back downstairs and out the gate to George's house.

He is an early riser, too. I ask him if he has any water.

"Nope, whole town's out," he says. "My compadre Vicente Pérez came over to tell me they hit a main while they were repairing last night. Could take two, three days." He begins to tell me that he has

lived through water cutoffs of two and three *weeks*. This morning I am
in no mood for old-time stories.

I reel back to our house. I tell Thia, just awakening, only that the
house is out of water and that a solution will be found. I choose not to
say anything about the town water. Thia is running on close to empty
herself. I summon up an image of my twelve family members, now no
longer waiting to use a single toilet, no longer just heating turkey slices
on their Sterno cans, but standing or squatting behind a tree—that is,
if we had any planted—then trooping indoors to wash dirty faces and
hands in the trickle from our single container of tightly rationed bottled water. I duck behind the house to have my first cigarette of the day.
It is going to be a long one.

CHAPTER 32

I Improvise . . . I Pay Out . . . I Hit the Wall

By eight o'clock on the morning of water cutoff, I have come up with a plan, my own improvisation. I remember that on the days when the town water goes out, there is a large tank truck I have seen rumbling around. It is a water truck, and I have heard that it can be expensive, but it is how the well-off gringos keep their homes hydrated at such times. Though I have never had to use it, and do not know how to find their number, I determine to track and intercept it.

I go outside, and about a half hour later, I hear the metallic rumble of a truck, catch sight of the large tank vehicle coming down the road, and flag it down. On the spot, I ask the driver to fill our aljibe. He follows me around the house, peers into the cistern, and whistles.

"It's big. You want it filled?"

"Filled," I say.

He tells me it will be at least fifteen hundred pesos, in cash, and I agree. Ten minutes later, his thick hose is lying across our rear (unfinished) terrace and is discharging water into our cistern. I am exceedingly pleased with myself. The cistern will take care of eight people for a week. Now all I have to worry about is the pool. The family is spending a lot of money to fly down here, and would be very disappointed to be unable to swim. They could go to the ocean, of course, but my father can not take the beach.

I ask the water-truck man how much it would cost to fill our pool.

He follows me to the empty tiled hole in our front yard, looks it over, and whistles.

"It's big. You want it filled?"

I ask how much. He tells me three thousand pesos, minimum. I make a deal for him to return tomorrow, when I have made clear to Beto that the pool equipment *must* be in. I am nervous that other gringos will make similar deals with him if the water cutoff persists. I am morally certain that our pool water is more crucial—on this important ceremonial occasion—than someone else's bath, shower, or toilet water. So I offer him a bonus to make certain he reserves enough for our house. He agrees, apparently agreeing with my moral stance. There may be a special devil god worshipped by the Aztecs that is waiting for me over this one.

The next day is T-minus forty-eight hours and counting. For the last several days, Beto has been spending less time, not more, on site. I don't like it, but I understand it. He has a new commission for a gringo house in San Pancho and has to spend some time there with his new owners. A contractor can keep his team working only as long as he has a commission, and there cannot be any dead time between an old and a new job; the team has to feed its families. But it means all the last-minute decisions must be made by Thia and me, neophytes who have never built a house before. An army of workers arrives, disperses to all parts of the property, and there is no letup for us for the rest of the morning.

You cannot choose your timing in life. It happens that I've been emailing an old publishing colleague about our plans after the house is finished. Out of the blue, my friend has announced that he is launching a New York–based travel website, and that I might be the right person to launch it for him. With my fresh appreciation of the state of our finances, it may be a lifeline. I am being asked to come up with a detailed plan for the site—and if I am to stay in the running, my outline is due today. Surreally, I take an hour this morning to finish it off at the computer. While sitting on an upended crate, I type out a proposal for an online array of luxury travel destinations. Every few minutes I have to stop to answer the latest in the flood of workers' questions, or to hand out money for some new appliance or material, then turn back to the screen to write about yacht charters, as cement dust and dirt swirl in through the open window.

By noon, giddy, I go up to the terrace to take a look around. Behind me, in the second-floor living area, Thia is in a frenzy, pushing furniture from one side of the room to another, at the same time working with Andy to hang Victoriano's huge pelican-and-coastline masterpiece. Down below, across the courtyard, this is what I see:

In one corner of the lot, Eduardo and his men are atop the pool cabana structure, finishing the palapa, fastening old palm leaves to the wooden poles that straddle the wall. One of the palaperos, sitting on the dry leaves, is tying off rope with a lit cigar in his mouth. Just beneath, a couple of men are carrying in the pool filter assembly. The equipment has at last arrived. By the far wall, Chava is finishing a pressure wash of the cantera tile terrace that was finished the day before. At the left corner of the lot, a large hose is snaked over the top of the wall and is dangling in the pool, whose tiling was finished a couple of days ago. Water is pouring in. The town water is still off. The bonus has been paid. We are going to be safe and moist in every available container.

Directly below me, four men are hauling a large date palm into place, as Benny and Hilda direct their work. Already, the garden section along the side wall has been planted with striking specimens: croton, ixora, copa de oro, and an assortment of ficus trees. As I became more stressed, Benny has reassured me that they could create the entire garden in two days—*one* day, if it came to that. If the grass is laid tomorrow, as promised, Benny will have been as good as his word.

Coming from the back of the house is the air-conditioning fellow, who has just now made the final connections and looks up at me with a nod. He—among others—is looking to be paid. Against one wall, screwing a lantern into one of our brick columns, are faithful Pablo and his two sons, who have indeed finished with the interior lights. Next to him, Pancho, making a final adjustment on the new sliding front gates. Beyond him is Roberto, picking up debris from the driveway, which was laid out and finished just yesterday, including a large, inlaid C and G in rose *cantera*, which I ordered when Thia was very, very tired.

Surrounding one of the arches in the fast-appearing garden are four men I have not met. They are hacking away at the aqueducts with chisels; one man is daubing paint on them. Benny walked in late the day before to tell me he had an inspiration. He is an old friend of Ropi, the local artist and muralist who uses just his first name. Ropi designed Hamaca, the elegant crafts shop, and, more recently, Raintree, the town's first nod to upscale dining. Benny happened to see Ropi on the street in Sayulita, and has enlisted him. Ropi owed Benny a favor, in the Mexican style. Now he is paying it off by doing a crash chip-and-paint job on our arches. I know that Ropi was once described by a Guadalajara art critic as Mexico's most celebrated unknown muralist since Diego Rivera. Out of the blue, we have a famous artist finishing our arches. Benny instructed him, "Make them look like we *found* them here, crumbling away, and we decided to build the house around them." As I look down now, Ropi, wearing a red shirt spattered with bright oil-paint colors, waves up at me. *"Antigüedad!"* he yells up. Antique!

As I finish my visual survey, I am flooded with a tingling, unexpected feeling of anticipation, the opposite of the heavy dread I have experienced these past two weeks. I feel, for the first time, that the impossible might indeed take place: we could pull this off. We could lurch our way to finishing this house in time for my family's arrival. No need for Sterno. No squatting behind trees. No rationing bottled water.

There is a glug sound from below. I glance down to see that the water-tank guy has finished filling the pool and is drawing up his giant hose. I am immensely satisfied. It was expensive—almost five hundred dollars—but now, even if the water cutoff goes on for a week, our first guests will be able to use the toilet *and* swim. I am happy to say that on this occasion I have been farsighted and resourceful.

I hear a voice from below.

"Señor Barry!" I look down. It is Pulido, looking up from a crouch. He is by one of the taps coming out from the wall. "The town water is back on!"

I am hardly fazed by the thought of what I have just paid out. Today, I know, as work begins to come to an end, most of our major construction fees will be coming due. The half-down deposits are about to turn into fully paid payouts. Because I am needed on site for my translation services, Thia must continue her daily drives into Vallarta. Today she must buy hinges, knobs, fasteners, a pump connector, more tiles, some handles, galvanized wire, a vacuum cleaner, porcelain hooks, and, in yet another nod to this house's plumbing idiosyncrasies, toilet seats.

It appears that in her enthusiasm to get toilets whose color matched the bathtubs, Thia neglected to ask if seats would be available for the models she chose. Yes, she was told, plastic seats. But, she had asked the local ceramics man, was it not true that in this sticky climate plastic seats tended to—and this she had to pantomime—adhere to one's bottom when rising from one's business? Would not a wooden seat serve better? *¡Cómo no!* the ceramics man nodded. Of course! Were any available in Sayulita? *¡Ah, no!* the ceramics man said.

So Thia has set off twice to Puerto Vallarta to hunt down wooden seats, our toilet tank lids rattling in the cargo hold for color matching. She finally tracked a few down deep inside a factory in Puerto Vallarta, where she attempted to further refine her search by inquiring whether they had seats for elongated oval toilet bowls, her preference. She explained in her Rome-inflected Spanish that such bowls were more sanitary, as they improved men's aim. The factory clerk, a helpful woman, inquired sweetly whether her husband had a problem. Thia pressed ahead and ordered seats specially made for our toilet bowls. As she was telling me about it later, I reflected that my wife, lately acting out the splatter effect of toilet bowls to a clerk in a Mexican factory, had not so long ago been hosting dinner parties in Manhattan.

Today, besides collecting the seats, her final errand in town is to stop at Lloyd's and pick up a check for $12,000 from Rosie, which she then will have to cash for a little over 130,000 pesos. Four hours later, dragging, she returns to the house. The toilet seats were not ready. But she has brought home the bills wrapped in little paper bands, stuffed far down into her purse. Feeling like a drug runner, she tells me she nearly froze passing by the soldiers at the checkpoint as she drove home. The trip has done nothing to lessen her increasingly jangled state of near-nervous exhaustion.

I am not much better. Unshaven, my Villa mustache wildly overgrown, I continue to try to grab some time at the computer, juggling the travel site proposal, the email logistics of our family arrivals, and the unending construction decisions that follow a shout of "Señor Barry! *Aquí, por favor!*" Though it hardly bears saying, during one of my swings between luxury-travel descriptions on the computer and going up to approve Pablo's use of a cardboard tube for a recalcitrant fan, it strikes me that this has turned into an extremely *active* retirement.

By afternoon, it is time to start settling accounts. I have the wad of pesos in a large Cheetos bag and have set up a pay station on the edge of the aljibe. The air-conditioning guy presents an invoice for 18,000 pesos, which I count out. The pool-equipment guys asks for 12,000 pesos, which I count out. Sonia, our accountant, needs 36,000 pesos for social security, which I count out. Pancho the wrought-iron man shows up, and his is a hefty bill: 24,000, which includes the extra ironwork he is certain I remember. I do, but vaguely, and count it out. Then comes Victor the carpenter, with the last portion of the bill that flattened our three-story house: we owe him 40,000 pesos, plus a thousand more for the hinges, which he is certain I remember saying I would pay for. I do not, but I am past negotiating. I am past asking for receipts. Indeed, I am almost out of cash altogether, and an image rises up of me skipping around my property, tossing peso bills around like confetti, calling out, "Hey, want some? *Take* it!"

I pull myself together and go down to give special thanks to Pablo, who has spent all those long overtime hours splicing wires on our behalf. He acknowledges it, mentioning that every morning he has to pass one of the projects he begged off on for us; he says he slides down beneath his steering wheel as he drives past. Pablo appreciates my thanks, but says diffidently that he is ready to be paid. I tell him I am sorry, he will have to wait until tomorrow, when Thia will have to make another trip into Vallarta. When he says apologetically that he expected to be paid today and is short of cash, I show him the empty Cheetos bag to show him that I am, too. I call over Beto, who has come back for a short afternoon look-see. I ask him if he has any money. He pulls out a one-thousand-peso note, and I borrow it from him, and hand it over to Pablo.

"Thanks for the loan, Beto," I say.

"Don't thank me," he says. "I won't have good news for you when we settle up." He says this with no satisfaction at all; he sounds, in fact, down.

Thia and I spend the evening hanging, banging, stretching, hooking, positioning, repositioning, drilling, yanking, nearly snapping. We get a visit from Cheryl, who leaves her marble-floored beach manor to volunteer as our bedspread laundress. Alone later that night, Thia and I have some good moments as the wrapping comes off the tapestries, and baskets, and dishes, and glassware. We have some less-good moments when the wrapping—and several skeleton arms and fingers—come off the Catrinas. It turns out toilet paper is overrated as a secure repository for dead dolls. But, thank the gods, Señorita Gala, our Juan Torres Catrina, is her saucy self, unblemished and unscathed.

In fact, as I drop off to sleep at four in the morning, Thia is still up, grasping one of her new Talavera cups filled with steaming coffee. She is chattering to herself animatedly and unintelligibly, and I do not take it as a good sign. When I wake up a few hours later, she is still up on a stepladder at one of our high niches, moving the big porcelain pineapple she got at the Pátzcuaro market an inch this way, an inch that way, speaking to it like a dog she is trying to train.

On this, our final day before the Thanksgiving arrivals, the grass turf is to be laid. Benny and Hilda have also brought along two round cement ponds to be placed near the courtyard and filled with water lilies and small fish. We had approved the lily ponds, but had nearly forgotten. "These are goo-pees," Hilda explains of the guppies she has brought in a plastic water bag, "and they will eat mosquitoes for you." Behind the pool and the aqueduct that arches halfway over it, is the "secret garden" they have promised Thia. We have bought a lovely cantera fish fountain for the corner, which will be shielded by flowering vines. It should be a garden spot for quiet repose, and I am enchanted as it all takes shape before my weary eyes. Benny *said* they could get it all done in a day if need be. And I did not believe him, I of little faith.

Meanwhile, his buddy Ropi is finishing up with the arches. They are now an antique terracotta umber, expertly carriage chipped and sponge painted to look four hundred years old if they are a day. (Which of course they are.) Ropi, wild-haired, orange-stained, wiping his brow, takes me aside. He has an artist's temperament and is given to grand gestures. Out of earshot of Benny, he grips me by the shoulder.

"This man did me a favor," he says. "I will *never* forget it. When my son was sick ten years ago, I had no cash. Benedicto gave me a thousand pesos for the doctor and never asked for it back." He shakes my shoulder. "A real man always repays his debts! I will never forget it." He looks over his shoulder at Benny. Benny has told me that this commission was between the two of them; I should not pay Ropi anything. "Of course," Ropi says confidentially, "you could pay me something for my workers," meaning the two or three apprentices who have chipped away these last few days. I hand him three thousand pesos and agree not to tell Benny. Having a major artist paint your arches in umber because of a Mexican debt of honor—cheap at any price.

As he is walking away, I say to him, "You could come back and sign the arch, if you like."

He grins and says, "I will do that. And I will write the date, too." He laughs, and shouts, "1652!"

By now Thia has returned from Vallarta with yet another bushel of bills, and—in the nick of time—the toilet seats. Though I know she is stretched as thin as a Catrina, she joins me for a few moments to watch our instant garden take root. She begins to sniffle as the bougainvillea is planted along the boxes at the top of the arches and as birds of paradise are set along the borders of her secret garden. Hilda is busily directing her workers, and Benny is positioning his ample self in one chair setting after another, gazing at his work. Benny gets up and signals for his workers to carry in his pièces de résistance: a pair of large square mirrors with iron grillwork soldered over them. He told us it is his best inspiration, and we're going along with it. He has his workers attach them to two sections on the inside of our perimeter wall, one inside the secret garden, one just beyond. The effect is striking, reflecting lush greenery or the pool's teal-blue water, depending on the angle of view, extending the horizon of the garden.

Pulido has just announced that the pool filter is working, so he and Benny and I go into the equipment room to study the valves and handles. Our main reason for doing this is a guy thing: as long planned in Benny's original sketch at Choco Banana, we built into the arch a recirculating tube that feeds water from the pool up through the arch and out a spout. The three of us men—Barry, the frazzled American owner, Benny, the Mexican architect, and Pulido, the loyal Bucerias plumber— watch our boy's electric train start off: the pump takes hold, sends water through its trestle to an ancient aqueduct, and from there to its terminus in the air, *chug-a-lug,* into a teal-blue pool. So cool!

The garden and lawn are embedded by the middle of the afternoon. Benny stands back, takes a sip from his oversized coffee mug, and gets off a practiced line: "Architects and doctors hide their mistakes the same way—with flowers." Hilda gives us instructions on how often to water the grass and the plants. Thia and I take a moment with our landscape wizards to thank them. The four of us embrace, and Benny turns to me and says, "Señor 'Worry.' Did I not tell you it would all work out?"

"¿*Yo?* Worry?"

* * *

Most of Beto's men have drifted away in the past couple of days, as the construction on the house was being finished, and we did not even get the chance to thank all of them individually. Only Govany, Chava, Pulido—still adjusting the plumbing—and Israel the painter are still around. Thia and I have plans to see the whole crew one last time, but for now it is just these few and Beto, who has asked that we find a quiet place to talk at the end of the day.

Beto and I sit on the edge of one of Hilda's planters. His face is dark, his mouth drawn.

"I hate, I *hate* to say this, but you should cash another check for one hundred thousand pesos. I have not worked out all the expenses yet, but I wanted to warn you."

I nod gravely, taking it in. It's all I can do. If true, it will take us to the very brink of our resources. "All right," I say. "let's talk about it and settle up. When?"

"In several days. I know your family will be here tomorrow. Why don't you have your day of thanks, and I will come by on Friday?"

We shake hands, a serious handclasp, and Beto walks out the gate.

Tonight Thia is a whirling dervish, spinning from floor to floor and room to room. She is working to bring two kitchens, two living rooms, two dining areas, a den, three bathrooms, and three and a half bedrooms up to her high level of decorating taste. She has been dreaming about it since we first sat down to plan our house. She expected to have three weeks to finish this and thought we had left enough time. Instead, she is doing it in three days. She has had almost no sleep. I have had just a bit more.

There are still, by her estimate, several thousand things left to do. It is going to be another night without sleep. We keep going, and then, suddenly, we don't. Thia is ricocheting from the extremes of crying at the sight of our new garden to resentment that I—who was supposed to manage the people we had hired—had let everything come crashing in at the same time. I am seething that the costs have ballooned and she is taking it out on me. I smash my thumb with a hammer. She lets a small pot shatter. We become churlish, then confrontational. We trade insults about competence and poor planning, follow it up with a few shouts about being fed up with both this country and each other. A couple of well-made parota doors experience their first full slamming.

Sitting in the den alone, plotting further revenge, I am not surprised to see her throw open the door for one last burst at me. She stands there, trembling with rage. We are both over the edge into hysteria. She points a finger at me and begins shaking it. I expect a final torrent about our rotten life, the holiday I have ruined for her, my shortcomings as a man. She says, "And worst of all! You're lower than the lowest! You've sunk to the bottom. You—*you stole the last cigarette I had out of my pack*!"

She is right. We *have* sunk to the bottom.

CHAPTER 33

An Official Visit . . .
The Family Arrives . . . A Toast and Wine

Thanksgiving week is a time for family and the warmth of reunion. Thia and I awake Monday morning giving each other the silent treatment. On two hour's sleep, we will have to balance our family's staggered arrivals with our need to create the illusion of a smoothly running, glittering new house in paradise. Andy is here early to put up curtain rods, and Thia and I communicate mainly through him.

I spend the morning checking that the water is indeed running in the bathrooms and sinks, flicking lights and fans on and off, and puzzling through the scribbled pieces of cardboard that Pablo has left to indicate breaker locations. Thia now has domestic help. She began searching for a part-time maid now that there is a house to clean, but the town's full employment has made for a novel concept of flextime. Several women came over for enthusiastic interviews; Thia hired them, made firm dates and then did not see them again—except when they waved at her cheerily in town as they passed by. Finally, she has found Esmeralda, a serious woman with the flat, handsome face of a Mayan totem, who has in fact come in the past couple of mornings within an hour or two of her appointed time. Good enough. No punch clocks here, God knows. Today she is helping to scrub down and sweep the interior of the house. It was swept out by Beto's crew two days ago, but dust has already settled everywhere.

The family is supposed to arrive this afternoon on flights from Oregon and California. My sister, Michele, and husband, Tom, from Washington, flew to Guadalajara a couple of days ago and rented a car, so they will be driving here on their own. The rest need pickups at the airport, forty minutes away. To give us a little space the first few days, my father and Bernadette have taken advantage of their time-share network to stay at a hotel in Puerto Vallarta, and they will need to be driven back and forth each day. My brother, Chris, and Kit will be flying in several hours later.

A couple of days earlier, from my dark perch at the computer, I emailed my father with the suggestion that they take a cab to their nearby hotel; that I would then drive in to pick everyone up at the same time. But my father is bringing us a special treat—a cured Oregon ham he and Bernadette found for us—and is concerned about keeping it refrigerated. Could I drive to the airport to pick up the ham and find refrigeration for it before making my other pickups? I am a dutiful son. I like ham as well as anyone. But I gently suggest that there are matters more pressing than ham that I must attend to, and that perhaps his hotel could stick the ham in a freezer overnight.

Having solved the ham problem, I am outside Monday morning sweeping the driveway, when two burly men in crested shirts walk up the driveway. They have serious expressions on their face; one is holding a clipboard, and the other has a piece of wide tape in his hands with some kind of printing on it. It looks like one of those yellow tapes police put up at the scene of an accident.

"Golson, Barry?" one of the men asks.

"Yes, how can I help you?"

"We are here to close down your swimming pool and back yard." He holds up the tape, which I can now see reads, *"Clausura."* Closed!

My stress level, which has lowered since last night's meltdown, shoots up.

"Why?" I say. "Who are you, and what's happened here?"

The leader, a strongly muscled hombre with a full, droopy mustache, explains that they are inspectors from the *Municipio* in Valle, the municipal seat I visited when we were obtaining our licenses. It appears that our plans did not include the swimming pool, and so no permit for it exists; the necessary fees were not paid. Our pool and the surrounding area will have to be cordoned off, and we will not be allowed to use it.

I politely protest that all our papers are in order. He points to a document on the clipboard, written in Spanish legalese, none of which I can understand—except for the word *clausura*. I tell him a mistake was made and ask if it is not usual to at least give a home owner a little advance warning and give him a chance to rectify it. Droopy Mustache says that he and his partner came by last week and handed just such a warning to one of our workers.

So there it is. How nice: my family will arrive to find that our garden and pool have been roped off as a crime scene.

It is again unsettling. Mexican enforcement, when it occurs, has a blunt directness that can be alarming to a foreigner. Like nonpayment for phone service or electricity, infractions are handled firmly, by shutting off access. But it is also understandable: a letter or a phone call would be more genteel, but where phone service is not universal, and postal service erratic, direct action gets a miscreant's attention.

I go into damage-control mode. I tell Droopy Mustache that the worker never gave me the warning and that my entire family is arriving in a few hours. I tell him that we will be celebrating the American day of thanks; is he familiar with it? No? Time for the heavy artillery. I tell him with a stricken look that my aged father, my very respected father, is coming down for the week, and he needs to be able to bathe his body for medical reasons—I even manage to come up with the word *hidroterapia*. Is it possible to postpone their clausura until I can contact the proper authorities and pay what I failed to pay?

Droopy mustache rubs his chin and looks at his partner, who shrugs.

"All right," he says. "I have a father too. We will give you two more days. But you must get the proper documents and post them on the outside of your house to avoid clausura."

Not a bad guy, Droopy. I thank him. They leave, and I go back inside to consider the next step. I recall now that when we made our permit application, we omitted mention of the pool to avoid environmental red flags. It is a perfectly legal pool, there are no restrictions against having one. At the time, we were simply doing a work-around. But we did not follow up later and modify our building permit, which requires fees based on the total number of square meters of construction, pool most definitely included.

I have to drive to Vallarta on airport duty. Someone else is going to have to step up to this. I make a telephone call and explain the situation. Twenty minutes later, arriving in his red pickup, our rescuer alights. Doffing his wide-brimmed hat, with his familiar sardonic smile, he says, "Aurelio Carrillo, su servidor."

As expected, Aurelio has the answer. There has been an election at the Municipio, and the new officials have reviewed all the most recent building plans. The treasury needs replenishing at the start of a new term, and this is a traditional opportunity for the local government to get off to a fresh fiduciary start. It will not be a problem, Aurelio says. He can drive to Valle, with the proper funding from me, of course, and straighten it out. As it happens, he says, a cousin of his has been elected to office, and he may be able to expedite things. Properly, of course.

I tell Aurelio that he is a good man to have in one's life, hand him a wad of my confetti from the Cheetos bag—five thousand pesos' worth— and he marches off with a snap of his hat.

Thia and I are speaking again, though many of her sentences are staccato and disconnected. She is still not far from the edge. I remind her that Michele and Tom should be arriving sometime after noon, but that the driving time from Guadalajara is uncertain, and it could be later. She certainly has enough time to finish the bedrooms and the den, which are still not up to her satisfaction, while I make sure everything has been picked up in the garden.

"Good. Go. Garden," she says, and disappears into the bedroom, caroming off the door frame.

Michele and Tom arrive a little after eleven that morning. I know this because I hear Tom's voice calling out the only two words of Spanish he knows.

"*Buenos nachos,* kids!"

They are *early*. Clearly they have no concept of Mexican time. (Beto's time, always, excluded.) Thia pokes her head out of the bedroom door, shoots me a hateful stare—it's my fault, I bungled the timing again— and we head out to meet them.

We hug Michele and Tom. We bring them around to the front door, lead them into the living room, which opens onto the garden and—

For the first time, I see our new house.

Through my sister's cries and whoops, through Tom's "whoa" and whistles, I see, in their eyes, what the year has wrought. Past the living room equipale couch, past the Aztec wooden table, in the sunlit open courtyard, a fresh lawn stretches around a lily pond to the pool, above which an old arch stands, with a stream of water pouring from its spout. A palm tree bows over the water, and there is a silver glimmer on the perimeter wall—a window, no, a mirror!—and a stand of colored vines shields what looks to be a small stone fountain. Is that a secret garden? All of it is framed, left and right, by the eaves of the red-tile roof slanting over the courtyard.

Leaning on me, knees wobbly, Thia lets herself go for a moment, taking it in.

The scene is repeated, with regional variations and accents, as the other members of the family arrive and take their turn coming in the front door: my brother Chris, toting a shiny new mammoth-lensed camera, clicking away as he walks in; Kit looking around with her blue eyes and her mouth open wide; Bernadette putting down her carry-on and clasping her hands in front of her; and my father, wheeling a small bag behind him (the ham, I believe) with one hand and a walking cane in the other, shaking his head with a smile, not expecting this.

Neither did we, frankly.

Looking ahead to this week, I imagined any number of scenes where the quirks and crannies of our new house would produce all manner of humorous little catastrophes. Of course, I would laugh when the lights shut off. This is the *fun* of being in Mexico—let's all light candles! Toilet overflowing? Just *look* how easy it is to mop up on this nice new tile. Window off its hinges? Don't even need to close it—this is the tropics! I had good reason to let my imagination run in this direction; there was every indication from the recent pandemonium that the week would be rich in calamities.

But none of these comes to pass. Incredibly, improbably, the house has come together and . . . holds. It works. It runs. Current and fluid course through its arteries, and the roof and walls shelter its new residents with professionalism and aplomb. In the next several days, my family eats and sleeps and brushes its teeth and cooks its meals and jumps in the pool and sits looking at the lanterns on the wall posts— *all on the dirt-filled lot with the chalk lines on it.* It is, I imagine, an excellent feeling to see a house that you have overseen go up in the States.

But I do not think the sense of wonder can be the same as it is here, watching your inspiration take shape, brick by hand-laid brick, from a dirt pile to a sturdy, gleaming hacienda in the sun.

For our first night, we have asked Conny down the street to cook for us. Conny will come to your house, but she prefers to cook at her own stove, so I walk down with Tom to pick up the dinner for eight that she has prepared. Crowded around our table in the open air, we dine on Conny's guacamole, corn tortillas, enchiladas, lemon chicken, and a great vegetable soup. It is a blessing that Thia does not have to cook. After a piece of the flan pie Conny has prepared, my wife staggers off to bed for her first full night's sleep in a week. She even pecks me on the cheek, resentment receded, not extinct.

The rest of us take a walk through the village, then we stay up to listen to a couple of my father's stories about his mining days in northern Mexico. Though he has trouble walking and has to read lips to help his hearing, my father's mind and memory are machete-sharp. He still lectures on history several times a week to senior groups in Oregon. Brother Chris, who is managing his own transition from tech executive to what he hopes will be a late career in photography, is busy taking candid shots, ordering us to pose against one or another of our Pátzcuaro prizes. Tom and the women try out the equipale easy chairs and couches, and Kit helpfully starts gluing fingers and hands back on our Catrina dolls.

Everyone goes to sleep tonight with their windows open.

The next day, Aurelio shows up, smiling his old smile, and hands me a sheet of paper with a bouquet of official stamps on it. It says our fees are now paid and "beseeches" those charged with enforcement to lift the clausura. I introduce him around as Maestro Aurelio and sit down to ask him what happened. He say there was nothing to it; not only was his cousin willing to help move things along, but his wife's brother-in-law now holds a post in the Municipio. I offer him a drink, give him a tour of the furnished house, and he is properly effusive. He leaves, reminding me that I must post the letter on our front gate to ward off further official visits.

After a couple of days of ferrying my father and Bernadette back and forth, they agree they will be more comfortable in our home, even if it is a little crowded. I get the feeling that they took the time-share hotel room not merely to give us more space, but because they wondered if our house would be ready. I take it as a quiet victory that, now that they've seen Casa Gala in all her down-to-the-wire glory, they are happy to make the move.

Thia, refreshed and once more cogent, is back to her enthusiastic self, beaming as our guests frolic in the pool, start up a game of tooth-pick poker, or lie on our Tonalá-bought beach chairs. She enlists Tom to help squeeze a huge pile of fresh oranges on our authentic native pull-down squeezer. (She recalls that at Rollie's, the women staff refused to use an electric squeezer.) In a few minutes, Americans that they are, Thia and Tom have come up with a new, improved system to increase productivity. While Mexican women at their street stands are content to squeeze oranges in the same, unvarying time-honored way, here an assembly line is established: Thia hands Tom an orange half; he pulls down the handle to squeeze it; she reaches in to spin the half to a dif-ferent position; Tom whomps down again to get added juice; then Thia tosses the first half and slips in a second; repeat and squeeze. Good old American know-how in Mexico. It probably saves a couple of seconds overall, and there's an extra quarter-glass of juice to boot. ¡Qué bueno!

The turkey is in the downstairs fridge. The upstairs fridge, of course, is devoted entirely to the ham. On Thanksgiving Day, Kit's daughter, Lisa, drives over from her hotel in Puerto Vallarta with three of her women friends, all in their thirties. It makes for a noisy, spirited atmo-sphere. Thia and Bernadette put the turkey into our new oven and set the heat to four. Thia has learned from the Mexican hot-water system that one is hottest and five is just warm. As we all know, a turkey must be cooked in low heat for eight hours. An hour later, Thia opens the oven, and the turkey is dark brown. In Mexico, the stove settings, it turns out, are opposite from the hot water settings. Thia grimaces, but the turkey looks all right to me. (At our poker game, Doc Forbis, who is now more Mexican than American, greets our plans for turkey with, "Oh, eating ethnic, eh?") Kit makes her southern stuffing, Chris has brought cranberry sauce, Jeanne has sent over twelve servings of choco-late mousse from the restaurant. Dad presides at the table, and at the proper moment, he lifts a glass of the French wine he has brought and offers a toast.

"I propose we give thanks for the completion of this elegant house and its beautiful garden, which just six months ago was dirt and shrubs. I give particular thanks that the crabs were not here to greet us. So let us drink to our family and to the future of this house in the Mexican way: *¡Que viva la Casa Gala!*"

We drink toasts as well to our missing family in El Norte: our two sons, so recently exposed to Mexico's pull; my youngest brother, Geoff, born in Mexico, but unable to get away; and Thia's sisters and brother and their respective families. I look across the Aztec table at my father, who brought us to Mexico fifty years ago, and I think of his being spirited out of Mexico in my grandmother's belly, on my grandfather's stagecoach, in the mountains of Chihuahua. I see my red-haired brother, also born in Mexico City, and my sister, who grew up with me in the hills above Chapultepec. I see my wife—my partner and ultimate good sport—who left New York City to become a waitress in a small town in Nayarit, had to struggle every day to make herself understood, and shared our folly almost to the breaking point.

I lean back in our tufted equipale chair, and take a sip of wine. Time has rarely seemed more fully rounded, or a circle more complete. In a word, I give thanks.

CHAPTER 34

Beto's Bill . . .
Three Fiestas . . . A Waltz

In the days following Thanksgiving, most people have turkey leftovers. Our turkey was only eighteen pounds, the biggest we could buy here, so there was just enough for our family dinner. We did, however, eat ham for a week: baked ham, fried ham, ham sandwiches, ham salad. When first Chris and Kit, then Michele and Tom, and then Dad and Bernadette left for the States, I felt a sadness, wondering if Dad would ever be down here again. And an emptiness, a sapping of adrenaline, like old rock-and-roll stars must feel when the concert at the end of their tour is over.

The day after my family leaves, Beto drives over in his white pickup. I show him into the living area and stand back to get his reaction to the way his house has been furnished and decorated. I do not expect anything flowery from Beto, not about decor, and I am right. He says, "So much furniture! You know the old saying: leave enough room between the chairs for a husband to get away." I do not know the old saying and am mildly surprised at his risqué remark. It is Beto's way of being breezy, and perhaps covering for an awkward moment I have created. I am not unaware that his own home is, by Govany's description, extremely spare and modest. There were one or two times when I offered to come by his house in Bucerias on some construction matter, and he always insisted he would come to us.

We go into the den, and I close the doors behind us.

We sit down and chat a bit about the little fiesta Thia and I want to have for his men. We would like them to come by after work at their new job in San Pancho, and share some food and drink with us. It is Thia's idea that we ask the men to bring their wives, girlfriends, and kids. We would like them to see the finished work their husbands and fathers have done. Beto nods appreciatively, but his mind is on other things.

He furrows his brow. He takes out his Daffy Duck notebook, opens it, and goes over his payroll expenses for the three weeks over deadline, and those of the unbudgeted construction in the garden and on the roof. He points to each expense item with his finger, explaining what it is for. There are no receipts, nor do I ask for any. We are past that, Beto and I.

"Once we pay for these," he says, "I will be even."

"You mean you have nothing left over for yourself? No profit at all beyond what you took out during the year?"

"That's the way it is."

I touch his shoulder. "Look, Beto," I say. "These cost overruns weren't your fault or mine; we have to share this problem. And I never intended for you not to make a profit from this. That's not right."

I am giving him an opportunity to tell me that it would be fine with him if I added a reasonable markup for him, and how much.

He is not about to say that. He says that he gave me an estimate and went over it, and he feels badly enough that it is going to cost me the extra hundred thousand pesos he estimated a few days earlier. He is clearly feeling some pain. I point out that in his original estimate, he had warned that he was figuring it at 90 percent, more or less. So it turned out to be more, I say. These things happen. And as I say it, I realize that I am the one consoling him, and am urging him to rationalize it to his benefit. Beto always *does* turn things upside down.

"I would not be happy knowing you haven't made a profit, Beto," I say.

He gives me a slightly lopsided grin. "Well, we worked together for six months," he says. "It meant my team had full employment. They had enough to eat and bring money home to their families. They did good work. As for me, it meant doing a good enough job that more work will come along. What more can you expect from life?"

I have a catch in my throat. "But it's still not right, Beto. You did a great job for us, far beyond what we expected. I think you should include something for yourself."

Beto will not budge. He has said his piece.

I follow my conscience and pay him.

"One fiesta was hardly ended when another began," John L. Stephens, explorer and author, wrote in 1841 about his stay in a small town in Quintana Roo. It is a nice fact about Mexico that no matter what a family's finances may be, whether work has been scarce or plentiful, if a fiesta is called for—as with a dress for a quinceañera—a way will always be found to pay for it. Mexicans are the ultimate showbiz pros: the fiesta must go on. Thia and I, who have been assimilated, agree. Our cash is low, but we will still spring for the fiestas that are our solemn responsibility as new home owners in Sayulita.

First, we will have our closest friends over for a housewarming. Then we will have that fiesta for Beto and his workers. And finally, we must have a party for the town, a tradition among gringos, and throw open our gates to the curious. Following which, we will have to get *out* of town to find a way to pay for it all.

We have already begun advertising our house online, and it looks as if we will have our fill of renters. But if we ever thought rental income would be enough to live on, the toting up of the year's expenses disabuses us of that. Like many of our age group, I suspect, we will not be retiring for good right away; it's going to be an on-off thing. Indeed, it is looking as if we will have to migrate back to the States for a time and somehow earn enough dollars to be able to afford to return to Mexico. How very Mexican of us.

But first our fiesta responsibilities. We ask Rollie and Jeanne, Bill and Barb, Bruce and Maggie, Dick and Cheryl, and Mike Scannell and his wife, Connie, to join us one early December afternoon for drinks and an early dinner. This will be perhaps our first meeting with any group of people in our home that will be free of stress, decision making, or cement dust.

The women wear flowing dresses in bright colors; the men have all put on clean sandals. As a departure from our staple Mexican food, we serve camembert and hummus, available from the new deli in town. Thia places our newest icon of the Virgin of Guadalupe, Jeanne's housewarming gift (and a sweet nod to my birthday a couple of days hence) atop the armoire. There is a blues concert on our satellite radio, whose antenna is aimed at the northern sky visible above the courtyard. Every-one here has built something in Mexico, and we tell each other our best stories. Ours are not yet as practiced; it's all pretty recent and raw. We again thank Bruce and Maggie, publicly, for the pioneering work they did for us. I give a little speech saying how grateful we are to this group, for their forbearance and generosity toward the new gringos.

We turn expectantly to Rollie. As a lay minister, he is called on to bless this union or that enterprise, and he has prepared something. From his seat on the equipale couch, beneath a wall lantern, he says a few words on the friendship of those present, and about our own jour-ney to this house, with its solid, welcoming walls. But, he says, it is not the walls, but the life inside, that will endure. He predicts it will be a place of love and of laughter. Then he pulls out a copy of a well-leafed book, and reads from the *Tao Te Ching:*

> *We join spokes together in a wheel,*
> *But it is the center hole*
> *That makes the wagon move.*
> *We shape clay into a pot,*
> *But it is the emptiness inside*
> *That holds whatever we want.*
> *We hammer wood for a house,*
> *But it is the inner space*
> *That makes it livable.*
> *We work with being,*
> *But non-being is what we use.*

Although this moment with our friends is as much about a widened sense of family as about the inner spaces of a house, I think it would not have had the same meaning elsewhere. In this town, it seems, everyone is related to everyone else, and we gringos have been borne by its currents.

The second fiesta is a low-key affair. Thia and I are perhaps oversenti-mental, but we wanted to show Beto's workers what their efforts had meant to us. Some time earlier, I ordered two dozen shirts with a special logo on them. *Equipo Beto,* it read—"Beto's Team." In smaller type, *Con-*

strucciones. Nayarit. Mexico. I had found an image of two hands clasping and had it pressed on the front of the shirts, beneath *Equipo Beto.* The shirts were late—no surprise—and were not ready for the fiesta.

We also had a lunch for the men, putting off for later the bestowal of the shirts. We reserved a long table at El Costeño's on the beach. On a weekday, just after one, twenty or so men arrived from San Pancho in two pickup trucks. Alejandro, with his van Gogh hat, and silver-haired Pablo, who had disappeared from the job once the heavy construction was done, showed up. So did Chava, and Roberto, and Govany, and Hugo. Thia hoped their wives and children would attend this lunch as well, but for once we did not heed Maggie and Bruce, who doubted they would come. They were right—on this occasion. But I could still make the gesture.

I stood in my sandals on the sand, as the surf broke in the distance behind me and the men found seats around the table. I said, "You served us for six months and built our beautiful house. Now it's our turn to serve you." With that, Thia and I first brought out the beers, and then the trays of cold ceviche, warm fish soup, and tostadas that Beto told us his men prefer. I served from the wrong side, which my wife, the newly expert waitress, corrected with a hiss, and the men dug in. We hovered, dishrags over our arms, listening politely to the inside chatter around the table. Beto was in an affable mood, and even called for a shot of tequila, which he mixed with grapefruit juice. It was the first time I saw him ask for anything other than a plain glass of agua. Finally, the men asked the waiters—us—to sit with them, and we did, finding seats next to Beto. It was a boisterous meal, and several of the men took off their shoes and went wading in the surf, holding cerveza bottles.

The lunch was a success, but it does not satisfy the sentimental education we now crave. We have the shirts to dispense and have saved them for when the work is truly done. Thia still wants to make the grand gesture: to persuade Beto's men to come by once more, this time with their families, to show them what their men have built. I call Beto to see if he and his crew can pick up some of their family members and swing by after work in San Pancho for a short little ceremony. Beto says he will talk to the team.

A single pickup truck arrives at the appointed hour at our house. It carries several of Beto's team, but no women and children. At least Victor the carpenter, who arrives separately, has his lovely young wife and a small boy with him. Beto's small group comes up the driveway and goes around to the front lawn, in front of the arches. They are still in their work clothes, and although they look around admiringly, I can see they are ill at ease. Thia makes what she can of it. She takes Victor's little boy by the hand. She shows him the dark and shiny wood doors on our handsome new downstairs bedroom, and says, in her charming Spanish:

"Look. Your father has built this. *Magnífico!* You should be"—she checked the word with me earlier—"*orgulloso*, proud." Victor's wife beams, and Victor coughs and smiles his melancholy smile.

But elsewhere, Beto's team, mostly his relations, are restless. Perhaps it is their dusty work clothes, but they are not at ease around Thia's artful centerpieces. Thia offers to show them upstairs, and they politely decline. I am beginning to understand that we have pressed our luck, and that our well-intentioned, if naive, sentimentality is colliding with their plain discomfort. So I decide to speed things up.

I duck into one of the bedrooms and emerge wearing one of the shirts. They are startled to see me, and it takes a few moments for it to register.

"I am a member of Equipo Beto," I announce. Govany pipes up, "*¡Qué bueno!*" The others look a bit bewildered. The gringo had one shirt made up for himself?

I plunge on. "My wife and I have been so very impressed by the friendship and loyalty this team shows for one another. So I chose the image of a handshake to symbolize your spirit." A couple of murmurs of approval. "But there is another reason as well. Beto and we built this entire house on a handshake. No contract, no lawyers, and not one misunderstanding in six months." There are several nods, though at least a couple of the guys have quizzical looks that say, "Yeah, no contract, so what's new about that?" "I hope you men will wear *yours* in solidarity."

Thia walks out of the bedroom with the pile of shirts, puts them on the Aztec table, and waves at the men to come find their size. This time there are pleased murmurs as they find a shirt their size. A couple of the men pull on their shirts and grin. Others do not. They do not want to soil them putting them on over their work shirts.

They thank us politely, shake our hands, and then begin to move out. I get the sense that they appreciate the gesture, but honestly, they'd like to be on their way now and get back on the pickup to return home. It would be a better story, it would have a better ending, if I could say that they had fallen in with our idea of bringing their families and girl-friends, if they had given a rousing cheer, if they had toured the house to see what their labor had produced in finished form. But I take Beto aside for one last chat, and he makes it all clear with one terse insight. "I appreciate what you did, and what Señora Thia wanted to do," he says. "But with us, work is work and family is family." He gestures at the men filing out the driveway. "When they finish one job, it is time for another job, nothing else. And when they are off work, they want to be with their families."

It has worked out all right. It always does. But this is one of those times in which I have never felt more like a gringo.

We choose to fulfill our third fiesta responsibility on Guadalupe Day. It dawns bright and noisy, with rockets shooting up over the palms. It is also yet another birthday for me, as I am reminded when Michele calls with her usual, "Hola, Lupe!" I have no time to be depressed about it. I have stayed up late on a couple of fresh assignments, and have been working on the travel site plans that will take us back to the States this Christmas. (Which, incidentally, is when we will get an excellent rental rate.) And now we have to prepare the house for the villagewide viewing. I go down to the pool, turn on the aqueduct spout, and take a morning swim.

Esmeralda is already at work sweeping out the dust that collects overnight. Two of her daughters—she has seven children—come over after school ends at noon and help their mother. Thia works harder than any of them, and it takes the morning and part of the afternoon to get the place ready. A new plumber, sent over by the property manager we have decided on, tells me the aljibe pipes have been installed wrong. I am less than competent to judge; my college major was literature. Today, I minor in pipes and water treatment.

By three, the drinks and canapés are set for our fiesta. Ian and Kerry are the first to arrive. It was they, one year ago, who first brokered the deal for this lot over dinner just down the street, at Terrazola. They pay Thia warm compliments on the decor, the first of a multitude this evening, and Ian ventures that we have set a record for building a house in this short a time. He talks about how fortunate we were, and mentions some of the town's stalled projects, and the season's real-estate scams. We both watch as the aqueduct begins to pour water out of its spout. "Neat!" he says, another guy.

Slowly the house begins to fill with people we haven't seen in months and many we have not met before. It is a nice crowd. The artist Evelyne Boren and husband Michael Sandler have descended from their majestic perch above Sayulita Beach to mingle with the north siders. Her legs are longer than ever, and she brings as a house gift one of her watercolors, a fishing-catch scene on the beach below her home. Larue and Caroline Shock, also from high on the hill, and among Sayulita's longest-settled gringos, tell Thia she has done a terrific job. Ismael and Adriána Sanchez, Jeanne and Rollie's restaurant partners, are here too. Eagle George, of course, wearing his Stetson, and Shirley.

The crowd of about forty is more gringo than Mexican, but I am pleased to see the local townspeople. For all the camaraderie in this village, there is less mixing of the nationalities at gringo dinners and parties than many American say they would like. It is the Mexicans who decline invitations, although they are hospitable enough about asking gringo friends to *their* family fiestas—mostly birthdays, weddings, and quinceañeras. A quiet dinner between gringo and Mexican couples is rarer, or at least is rare for newcomers like ourselves. We are pleased to have our friendship with Benny and Hilda, who are away on a trip today—Hilda dropped in yesterday to check on the "goo-pees"—but we know that we will have to live here a while longer to be accepted by the local gentry. That will come.

Our close friends are here, of course. Dick has a new book I've *got* to read; Cheryl is bubbling over her latest passion: day-trading online. Jeanne has brought a fresh nosegay of anecdotes from the serial drama inside Rollie's kitchen. And Barbara is in fine fire-eating form, citing a rough patch with their partners at Obelisco. It is tough enough for two people to live and run a service business from home; four people on the same piece of paradise can bump wings.

Thia leads our new visitors on tours of the house, raising a hand as if she has a sign, shouting, "Walking! Walking!" An artistic gay couple recently arrived from New York notices *everything* she has done—her napkin arrangements, the spotlighted Catrina—and compliments her fulsomely. When she gets to the roof, where the wooden beams were finally laid across the columns and where white muslin curtains flutter in the light breeze, she leads the group to the railing, and waves at the sky above Sayulita's hills. The sunset is bright ginger, streaked across the low cirrus clouds.

"*Ta-da!*" she says, taking credit.

As the coach lights go on below, and the party ebbs, we do our post-mortem with our pals. From the comments we collect, it is clear we have a hit on our hands. We began by wanting simply to acquit our-selves in the dream-home stakes: something that would please us, not look ungainly or graceless, not break our bank. But in fact, if the wine-fueled compliments are sincere, we have built a real showcase. Our property manager, Jocelyn Guzmán, who handles the fanciest places in town, quietly tells us over a drink that she thinks it's one of the best-designed house and gardens in Sayulita. Bliss! Tequila and bliss, but bliss nonetheless.

The Guadalupe Day fireworks are getting serious over in town, and the crowd drifts away to watch them. Closing the gates behind us, but leaving on the house lights from garden to roof, Thia and I stroll into the village. We know the dirt roads, and the ruts to avoid, just as well as the horses that canter by each morning. Christmas lights are already up in some of the homes and shanties along the way—some are now the little elegant white lights once disdained as not colorful enough. The roads are still atrocious, but the town is definitely on its mucky, bumpy way to upscale. A couple of last year's grocery stores have become clothing boutiques. At a corner of the plaza, someone's weed-tangled backyard has become an espresso bar.

Earlier that day, I had gone into town to pick up party staples. Like all express routes in Sayulita, it turned into a local, with multiple stops. I had been so engrossed in finishing the house, I had not really seen the changes in town since the new season began. Over at the laundry, our *Sierra Madre* friend, Mr. Gonzales, had raised his prices. Annie Bananie had moved her jewelry in from a street stall to a bright new store on the main drag. Across from Rollie's, a couple of doors down from the butcher—where live chickens are still dispatched—a new art gallery was opening. Then I saw a familiar round-bellied figure tooling down the cobblestones, perched like a large egg on a new bright-green motor scooter. I flagged Gaby down, asked about his parents, wife, and daughter—all well, but his father's *pinche* leg!—and he told me business is good, very good. The parrot as well. A block down, as I rounded the corner, I caught a glimpse of Aurelio, driving a new Jeep Cherokee. I could see that he had an American couple in the car with him and was talking animatedly. I wondered if their horses would soon be running free.

Only Doña Lety, her sandwich stand open again after a three-month "vacation," seemed unaffected. We greeted each other, and talked, as we always had, about change in the village. Real estate prices are higher. I mentioned that one of her neighbors had sold her house; a new dress shop has been opened up. "Yes, the prices keep rising, and so does the temptation," she said. "It can be a good thing, but I tell them: it does not guarantee happiness." She herself is going nowhere, she said. We talked about the death a few days earlier of a local teenage girl, who drove herself and three friends into a tree just past the highway turnoff. A second girl died later. Alcohol was involved. Another traffic fatality, another procession to the cemetery. I asked Doña Lety if she thought this would have happened before prosperity, before gringos, before there were cars for teenagers to drive. She wrapped my lunch torta and thought for a moment. "There is a saying," she said. "It's not the fault of the mouse but of the one who offers him the cheese."

Tonight, lightly buzzed, Thia and I grab some dinner, then walk to the plaza. There has been another running of the fireworks bull, and the sparks are still sputtering on the plaza paving stones. We pass the gas-station store, with its open jerry cans waiting for their Coke-bottle funnels, and a fiery spark whistles close—very close—by. On the park benches, very young couples caress each other. An old Huichol couple walk by, clutching their cases of ornamental wares. Children scamper up the bandstand; more of them are now driving new electric tricycles in the plaza.

At one corner of the square, a brass band is playing, trombones in the lead. Next to them, in a small circle in the street, are a group of men in cowboy hats, tapping their boots, drinking cervezas, and their women, done up in their spit-curl best. In the middle are three or four charros in their saddles, rein guiding their horses into the sideways prances I loved seeing at the Sayulita rodeo. In fact, I realize, these *are* the rodeo buckaroos, out for a Guadalupe Day jam session with spurs.

I recognize them by the Modelo beers in their hands, which they cheerfully toss into the street to be crumpled by their steeds' hooves. They're
not part of any official holiday event, as far as I can see. They appear
to be out on a joyride on a good evening for celebrating. Several of the
cowboy señores twirl their señoritas on the cobblestones in the familiar two-step. I feel Thia sway beside me, but she knows better than to
nudge me to dance. Horses do it more gracefully than I.

We return to our home. Next door, Casa Aguila is dark; the Eagle
sleeps.

We walk past our driveway, so handsomely engraved with hand-laid
initials. My wife has asked several times how they happened to be there,
and I cannot tell a lie. I say they were Benny's idea.

We pass beneath the arch that Beto built, scraped away by ancient
carriages. We go into the living room, out Victor's door, and up the staircase that Aurelio wanted to build as high as an Aztec temple, which we
foreign invaders so cruelly reduced. Just inside, by the moonlit terrace,
we see Victoriano's bright seascape on the wall, framed by Armando's
teakwood. We climb the spiral staircase, take the turn on Pancho's over-
pass, and step out onto the roof.

I have left the satellite radio up here, antenna facing north. The
moon is above the palms, and I can hear the waves. I reach down, find
a light classics channel, and hear a waltz. Pretty old-fashioned. Even *I*
remember, barely, how to step through one of those. Mrs. Plum's dancing classes in Chapultepec.

Tonight, on our roof, I hold out my hand and ask Thia for a waltz.

"Señora?" I say.

"*Signor,*" she says.

APPENDIX: 10 GRINGO MYTHS ABOUT RETIRING IN MEXICO

... and a Few Suggestions Before You Pack Your Sandals

1. **You need to speak Spanish to get by.**
   Not really.

   It's a shame not to at least try to learn the language, but I've met few non-Spanish-speaking retirees—including my wife—who say it's been a big problem for them. Mexicans have lived cheek by jutting Anglo jowl with us throughout their history and are more skilled at interpreting hand signals and foreign gibberish than are most monolingual Americans. (Gibberish = Greek = griego = gringo.) Except for remote venues, there will usually be some Mexican nearby who has worked with Americans, has learned some English from TV and movies, or has spent time in El Norte. On the other hand, any effort to speak Spanish is usually appreciated, not mocked, and your experience can be exponentially richer if you add a new language to your life.

2. **Serious crime is rampant.**
   With few exceptions, not against tourists or foreign residents.

   Nothing causes greater fear among Americans or Canadians than reports of violence, armed robbery, and kidnappings in Mexico, or of the culture of police and government corruption. It's true that in Mexico City and in the border cities, crime of all kinds is high. Incidents along the Baja coast have affected the tourist trade. But in

smaller locales in the interior, and in most places that Americans
have chosen to live, retirees say they feel safer walking around at
night than they do in the States. (A recent poll of Mexican immigrants in the United States found that fewer than half found "safety
from crime" more effective in the United States than in Mexico.)

Petty thievery and traffic bribes in Mexico *are* a part of everyday
life. Like anyplace where richer people live among poorer folk, the
rich can be a target. But when it comes to the big stuff—personal
safety and everyday honesty—I have felt more, not less, secure than
I do in the States. Despite the shoot-'em-up movies and news
reports, owning a gun in Mexico is a serious crime, and there are far
fewer of them than in the United States. If nothing else, there's
widespread agreement among Mexico's local authorities and communities that crimes against gringos are bad for business. Less cyn-
ically, the honesty of the average person we met in Mexico,
whether a contractor handling thousands of dollars in cash or a
shopkeeper returning a few centavos of overpayment, was for us a
constant source of reassurance and satisfaction.

Americans seem more susceptible than most to anecdotal paranoia: a single kidnapping in a city of twenty million, and tourism
plunges. A backpacker gets robbed, and no foreigner in the country
is safe. A traffic cop solicits a bribe, and no policeman in Mexico is
to be trusted. But twenty million Americans visit Mexico annually,
and the vast, vast majority return unscathed. The same underpaid
cop who takes twenty dollars for a speeding ticket can be extraordinarily helpful to a visitor in real trouble. It is probably true that
most official crime statistics are not to be trusted because so much
crime goes unreported. Mexicans tend to solve things through personal negotiation, by the intervention of family and friends, not by
appealing to authorities. But by any measure of everyday life as
lived by American residents I've come to know, the incidence of
major crime is extremely rare. We do lock our doors, but we don't
live in fear.

3. **You can't buy American stuff or high-quality goods.**
   Not true since NAFTA and the arrival of the Big Shops.
   That's the good news *and* the bad news. There are Mexican farm-
ers and merchants whose traditional ways of doing business have

not, to put it mildly, prospered under "free trade." And some argue that the Wal-Marts and Costcos have wreaked the same kind of havoc on mom-and-pop businesses in their neighborhoods as they have in the States. But the fact is, you can now find a rich, wide variety of merchandise and products—American-made or close Mexican approximations—that were unavailable just a few years ago. On a day-to-day basis, we patronize local merchants; unlike Americans, the vast majority of Mexicans cite the "corner store" as their main shopping outlet. But the new Big Shops provide greater diversity and better prices, and that's where we go on our major shopping expeditions. And so does every other American and Mexican we know. Whatever harm Wal-Mart did to small local businesses, it sparked a revolution in shops and shopping. Big, decrepit, lackadaisical Mexican department stores and grocery stores had to stock up, spruce up, and step up to stay in business. In Puerto Vallarta, to name one city, big stores like Gigante, Sorrano's, and Mega became competitive with the looming likes of Wal-Mart and Sam's Club, and we gradually found we were as happy to stock up there as at the American-owned emporiums.

Just a few years ago, a typical retiree considered it impossible to build and furnish a house without trips to stateside malls and elaborate stratagems to get things back across the border. Gringos claimed it was difficult to find household essentials of high quality: appliances were shoddy, fixtures fell apart, tools didn't work. No more. My wife and I built our home by shopping entirely in Mexico, and with a few exceptions like linens and towels, we found what we needed here. Mexican quality is improving, and not just because of competition from the North. Our lawn chairs, bought in Guadalajara, are made in China.

And, oh: the things we bought that we cherish the most—our furniture, our dishes, tiles and glassware, the art on our walls—are all made in Mexico.

4. **You're cut off from family and friends.**
Not as much, since discount airlines, cheap phones, and the Internet.

Most Americans retire within a few miles of where they last lived, presumably because they want to stay close to their children

and grandchildren and the comfort of close friends. Among retirees
of past years, this was the great lament: what price an exotic locale
or a princely lifestyle if you cannot spend the years you have left
with your family or those you love?

Now you hear something else. Retirees in Mexico are saying they
have found a way to balance the adventure of living abroad with
seeing *just enough* of their stateside family and friends. They have
funds put aside to take cheaper air flights back to the States several
times a year and to fly the kids down another several times. They
have an inexpensive callback phone service, or better yet, an Internet phone, and can have long, daily, stay-in-touch conversations
with sons and daughters and old neighborhood pals. They have
email alerts set up with one of the web travel services, to let them
know when there's a special airfare home. (My wife and I bought a
round-trip fare from Puerto Vallarta to New York, on a special deal
from Travelocity, for three hundred dollars.) And to judge by the
many silver-haired heads tapping away at Internet cafés, or over key-
boards in their casitas, email has added a new dimension to the way
we stay in touch. Some even claim they see *more* of their kids and
friends in Mexico than when they lived a few states away: having a
home in a tropical or colonial locale can be a wonderful incentive—
sometimes *too* tempting an incentive—to pay the older folks a visit.

5. Mexicans are hostile to Americans
Mostly untrue, survey says—unlike elsewhere.

During a decade in which regard for America fell nearly everywhere in the world, a poll showed that Mexican attitudes toward
America and Americans remained positive. In 2008, there were
some protests from politicians in Mexico City responding to the
conservative anti-immigrant agitation in the States, and the
renewed construction of the border wall, but overall Americans
report no anger directed at them personally. Over half of all Mexicans report that they know or are related to someone in the United
States, and that number has been growing as tourism and immigration in both directions has increased.

In our own travels and residence in Mexico, we did not see a single incident I would regard as hostile to us as Americans. Toward
our government, yes, but far less than what I've encountered in

Europe and Asia. Mexicans are highly patriotic, but they also have a healthy skepticism about their own government, and that may make them less likely to cast stones. That's not to say that some Mexicans don't see gringos as marks; they do, but no more so than other visitors. In general, the hospitality and warmth accorded by Mexicans to Americans greatly exceeds anything I've witnessed among Americans toward Mexicans in our country. Individual cases, as always, excepted.

6. **Mexicans are lazy.**
   Untrue, and a blood libel at that.
   If there's a calumny that deserves to be put away forever, it is the stereotype of the lazy Mexican dozing beneath a sombrero. I've traveled through much of Europe and parts of Asia, and, even as compared to the Japanese, I do not believe I've seen a more industrious people than Mexicans. (A related myth is that most Mexican immigrants come to the United States because they are unemployed in Mexico; studies show that most have jobs, but want to advance themselves and do better by their families.) In Mexico, whether it was lawyers or doctors or architects or accountants or construction workers or maids, the people I came to know worked as long hours, with as much or more diligence, as the hardest-charging citizens of the land to the North. Siestas are a smart, healthy corrective to the searing climate; fiestas are a life-affirming corrective to drudgery that too few Americans (or Asians) know how to escape as joyfully. While it's true that time schedules and appointments are hugely flexible, in the long run, most Mexicans will eventually show up, in their own time, ready to put in a long day's work. That they also know how to slow down and how to celebrate often, is something we might consider importing, duty-free.

7. **Mexican medical care is inferior.**
   Not necessarily. You can pay, modestly, for excellent care.
   The Mexican government has an enlightened, humane, and progressive health policy—subsidizing doctors' educations, mandating health clinics in nearly every town and village, supporting major hospitals and health facilities. While its medical technology

and resources are not generally up to the standards of America's top hospitals (with some notable exceptions), patient care can be an astonishment to Americans long resigned to HMO-type assembly-line office visits. Doctors still make house calls, give out their cell-phone numbers, and take time to get to know their patients. Nurses will spend nights on cots beside their patients. Most drugs can be purchased without prescriptions.

Medicare is not valid outside the U.S., but American retirees have options: There is a national-health insurance system, open to foreigners of any age, and although it is basic and primitive by American standards—a patient brings his own blankets and pillows to a hospital and sends out for his medications—it can theoretically serve as a reassuring catastrophic backup. In practice, because of the maddening bureaucracy, basic service, and waiting periods, most gringos buy private insurance, which is generally inexpensive (but will not cover pre-existing conditions), or sign up for an international traveler's insurance program, or pay reasonable out-of-pocket costs.

Like real estate, the most important consideration in Mexican medical care is location. Mexico City, Guadalajara, and Monterrey are known to have hospitals and physicians of world-class caliber, including state-of-the-art facilities. Some resort cities, such as Puerto Vallarta, have good hospitals. Others, such as Cancún, at one point were reportedly beset by corrupt kickback schemes. An Arizona team of doctors set out to rate doctors and hospitals at a number of resort and retirement locations throughout Mexico. Their findings were published in an extraordinarily helpful book listed at the end of this section.

8. A) **Americans cannot buy land in Mexico and . . . B) Americans** *can* **buy land in Mexico, but it can be taken away from them.**
A) *Mostly untrue, and where true, it's a technicality.*

Aside from narrow strips along border and coastal areas, foreigners can buy land in their own names. Both mortgages and title insurance, once almost nonexistent, are beginning to be available, though mostly for developments. (A number of American title-insurance companies have begun to clear titles for Mexican properties.) Ownership works the way it does in the States, although capital gains are more complicated when you're ready to sell. Simplified, if you have a resident visa and observe certain regulations, you are exempt from capital-gains taxes on a home in which you have lived. Speculation in raw land can be heavily taxed.

As to property along the ocean, where many Americans want to settle, foreigners may not own land within fifty kilometers of a coastline; nor are they permitted to buy land within one hundred kilometers of a border. However, they may buy a "beneficial interest" in a bank trust that holds the legal deed to the land. This trust gives the buyer the right to "hold, occupy, use, improve, develop, rent, and sell" the real estate. The trust may be used as collateral for a loan, and may be passed along as an inheritance. Known as a *fideicomiso*, it is the instrument used by tens of thousands of foreign "owners" of beachfront property. To my knowledge, properly executed fideicomisos can neither be revoked or otherwise rescinded.

B) Also mostly untrue, and where true, the land was never "owned."

Where things *can* get dicey is "purchasing" property owned by an ejido, the communal land system created to keep and develop property in the hands of the Mexican peasant population. The ejido was once the proud end result of efforts of reformers ranging from Emiliano Zapata to Lázaro Cárdenas, as much a correction to rapacious homegrown land barons as a defense against foreigners. In recent years, the system has fallen prey to corruption, especially as rising land values became a greater temptation to ejido leaders. As a result, ejidos are now undergoing "regularization," whereby former communal land is converted to private property purchasable as a trust.

The land we originally bought in Sayulita had undergone such a change, and it was the growing pains and vagaries of this new system that made the experience stressful and uncertain. I never thought I might lose the land; I had it checked out by my own Mexican lawyer, and by a notario público, a government-appointed attorney (quite unlike an American notary public) charged with verifying that all the formalities have been observed. Our concern was that there was so much red tape and paperwork, not to mention casual surveying techniques, that we might get snarled up in its technicalities, as we did.

For years before regularization appeared on the scene, Americans and Canadians found a way to "buy" ejido land—and that is where most of the wild stories spring from. Since the accepted (but not strictly legal) practice was that ejido property could be deeded to a Mexican citizen, foreigners would get a local person that they "trusted" to purchase the property and hold it for them, usually for a small fee. In time, that became its own temptation, leading to at least some costly confrontations between "owners" and their prestanombres, or "name-lenders." The interesting thing is that by and large, the system worked and the vast majority of foreign ejido land owners built their homes, lived in them, and even resold them to new "owners" without incident. Mexicans, these owners will tell you, are honest people. But there were exceptions.

Some years ago, a number of ejido property "sales" in Baja California were found to be illegal, and the American owners were indeed dispossessed. From this one event, painful for those involved, but largely isolated to this incident, came most of the anecdotal bad press about land ownership in Mexico. So although the prestanombre practice continues, for most quite successfully, my general advice would be: You can certainly trust a trust, but do not approach the undeeded ejido unheeded.

9. **Foreign women will feel unwelcome in a macho society.**
   Untrue, if paradoxical.

Machismo is *not* a myth. Many Mexican men grow up to think that the male is ordained by nature to be the "head of household," and may enforce their domination over their wives or sweethearts, sometimes by physical means, especially when there's drink involved. The male macho syndrome goes back to the Spanish conquistadores, and before that, to the Moorish influence when the Arabs ruled Spain for six hundred years. That this coexists with an exaggerated, romantic exaltation of women, especially mothers, is the first part of the paradox.

But the second part is that, in the main, expatriate and visiting women report being treated with respect and dignity by Mexican men, often with a certain level of discomfort that affords distance. Though it can still be a feather in a young Mexican man's cap to bed a gringa, to the extent that a foreign woman is seen as more prosperous and better connected, she may be seen as untouchable, if only because she may not be worth the trouble that may ensue. And for the potential woman retiree, age and the aura of motherhood (or beyond) put her further out of bounds. There are always isolated exceptions, as was the case when several American women were assaulted in San Miguel de Allende. But far more common is the sight of Mexican men at fiestas making certain that all single gringas—of any age—are asked to dance.

At any rate, the fact that in some communities American and Canadian female retirees outnumber their more rapidly depleting male counterparts attests to women's comfort level in Mexico. In Lake Chapala, among other venues, women say they feel a sisterhood and support network they have not encountered elsewhere. Though our married female friends say that Mexican men often prefer dealing with their husbands, they have nevertheless been treated with deference. Single female friends of a certain age said they felt highly secure and comfortable in their Mexican communities, though they used common sense—for instance, staying out of Mexican taverns alone. There is a literature of, and by, women living single in Mexico, a couple of which are noted at the end of this section.

10. For the most part, the tap water is not safe to drink.
    True.
    Nine out of ten ain't bad.

RESOURCES

Because this is not a guidebook, I'll limit myself to listing some of the websites and books that I found useful in our own experience as novice retirees. They are neither exhaustive nor representative of Mexico as a whole. We spent our time in central Mexico and claim no special expertise as yet in other areas. As to phone numbers and websites, I suggest caution in relying on lists in print; even in recently published books, a surprising amount of information becomes quickly obsolete. Even consulates and tourist bureau information change often, and are more efficiently found online. Tourist and travel sites are also beyond the scope of this book. Because of frequent change and the difficulty of figuring out who is pushing what online, I mention just a few sites I think will be around for a while. For updates, I have a website that I hope to keep fresh with helpful resources. Point your browser to www.gringosinparadise.net, and I'll do my best to stay in touch.

WEBSITES

www.mexconnect.com Subscription site, but lots of good free content. A portal of useful articles and links, it encourages its users—many are long-time expats—to help one another out in their forums. It tends to be Chapala-centric.

www.mexonline.com It's been around a long time, and has helpful general content

www.virtualmex.com Lots of tools: driving-distance maps, currency converters, and so forth.

www.internationalliving.com These folks are a busy enterprise, publishing newsletters, holding seminars, and brokering real estate. Their reporting and ranking of retirement venues produce lots of useful first-person information. www.mexinsider.com is a partner.

www.escapeartist.com Lots of real estate being sold here, so you have to judge the ads for yourself, but it has a wealth of helpful resources.

www.aarpsegundajuventud.org AARP's bilingual Hispanic site has good basic info.

www.state.gov and **www.cia.gov** The State Department and the spooks: for travel alerts, visa information, emergency numbers, and hard-nosed basic political information.

BOOKS

The major guidebooks—*Fodor's, Frommer's, Lonely Planet, Rough Guide*—all have information useful to the potential retiree, even if they're not aimed at the general demographic. For my purposes, *The People's Guide to Mexico* (listed separately below) was the most usefully plainspoken. Always check for publication dates; there are still books available on Amazon.com promising you retirement in Mexico at four hundred dollars a month. An online search will often get you to a book's updated site. Regional books listed here are biased toward central Mexico.

Adams, Don. *Head for Mexico: The Renegade Guide.* Self-published, 2003. Funny, utterly irreverent with great tips from his resident gang.

Blue, Karen. *Midlife Mavericks: Women Reinventing Their Lives in Mexico.* Boca Raton, FL: Universal Publishers, 2000. Anecdotal, inspiring stories.

Cohan, Tony. *On Mexican Time: A New Life in San Miguel.* New York: Broadway, 2001. The book always cited as I was writing mine—a lyrical account of a California couple's move down to San Miguel de Allende.

Dean, Archie. *Insider's Guide to San Miguel.* Self-published, 2nd ed., 1995. My personal favorite of the genre—unbiased coverage by a longtime expat.

Doerr, Harriet. *Stones for Ibarra.* Penguin, 1984. First published 1984 by Viking Press. Exquisite, timeless fiction about an older couple's move to rural Mexico. Doerr wrote this, her first book, in 1978 at age sixty-eight—hurrah!

Franz, Carl. *The People's Guide to Mexico*. Edited by Lorena Havens and Steve Rogers. 12th ed. Emeryville, CA: Avalon Travel Publishing, 2002. This classic, chatty, entertaining book, regularly updated and loaded with info, is widely regarded as the best guide to Mexico ever. I agree.

Howells, John, and Don Merwin. *Choose Mexico for Retirement*. Insiders' Guide. 9th ed. Guilford, CT: Globe Pequot Press, 2005. One in a series, lots of practical information; be careful to buy the latest edition.

Jennings, Gary. *Aztec*. New York: Tor, 1997. First published 1980 by Atheneum. Epic novel about the Mexica and the bloodiest book I've ever read.

Kamen Henry. *Empire: How Spain Became a World Power, 1492–1763*. New York: HarperCollins, 2003. Fascinating account of how Spain took over a continent.

Kendrick, Theresa. *Mexico's Lake Chapala and Ajijic: The Insider's Guide*. 2nd ed. Austin, TX: Mexico Travelers Information, 2005. At over 400 pages, you wouldn't leave for Chapala without it.

Krauze, Enrique. *Mexico: Biography of Power: A History of Modern Mexico, 1810–1996*. New York: Harper Perennial, 1998. *The* book to read to understand Mexico's history and politics.

De Mente, Boyé Lafayette. *There's a Word for it in Mexico: The Complete Guide to Mexican Thought and Culture*. New York: McGraw-Hill, 1998. First published as *NTC's Dictionary of Mexican Cultural Code Words*, 1996 by NTC Publishing Group. Provocative, slanted essays about Mexican expressions and culture. Conversation stokers.

Luboff, Ken. *Living Abroad in Mexico*. Emeryville, CA: Avalon Travel Publishing, 2005. Lively resource guide, by the late, longtime Mexico expat expert.

Michener, James A. *Mexico*. New York: Fawcett, 1994. First published 1992 by Random House. From the land mass formation to piñatas, the epic storyteller's usual sweep.

Nelson, "Mexico" Mike. *Live Better South of the Border in Mexico: Practical Advice for Living and Working*. 4th ed. Golden, CO: Fulcrum Publishing, 2005. Fact-filled, easy-to-read pros and cons.

Page, Robert H., M.D., and Curtis P. Page, M.D. *Mexico: Health and Safety Travel Guide*. Tempe, AZ: MedToGo, 2004. Very helpful expert reviews of Mexico's medical facilities.

Paz, Octavio. *The Labyrinth of Solitude: Life and Thought in Mexico*. Translated by Lysander Kemp. New York: Grove Press, 1962. Poetic and profound, the Nobel winner's masterpiece on understanding Mexico.

Ross-Merrimer, Ruth. *Champagne and Tortillas*. Self-published, 2001. Expat life in Lake Chapala turned amusingly into a mystery novel.

Smith, Jack C. *God and Mr. Gomez*. Los Angeles: Los Angeles Times Books, 1997. Originally published 1974 by Reader's Digest Press. Classic comic tale of house-building in Baja California, circa 1974.

Thomas, Hugh. *Conquest: Montezuma, Cortés, and the Fall of Old Mexico*. New York: Simon & Schuster, 1993. The definitive story of Cortés and Moctezuma.

ACKNOWLEDGMENTS

Many of the people I wish to thank are already named; they are the protagonists of this story. But I want to single out Barbara Hart-Kirkwood and Bill Kirkwood, and Maggie and Bruce Nesbitt of San Pancho, and of course Jeanne and Rollie Dick, Cheryl Vaughan and Dick Dobbeck, and Shirley and Eagle George Newman of Sayulita, for the uncountable hours of advice, stories and friendship they shared with us. Also gracias to Triny Palomar Gil and Gloria Honan, Reyna García, Doc Forbis, Harvey Craig (I kid him, but he worked hard and loyally on our behalf), Flip Baldwin, Kerry and Ian Hodge, Teke and Chuck Mohill, Joanie Cartal, Judi and John Levens, Mike Scannell, Dr. Mauro Malja, Kathy and Bill Glaysher, Cheri and Patrick Hasburgh, Andy Mehl, Jesse Hendry, and our early guide to Puerto Vallarta, Patricia Mendez. I owe as well a debt of gratitude to our other Mexican colleagues, sages and craftsmen: Aurelio Carrillo, Beto Ramos Balcazar, Armando Vasquez, Doña Lety, Benny and Hilda Flores, Jocelyn Guzman, Concha Patrón, Sergio and Jose Luis Barrios, among many others.

My family is for the most part also named in the narrative, but I nevertheless thank my father and Bernadette for making not one, but two trips on bumpy cobblestones to visit us; sister Michele and "Uncle" Tom for their enthusiasm and help in our travels; brother Christopher and wife Kit for their encouragement and his photographs; the moral support (and umbrella hat) we got from brother Geoff and Laurie; and *hola* to sister Cecile. Thia's far-flung clan, the MacKenzies, helped us through the lean months by putting us up, bucking us up, and picking up a lot of checks. Thanks, John and Laura, Julie and Larry, Merrick, and Linda and Robie. Same goes for our friends Mady Brown, with whom we camped out; early manuscript readers Harry Stein and Priscilla Turner; Peter Ross Range; Ingrid Von Eckert and John Blumenthal; Jeri and Nick Bryan; Linda and Andy Garvin; Narda

Zacchino and Bob Scheer; and particular thanks to our traveling companions Dr. Paul and Cindy Prewitt. Paul also took many of the photographs that are used in the book.

On the publishing front, I'm grateful to to Lisa Drew, legendary editor, who responded with such *cariño* to my proposal and streamlined the manuscript with such *elegancia*. I don't know how affected she was by our experiment in retirement, but I note that she announced *her* retirement immediately after editing *Gringos in Paradise*. And an *abrazo* to my agent Ellen Geiger, who helped shape the original proposal and served as able negotiator and hand-holder. Huge thanks to Samantha Martin at Scribner, who worked devotedly on this book. Gratitude as well to copyeditor Nancy Inglis, and by the time this is published, I will of course be grateful to my new editor Beth Wareham, who is taking me the rest of the way.

As to Thia, Blair, Tyler, and the memory of my beloved mother—originally Beverly Barry, known as Gala—the book's dedication says it all.

INDEX

environmental-impact study, 135,
145, 146, 152, 154–55, 162–63,
168, 269
equipale furniture, 222–23, 234,
236–37, 271, 272, 274, 278
expatriates
assimilation of, 71
criticisms of Mexico by, 80
as risk takers, 20
satisfaction with Mexican life of,
54
See also gringo-Mexican relations;
gringos; retirees, American

feminism, 199, 203–4
fiesta
for construction workers, 275–76,
277, 278–81
housewarming as, 277–78
importance of, 277
for town, 277, 281–83
*See also specific town, village, or
occasion*
Flores, Benny. *See* Aristedes Flores,
Benny (Benedicto)
Flores, Vicky, 136–39
Forbes, Michael, 15
Forbis, Doc, 89–90, 91, 273
Four Seasons Resort (Punta Mita),
109–14, 135
Fourth of July, 198–99
Fox Quesada, Vicente, 67, 135
Francisco (subcontractor), 243–46,
248, 253
Frank, Waldo, 229
Fuentes, Carlos, 10, 191
furniture, Casa Gala, 222–23, 234,
236–37, 251, 252, 253–54, 271,
272, 274, 278

garbage collection, 36
García, Reyna, 89–90
García Realty, 58, 90
Gayosso, Estela, 74, 75, 144
gender relations, in Mexico, 80–81,
90, 203–4, 294–95
Glaysher, Bill and Kathy, 143–44,
155
God and Mr. Gomez (Smith), 180
godparents, 150–52
golf, 109, 114, 124

Golson, Barry
birthday of, 94–95
broken-toe period of, 46, 47–51,
57, 61, 63, 66, 68, 69
childhood and youth of, 7, 11, 14,
25–26, 63, 65, 67, 74, 94–95,
219, 285
education of, 25, 63, 65
family background of, 7, 25,
212–14, 215, 230, 274
income of, 126–27, 135, 136, 258
professional background of, 2
Golson, Bernadette, 243, 268, 271,
273, 275
Golson, Bernard, 212–14, 215
Golson, Blair
car accident of, 185–86
and Christmas holidays, 99, 100,
102, 115, 116
decision to live in Mexico with
parents, 99, 109
e-mail from, 128–30
as family chef, 106, 197
Mother's Day visit by, 199–200
and Pilar, 148–49, 152, 170–71,
185–86, 190, 199
as reporter, 99
speeding by, 170–71
Golson, Chris, 124, 243, 268, 271,
272, 273, 275
Golson, Geoff, 198, 274
Golson, George, 7, 243, 247, 268, 269,
271, 272, 273–74, 275
Golson, Kit, 124, 243, 268, 271, 272,
273, 275
Golson, Laurie, 198
Golson, Michele, 26, 94, 123–24, 243,
268, 270–71, 274, 275, 281
Golson, Thia
birthday of, 199
construction crew's relationship
with, 197–98, 203–4, 215
fears about leaving U.S. of, 10
hair washing by, 37–38
as helper in Rollie's at Night, 38,
45, 55–56, 73, 87, 100, 123,
134, 163
as La Luz, 87
professional background of, 2
Golson, Tyler, 99, 102, 109, 110, 111,
115–16, 181, 193, 208, 274